"This is as clear and thought provoking a statement as I have seen yet of a theology of Scripture for emergence Christianity. Conversational in tone, these pages are filled with the practical implications of the possibilities and ideas being presented. As cofounders of Emmaus Way, Conder and Rhodes speak with the authority of lived experience as well as out of their own deep faith."

Phyllis Tickle, author, *The Great Emergence*

"The Bible is the product of the believing community, and it is meant to be read in community. Solitary reading of Scripture has gotten us into all manner of difficulties. Now Tim Conder and Dan Rhodes discover the fruitfulness of reading the Bible together. This book is a wonderful exercise in biblical hermeneutics by two of the best representatives of a younger generation of pastor-scholars. Weaving in popular culture, well-informed Christian theological insight, and excitement for the Bible as uniquely revelatory, Conder and Rhodes lead us into a fresh new encounter with Scripture—the church's book—speaking anew to the church for the salvation of the world."

Will Willimon, bishop, the North Alabama Conference of the United Methodist Church; author, *Conversations with Barth on Preaching*

"With profound pastoral care, sensitivity, and wisdom, Conder and Rhodes disclose a communal hermeneutic that arises out of the real-life struggles of reading Scripture in the midst of the Emmaus Way community. In this rich and suggestive book, we are called beyond the culture of ideological, political, and spiritual fear, and beyond a homogenizing and dogmatically absolutistic biblical interpretation into the liberated imagination of the counterstory of Jesus. There is, in this book, good news for those of us who are passionate about

Scripture, deeply committed to community, and longing to experience the power of both with candor and openness in the midst of our pain, confusions, and disappointments. Never falling to the temptation of writing a how-to book, Conder and Rhodes simply bear witness to their experience of creative reading and living of Scripture in a particular communal context. And they do so with generosity and grace."

Brian J. Walsh, coauthor, *Colossians Remixed*
and *Beyond Homelessness*

"It's not easy to make the familiar odd, but Conder and Rhodes accomplish that feat by helping us recover what it means to read Scripture in communion. This is not another book that recommends a communal interpretation of Scripture, but it is a book that exhibits such readings by close analysis of texts. This book will be widely read in congregations and classrooms."

Stanley Hauerwas, Gilbert T. Rowe Professor of
Theological Ethics, Duke Divinity School

"This is an excellent guide to recovering the place of the Bible in the life of Christian communities. In a lively and informative way, it reminds us that biblical interpretation is not the province of a few who tell the rest of us what the Bible means, but it is instead a profoundly interactive communal activity that involves everyone. Following the wisdom found in these pages can help unleash the transforming power of the Bible in the church and in the lives of those who read it."

John R. Franke, Clemens Professor of
Missional Theology, Biblical Seminary

Free for All

Emergent Village resources for communities of faith

An Emergent Manifesto of Hope
edited by Doug Pagitt and Tony Jones (April 2007)

Organic Community
Joseph R. Myers (May 2007)

Signs of Emergence
Kester Brewin (July 2007)

Justice in the Burbs
Will and Lisa Samson (August 2007)

Intuitive Leadership
Tim Keel (October 2007)

The Great Emergence
Phyllis Tickle (October 2008)

Make Poverty Personal
Ash Barker (February 2009)

The Justice Project
edited by Brian McLaren, Elisa Padilla, and Ashley Bunting Seeber
(September 2009)

Thy Kingdom Connected
Dwight J. Friesen (November 2009)

Formational Children's Ministry
Ivy Beckwith (January 2010)

www.emersionbooks.com

Free for All

Rediscovering the Bible
in Community

Tim Conder
and Daniel Rhodes

BakerBooks
a division of Baker Publishing Group
Grand Rapids, Michigan

Published by Baker Books
a division of Baker Publishing Group
P.O. Box 6287, Grand Rapids, MI 49516-6287
www.bakerbooks.com

Printed in the United States of America

Library of Congress Cataloging-in-Publication Data

Conder, Tim.
    Free for all : rediscovering the Bible in community / Tim Conder and Daniel Rhodes.
        p.   cm.
    ISBN 978-0-8010-7147-8 (pbk.)
    1. Bible—Criticism, interpretation, etc. 2. Bible—Study and teaching. 3. Bible—Hermeneutics. 4. Small groups. 5. Church group work. I. Rhodes, Daniel, 1976– II. Title.
    BS511.3.C654 2009
    220.071—dc22   2009012942

In keeping with biblical principles of creation stewardship, Baker Publishing Group advocates the responsible use of our natural resources. As a member of the Green Press Initiative, our company uses recycled paper when possible. The text paper of this book is comprised of 30% post-consumer waste.

ēmersion is a partnership between Baker Books and Emergent Village, a growing, generative friendship among missional Christians seeking to love our world in the Spirit of Jesus Christ. The ēmersion line is intended for professional and lay leaders like you who are meeting the challenges of a changing culture with vision and hope for the future. These books will encourage you and your community to live into God's kingdom here and now.

Free for All is the perfect book for this endeavor. The ēmersion line of books is all about conversation between people, between faith traditions, and, as this book shows, between our communities of faith and the Bible. *Free for All* will certainly make us think—and think all the better—about the role of the Bible in our faith and the role of our traditions in the reading of it.

This book will introduce a conversation about the Bible that is new for some, and for others will bring to the forefront a long-awaited conversation. And all of us will find our communities of faith strengthened, invigorated, and deepened by the call to develop a communal understanding of the Bible.

Emergent Village resources for communities of faith

This book is dedicated to the Emmaus Way community—a fellowship of faithful friends who have inspired and compelled us to continually read the text of God's revelation with mystery and confidence, penitence and peace, lament and laughter, and an unquenchable hope in the completion of God's grace and redemption.

Contents

Introduction   11

Part 1: Embracing the Text

1. Boundaries and Biases: The Lenses of Interpretation   21
2. Recovering the Word in the Bible: A Living Word   43
3. Let the Chaos Begin: The Hermeneutics of Peoplehood   65

Part 2: Turning to the Text

4. An Interpreting Community   83
5. The Word in the Obscure—Genesis 34: The Rape of Dinah   89
6. The Word in Pain and Joy—Psalm 22: The Cry of Dereliction and a Song of Deliverance   109
7. The Word in the Familiar—*The Gossman Passion*: An Artistic Engagement   122
8. The Word in Controversy—Romans 1: Asking and Telling in the Church   131

Part 3: The Intersection of Text and Community

9. Proclamation: The Liberation of Our Voices   153
10. Ethics: Practicing New Creation   176

11. Hospitality: Setting a Subversive Table   194
12. Mission: From Defense to Offense   210
13. Imagination: Exploding the Bounded Set of Our Minds   231

Notes   249

Introduction

Free-for-all is a description that we often reserve for the likes of hockey fights, wrestling on TV, fraternity boys around a tapped keg, the hungry (and impolite!) around a full table, or an argument without boundaries. What good can come of it? One might secretly enjoy a bloody cage match on TV, but this is a guilty pleasure rarely admitted in polite or sophisticated society. Such melees are to be meticulously and persistently avoided rather than recommended. But this is a book that recommends, in a way, a melee that many faithful persons strive to avoid or even impede. One can understandably be fascinated by the destructive aftermath of a great storm, but this admiration surely exists without wishing for the storm to occur. This is a book that openly solicits the approach of a storm.

Naturally our fears of chaos should be exponentially compounded when applied to the Bible. For many of our readers, and certainly for us, the Bible is revelation from God and a trustworthy guide to a life in the way of our Savior, Jesus Christ. It seems only appropriate to respond to this record of God's gracious speech with great respect, diligent study, and prayerful contemplation. The Bible—by virtue of its sacred content, its long history of interpretation by the church, and the development of sophisticated theological systems—should certainly be above and safe from chaotic meddling and unrestrained interpretation by the masses! Shouldn't the Scriptures be the sacred domain of scholars and well-trained pastors with the faithful operating within the boundaries well marked by these experts?

Despite this apparent wisdom, we passionately beckon the storm that comes with placing the Bible in the hands of the great and diverse community of those seeking the good news of Christ and those faithfully practicing Jesus' way. We want to place upon this community of critics, doubters, seekers, followers, and faithful ones the mantle of reading, interpreting, and embodying God's Word.

Certainly our enthusiasm for this community hermeneutic, our trust in the coming storm, is rooted in the gift of God's Spirit to guide us to faithful interpretation that moves past the limited possibilities, biases, and flaws of its human readers. But we don't want to just leave it at that—that the Spirit will guide us. Exploring further the idea of community interpretation reveals many other wonderful and unexpected gifts besides fellowship in the Spirit.

We believe that the Bible was inspired and graciously given for exactly this purpose. The Bible was written by a community of inspired authors telling a corporate story of redemption for the community created by God—a community text revealed as a gift to the human community. *We* are its intended audience. To this point, nothing we have said here could be construed as radical or even insightful to the historical church. The community origin and destination of the Scriptures has long been an assumption of historical orthodoxy. Unfortunately, this assumption has been largely forgotten in many portions of the contemporary church.

The Great Reformation brought many gifts to the church, not the least being a passionate redirection of focus back to the text. This move not only corrected excesses and corruption in the church, but it put the Bible in the hands of the public. The invention of the printing press, as well as the educational acceleration toward far greater literacy, in many ways sealed the deal. The Bible would be as it was intended, a sacred text in the hands of not only the institutional church but also the public.

The attention given to the Bible and the technology that put it in the hands of the people were fuel for the conflagration that we call the Great Reformation (which swept across Europe during the end of feudalism), for the rise of the nation-state, and for the waning of the influence of imperial Catholicism. This Reformation collided not coincidentally with the advent of the Enlightenment and modernity. This constructed a passionate individualism that would inspire the revolutions to topple aristocracies, write constitutions establishing and protecting personal rights and construct the tenets of capitalism, and form a whole new economic class in Europe and eventually America.

But after a few hundred years under the dominion of modernity, we now live in a time of hyper-individualism. Especially in an American context, individualism is an omnipresent norm, the oxygen we breathe. "Rights" language is ubiquitous. The language and assumptions of individualism permeate our speech on economics, recreation and lifestyle, politics, relationships—and faith.

We now think of the Bible as "my Bible." And why not? Many of us own numerous versions. We carry them in our briefcases and have downloads on our laptops, PDAs, and iPods. It is only a small jump, a hop if you will, from "my Bible" to inflexible and authoritarian interpretations. Since it is mine, certainly I can tell myself—and you—what it means. Of course, some of us are better, more clever, and more skilled in reading the text and communicating interpretations. Some, due to skill or the simple luck of being in the right place at the right time, have far greater platforms from which to communicate their interpretations. Technology and media exponentially multiply the size of those platforms. In many ways, we live in an era of rival, authoritarian proclamations about the message of the Bible. There is an abundance of loud voices in the air telling us "the final word" about the Word.

That final word—regardless of whether we add a twist of prosperity, a slice of Calvinism, or an umbrella of Pentecostalism—is typically a word of personal salvation, personal intimacy with God, and individual rights. The descent toward such an individual gospel told as personal story by isolated authorities didn't happen in a century or even a single era. It has been happening for generations.

We resonate with William Cavanaugh's telling of this history in *Theopolitical Imagination*. In short, he contrasts this gospel of individualism with a Scripture story told historically by the church that describes a created humanity intimately joined to God and joined to each other. When sin infects humanity, it not only separates humans from God, it separates humans from each other. In essence, sin creates individuals.

The nation-state (and its companion church), which takes form in the Enlightenment, tells a different story. This narrative, enforced by the works of Locke, Hobbes, Rousseau, and others, describes human beings born free—free from each other. The state, formed by social contract, protects the rights, property, and freedoms of individuals. Accepting the social contract and story as told by the state, the church makes a reactive move. Thankful for the freedom of religion given by the state, the church accepts the dictum that religious discourse should not enter the public realm (and hence threaten the equilibrium of the contract or the freedoms of others). With the public square monopolized by the state, the turf of the church becomes the interiors of the human soul and the private lives of its members and converts. Ultimately the Bible becomes an authoritative word of personal salvation and an ethical manual to better living and improved life.[1]

We lament this alternative narrative not only because it reduces Jesus' gospel, but also because it domesticates the church we love and incarcerates the text that inspires us. We desperately want to liberate the Scriptures from the prisons of individualism and contesting authorities. This book is not only about a community hermeneutic or methodology of interpretation that works toward the liberation of the text; it is about the communities who receive the text as God's Word. Scriptural interpretation and Christian community have always had an enmeshed relationship. When we read the Bible as a personal salvation story and a self-improvement text, the church becomes a sanctuary for spiritual entitlements and an advocate for personal religious experiences. The Bible read as the cosmic metanarrative that describes God's intimate activity of the redemption of humanity and creation catalyzes communities with indefatigable hopes and bold embodiments of Christ's story. Throughout this book, we will stress the intimate and reciprocal causalities between Scripture reading and faithful communities.

The time is ripe, even urgent, both for the liberation of the text to once again reclaim its heritage as the cosmic story of hope, and for communities of faith to eagerly accept the mantle of cooperative and dialogical interpretation. Phyllis Tickle, in *The Great Emergence*, tells us that we are in the midst of another great rummage sale of ecclesial transition. Modernity and the Enlightenment are yielding to another season in the life of humanity and the church. The time is rife with new possibilities and new perils.[2] One of the great possibilities we pursue is a Bible received as God's Word for the church and the culture during this season of change.

We will present our thesis of and methodology for community hermeneutics in three distinct sections of advocacy, demonstration, and community practice. The first section, "Embracing the Text," advocates for the communal nature of the Scriptures. In individual chapters, we expose some of the biases that individuals bring to the text, argue for an understanding of the Bible as a living Word to be received and embodied by living communities of faith rather than a static text of abstract propositions, and advocate for a hermeneutics of peoplehood that transcends our fallibilities as individuals and receives the Scriptures in their fullest measure and grace.

The second section, "Turning to the Text," is a demonstration of a community in dialogue vulnerably accepting the call to interpret together. For this, we turn to the community we pastor, Emmaus Way, to model dialogue and the hermeneutics of peoplehood advocated for earlier. We will take four texts—an obscure text, an emotive text, a familiar text, and a controversial text—to show the full range of possibilities for this method.

In the third and final section, "The Intersection of Text and Community," we focus on five essential, sacred, and even sacramental community practices that are imagined, formed, inspired, and sustained by our reading of the Scriptures. The relationship of these practices to the text, though, is truly reciprocal. Each practice in turn shapes and informs our continued interaction with the text. The practices we explore are proclamation (sacred conversation), ethics (new creation declared in baptism), hospitality (the subversive table of the Eucharist), mission (the possibility of martyrdom), and imagination (the invitation to prayer).

In the end, we hope that we have sufficiently invited you to challenging labor and an exciting process of Scripture reading in community. But this is far more than a process. It is a conception of the identity of the Bible as a community text and a lifetime of community practices that keeps us intimate with God's revealed speech.

Ever since I (Tim) received that Tyndale *Living Bible* in the eighth grade, I have been a passionate reader and interpreter. It was truly frightening the first time I made the journey through the text alone.

I vividly remember thoughts of turning back in Numbers and abject terror when I got to Matthew 24. When I read this passage for the first time, I was scared and confused:

> So, when you see the horrible thing (told about by Daniel the prophet) standing in a holy place (Note to the reader: You know what is meant!), then those in Judea must flee into the Judean hills. Those on their porches must not even go inside to pack before they flee. Those in the fields should not return to their homes for their clothes.
> And woe to pregnant women and to those with babies in those days. And pray that your flight will not be in winter, or on the Sabbath. For there will be persecution such as the world has never before seen in all its history, and will never see again.
>
> verses 15–21, TLB

I started asking lots of questions. I began with my parents and moved rapidly to my church. Still dissatisfied, I started reading—and reading.

When I met Dan a few years ago, even before inviting him to join me in pastoring Emmaus Way, I was amazed by his love and passion for the text. Both of us have been gladly and frightfully formed in our interaction with the Bible. Most graciously, our passion for the text has driven us into the arms of the Christian community. If you knew us well, as passionate, strong-willed, overly confident individuals, you would know that our movement to community was at best a possibility and at worst a long shot. But Dan and I have both been asking questions and reading for a long time, and we are grateful that we don't do it alone. We are thankful for the communities that have received us and inspired a lifetime of dialogue with the text.

First and foremost among those communities are our friends at Emmaus Way. This book could not have been written without them. They are the true coauthors of this book. We have never met a more honest community. Each week we are inspired by their passion for dialogue, their vulnerable engagement with the text, and their graciousness directed toward us. Sharing the table of God's provision and grace with these friends has been a pure gift to us.

We want to thank our families for not only enduring the labor of writing but also contributing passionately to the thoughts in the book.

Elizabeth (Dan's wife) literally married right into this project. She has been an ever-gracious supporter and encouragement to Dan. If you knew Elizabeth, this would come as no surprise. My (Tim's) wife, Mimi, Keenan (our eighth-grade son), and Kendall (our sixth-grade daughter) have enthusiastically embraced another writing project and contributed to it with constant conversation and by offering me the freedom to retreat and write, even at great cost to themselves. Where the two of us are rich beyond measure is that Elizabeth, Mimi, Keenan, and Kendall "get" the hermeneutic we advocate without needing to be coerced. They practice hospitality, dialogue, and mission every day.

We also want to thank three communities that have greatly influenced our thoughts: our friends at Emergent Village, Duke Divinity School, and Mars Hill Graduate School. Baker Books has been a wonderful partner to Emergent Village, and it has been an honor not only to write in the ēmersion line but also to serve on its editorial board. Chad Allen is to be thanked for believing in this project—and listening to me talk about it for years. Carla Barnhill and Doug Pagitt, both true friends, have worked kindly and diligently to get this book to publication. Carla's editing of this text was absolutely stellar. Like so many other books before it, this manuscript became so much more with Carla's attention and guidance.

Tonight, we'll once again begin the long road to Easter by sharing in the liturgy of penitence, ashes, and hope in the embrace of a community that eagerly seeks to live passionately and missionally in the living Word of God. In confession, we'll be reminded that we don't have a full vision of God's grace and mercy and have often fallen short of those gifts. But at the Eucharist table, we will join our community and the whole body of Christ in receiving God's gifts and constructing shared lives that proclaim this hope. We humbly hope that this project will offer a small gift in our shared lives as readers of God's Word and living embodiments of its message. May God's Word truly be "free for all," a text liberated in hopeful communities.

Tim Conder and Dan Rhodes
Ash Wednesday, 2009

Part 1

Embracing the Text

→ 1

Boundaries and Biases

The Lenses of Interpretation

My (Tim's) childhood home sat on an outer acre of my grandfather's farm. Living in the country in a far more innocent time, my brother, my cousins, and I were allowed to wander the farm at will. The numerous outbuildings, parked farm machinery, cow pastures, dog pens, and central orchard functioned as an inexhaustible playground of discovery, adventure, and imaginary play. As our teenage years approached, even my grandfather's old blue pickup—with the Swisher Sweets cigars in the familiar red box "hidden" under the front seat—became the site of mild rebellion.

This was our world. In the winter, when the trees were denuded of leaves, I could look across the soybean fields to a series of fence lines that marked the outer boundaries of the property. Even now, I can close my eyes and recall the jagged journey the barbed-wire fence—covered in tangled vines, kudzu, and blackberry-laden briars—made around the property. I remember the path of the low electric wire that dissected the farm, kept the cows in the pasture, and brought a rude awakening to more than a few young boys playing baseball in those same fields. I can see the gentle slope of our yard, the gravel driveway down to the ditch, and the country road that marked the impenetrable line between "us" and "them."

It's not entirely surprising that my memory of the farm and our modest home seems to focus on the fences and boundary lines. These boundaries defined our space. They were stable memorials of the familiarity, safety, confined exploration, and identity of a nurturing and sheltered childhood. Knowing the boundaries made me feel safe. It made life a little more predictable. It gave me a clear sense of where I belonged.

After many years of pastoral ministry, we are fully aware that fences and boundary lines are eagerly sought out within the realm of faith (even by self-proclaimed "rebels"). The community we lead constantly engages questions about artistic, ethical, missional, and personal boundaries. Our old day-timers and PalmPilot files are littered with pastoral appointments driven by questions like, "What are appropriate sexual boundaries for my life?" "How much money and time should I contribute to this fellowship?" "Is that interpretation of a specific biblical text consistent with our beliefs or doctrine?" "How and how often should I pray?" "How can we justify the existence of a loving and gracious God given these circumstances?" Each of these questions is a request for borders to define and shape one's identity, belief structures, ethical choices, activities, and sense of security as a Christian. Even those who like to journey far afield in their faith, often do so with a clearly defined sense of non-negotiables.

The people in our churches are prone to think about their Bibles the way I remember our old family farm. Those who have read these sacred texts their whole lives find warm familiarity, tangible safety, and a distinct identity in the words of Scripture. The Bible's well-worn pages, creased bindings, and aged markings become elements of a personalized version of the text, one that produces a secure treasury of spiritual conceptions, an established code of morality and spirituality, and a confined set of possibilities. It not only inspires us but also keeps us within the pastures of right living.

If only it were that simple.

Over and over, we find that the Bible simply refuses to be *our* Bible. The Scriptures repeatedly leap beyond the boundaries of safety into uncharted lands of mystery, irresolvable tension, and offended propriety. Just as the fence line of my grandfather's farm didn't ultimately keep us "in"—I don't live there anymore—an honest reading of the Bible eventually forces us beyond the confines of interpretation that we so habitually employ. In this straying, the adventures of transformation and the debates of orthodoxy rage in perpetual struggle.

But we're getting ahead of ourselves here. Before rushing headlong into this passionate adventure of interpretation, before we begin to press for a new *modus operandi* of reading the Bible, we want to ask you to examine, as we also continue to do, the biases that shape your interpretation of these sacred texts. We will argue that any reading of the Bible is inextricably linked to the boundaries and biases created by our experiences (our wounds, joys, and life stories) and the specific contexts in which we read the Bible (our geography, our relational background and associations, and our educational training, to name a few).

This assertion doesn't need to be a calamity or a scandalous admission. In fact, the purpose of this book is to invite you to realize how the experiences, knowledge, perspective, and insight of a diverse community can liberate the Bible from unnecessary confines and unleash its transformative narrative in your life and the life of your church. If you'll offer us the gift of patience, we believe you too will see the wealth of power the Scriptures can have for your church by reading the text with and in a diverse, practicing community. Exposing the fence lines of our biases, predispositions, experiences, and contexts requires an admission that these boundaries exist and that they exert some authority over our reading of the Bible. Only when we acknowledge the boundaries we place around the text can we begin to understand it in deeper, fresher ways.

We actually bring these biases to nearly every part of our lives. Consider our belief in medical "expertise." Just the other night while I (Dan) was watching television, a commercial came on for Requip (ropinirole HCl), the newly FDA-approved medication to treat Restless Leg Syndrome. With the assuring image of what appeared to be many well-trained experts in white coats attesting to the truth of this disease, I began to pay closer attention; perhaps I was suffering from RLS without knowing it. A woman's voice on the commercial asked: "Do you sometimes have a compelling urge to move your legs?" *Well, now that you mention it* . . . The commercial continued: "Does moving your legs provide temporary relief?" *It kind of does* . . . The commercial asked: "Do your leg symptoms begin or get worse when sitting, lying down, or trying to rest?" *They must because I didn't even notice the pain until I sat down to watch TV.* Finally, the commercial inquired: "Does your pain get worse at night?" *Absolutely, I definitely have this condition because I'm always more sore at night, like right now, than during the working day!* My hypochondriac brain quickly moved from the belief I was reasonably healthy to a state of near-panic over a disease that's been diagnosed by a TV commercial.

It's amazing what we can find when we are told what to look for. Sometimes even a simple suggestion can lead us to misread common ailments as the "symptoms" of a horrible disease. It just goes to show that we humans often find what we are looking for; we see what we think we are going to see, and we read exactly what we expect to read.

Anyone who works in or keeps up with the field of scientific research understands that this happens all the time. Scholars pen article after article in journals challenging the findings of the latest experiment, claiming that the former researcher manipulated the data so as to discover her own hypothesis. Some scientists look at the fossil record and see indisputable evidence of evolution; creation scientists look at the same fossil record and see the undeniable truth of creation. One need not argue for the complete relativity of truth to realize that we often do find exactly what we are looking for, even when we are trying to be completely honest and objective. This tendency isn't bad; it's just part of human nature and the way we make sense of the world.

When it comes to reading the Bible, things are no different. We have all learned to read the Scriptures in a particular way. Many of us learned to interpret Scripture by listening to our preachers or by becoming involved with in-home Bible studies. Some of us learned how to find the meaning of a text by taking classes in colleges or seminaries. Still others of us learned specific methods by using popular study Bibles or devotional guides. We even pick up messages about how to read the Bible from our families, careers, or hobbies. Each of these influences passes on certain rules and regulations we are meant to use when interpreting what we read in the Bible; they function as an authority (occasionally visible and recognized, but usually invisible) in guiding and disciplining our reading of Scripture. In a sense, they give us a prescription for interpretive "glasses" through which we read the text from then on. We had a vivid experience recently that demonstrates the magnitude of our biases in judgment (and anticipating a critical point we'll make later—the importance of community in confronting our biases) when we acted as pastoral support for a friend of ours. He was going through an ecclesial "trial" where he faced excommunication from his former denomination—in which he had served as an elder—due to his recent divorce.

Like most divorces, his included much failure and blame on both sides, a volume of "facts" that were easily disputable based on perspective, and some very deep wounds. He had become a part of our church community just as his marriage was beginning to unravel. He had spent many hours with our staff tearfully confessing his failures, sharing his wounds, looking for signs of forgiveness, and hoping to see the marks of God's redemptive presence in his life. After long reflection, he felt that it was a critical step in his confession and absolution to attend the trial, even though he had already resigned his eldership and hadn't attended a church in that denomination for more than two years.

During the examination, one of the accusing council members kindly introduced himself to us as an engineer, presumably to expose to the council his rational problem-solving skills. From his perspective, the case appeared to be a matter of sharply contrasting binaries— sin or the absence of sin, guilt or the absence of guilt, failure as a husband and elder, or the failure of his former spouse. The task of the council was to consult the teaching of Scripture, and then apply proper blame and consequence on the offending person. There was more than a presupposition about the nature of marriage and human relationships in this statement. There was also an assumption that when properly interpreted, the Bible comfortably supports this view and the judgments demanded by it.

His bias jumpstarted our bias as pastors who constantly traffic in the broken spaces of life and faith. We constantly deal with the wheat-and-tare complexities of sin, brokenness, and God-spoken mercies in the lives of our community. (Many weeks end with us wishing there *were* simply binaries or quick fixes we could apply to some of these situations.) We have a hard time saying that the demise of any relationship breaks down to a simple binary of who's right and who's wrong. In our opinion, the lives represented in this case did not fit well in closed-set binaries. The situation was a horrible mess of "both/ands," a complex web of damage, heartbreak, sin, and anger.

Our pastoral bias naturally catalyzes reactions of compassion and empathy, but we are aware that it can in turn be a barrier to making hard decisions. Our vantage point also reveals a presupposition that the Scriptures are filled with wisdom, that they dramatically describe the human plight, and that they tell the story of God's redemption of humanity but often do not yield hard-and-fast criteria for judgments such as this.

In this case, the confluence of our biases and interests, the council's need for sound judgment on a delicate matter that their polity demanded they address, and our desire to reveal the complexities of the lives represented and to care for our community member, yielded a gracious outcome. The council decided the best jurisdiction in the matter was our community, which cleared the way for us to continue on our path of care for our friend.

No matter how we obtain our interpretive lenses, each of us has them. They shape the way we interpret the Bible, leading us to emphasize certain conclusions and assertions while virtually ignoring other possibilities. In the remaining pages of this chapter, we will expose seven biases or lenses that, although we may not realize it, often fence us into a particular reading of the text. This list is clearly and intentionally incomplete. But we think many of these perspectives will resonate with you as the reader.

The Lens of Systematic Theology

One of the main forces at play when we read the Bible, whose presence strongly influences the meaning we find in the words of Scripture, is that of a systematic theology. Systematic theologies, as the name implies, are organized systems of belief that offer coherent structure to the perceived message of the Scriptures.

One of the great urban legends from my (Tim's) seminary days includes an in-class episode involving a student asking a "forbidden" question. The professor allegedly in the middle of this story was a distinguished scholar and regular visiting lecturer. The professor had garnered a reputation for giving students A's when they replicated his theology on tests and giving F's to those who took divergent views. And whether that was true or not, the following story was religiously told as a warning to first-year seminarians who were about to take his introductory survey class.

As the story goes, a student asked a question that whimsically implied some limits to the sovereignty of God (an indispensable element of this professor's theological system). The quick and fiery response from the podium was, "Only Satan would ask that question! Next question—please!" As you can imagine, few hands were raised in the class from that day on.

The systematic theologies we affirm tend to police and limit the possible ways of understanding what we read in the text. Systematic theologies act to regulate and define a legitimate way of reading the text even before we approach the Bible; we might even say these theologies create an understanding of the text before we read it, determining beforehand what we will find there. Anyone who attempts to read outside the lines of the theological system accepted and assumed by their community or context will be sure to feel tension and perhaps even the full wrath of formal or informal authorities. The power of a systematic theology determines what we are allowed to find and how we are to read, often taking the bite out of tough texts and rendering banal even the most exciting and enigmatic of passages when they appear to threaten the system.

For example, Romans 7 is one of the most visceral and seemingly relevant passages in the New Testament to readers of any era. The apostle Paul, a man with seemingly limitless faith that persevered through shipwrecks, personal pain, brutal beatings, and incarceration, makes a startling confession about moral failure: "But I am unspiritual, sold as a slave to sin. I do not understand what I do. For what I want to do I do not do, but what I hate I do. . . . For I have the desire to do what is good, but I cannot carry it out. For what I do is not the good I want to do; no, the evil I do not want to do—this I keep on doing" (Rom. 7:14–15, 18–19).

These are fresh words, unexpected and deeply encouraging to most readers, especially us! It's like the "perfect" kid in the church youth group
whom your parents constantly badgered you to emulate is admitting
that she steals cigarettes from the convenience store. The valedictorian
is telling us that he cheated on a couple exams. Whew! All this time we
thought we were the only ones messing up this faith thing.

Most of us love this text because it not only humanizes Paul but also
gives us a little personal grace. But is this what the passage means? Some
commentators read the text as an admission from the great apostle
of the difficulty or impossibility of living without sin. But others adamantly state that this is Paul's description of his past, pre-conversion
life when he was under the rule of law. The difference between these
two possibilities is substantial and is largely due to the theological
system to which the interpreter subscribes.

Even the great Martin Luther was not immune to letting his systematic theology determine his reading of Scripture. Luther's theological
conclusion on the issue of works and faith led him to refer to the whole
book of James as "the Epistle of Straw."[1] The strong emphasis on the
actions of faith in James did not easily align with Luther's understanding of faith, and his systematic theology gave him great disdain for this
letter to the point of wishing to have it removed from the canon.

Systematic theologies are not inherently wrong. After all, it was the
formation of basic theological understandings that assisted the church in
selecting which texts to include in the canon of Scripture. But theology
must always be understood as the servant of the gospel, a tool for the
preaching and practices of the church community. Our organized theologies can bring with them the danger of forcing our interpretative decisions
to work along the system's prescribed outline. And that is when we begin
to read the text in order to support a theology we already hold, rather
than letting the Scripture form and move our theology.

The Lens of Science and Scientific Method

In the early part of the nineteenth century, Thomas Jefferson declared
that true religion was devoid of all mystery. Steeped in the scientific
prejudice of the Enlightenment, Jefferson composed his own version

of the Bible, cutting out all the miracles and miraculous stories. In his mind, science determined what was historically possible and anything that could not be proved by science was to be left to the arena of ghosts, goblins, wizardry, and mythical inventions.

A few years ago I (Dan) had the opportunity to visit Tunisia, a small country on the northern coast of Africa. Set against the magnificently blue waters of the Mediterranean Sea, Tunisia is home to the ancient city of Carthage—one of the largest cities in the ancient Roman world and an important location in the history of the Christian church. Just south of the ruins of Carthage lies Tunis, the capital of Tunisia, an old trading city founded by the Berbers sometime around 2000 BC. In the seventh century AD, this old city came under the control of Arab Muslims, and it was at this time that the medina was built. The medina, in the center of the current-day sprawling metropolis, is the old city, a trading center with extremely narrow streets, fantastic smells, large mosques, crowded shops, and bustling business. Needless to say, it is an extremely hard place to navigate.

During my trip there, while touring the medina, I wandered off to shop for gifts to bring back to my friends and family. Map in hand, it didn't seem to be a big deal to head just down the narrow corridor of a street to find that perfect object conveying the beauty and history of North Africa. Rather quickly, however, I became disoriented, losing my bearings and not knowing how to return to the tour group. It was at this point that I discovered my map to be completely unhelpful. Barely able to read a word of Arabic, I had no idea where I was and therefore had no idea how to locate myself on the map. After a deep and anxious prayer for help and a quick confession of every sin I could remember having committed in the past year, I tried—in broken and Spanish-sounding French—to ask one of the shopkeepers how to get to the North Gate. Realizing this was going nowhere and feeling an overwhelming sense of desperation rising in my stomach, I turned around, thank God, to see the tour group passing right behind me.

In recent decades, a great deal of our reading of the Bible has followed in the wake of Jefferson, the Enlightenment, and philosophies like Scottish commonsense realism. Those influences work like a map written in a foreign language. They are meant to navigate a world that is very different from the world of faith and when we follow them blindly, we end up dreadfully lost. While we don't believe science is anti-Christian, we do think it's important to remind ourselves of what scientific method was first developed to do. Using scientific method as a lens for reading Scripture does not often lead to faith in God, because this is not what scientific method was developed to do. The roots of scientific method developed during the sixteenth and seventeenth centuries in response to the perceived problems with theology and humanism. Instead of focusing on humans or on God as the basis for understanding the world, scientific method turns its attention to nature, focusing not on what things are but on how things work.

Yet armed with a method focused on how nature works, Christians, both liberal and conservative, have had extreme difficulty trying to answer theological and anthropological questions, which seek to tell us who God is and who we are as human beings. We've found ourselves lost in the city of God, trying to find our way out with a map of the city of nature.

For many liberal (a word we use in its most generic sense) Christians, the domination of the lens of scientific method has tended to lead further and further down the path toward a Christianity defined as "religious experience," meaning a private feeling that each person possesses as a sense of the transcendent. Hence, God's interaction with the world tends to look more like a revival of humanism—a celebration of human potential at the expense of any real need to speak of Christ's death, resurrection, or return.

A reaction to this type of prejudice emerged in conservative (also the generic sense) Christian thought. Unfortunately it was a reaction that bought into the same scientific presuppositions. For conservatives, the application of this method led to a solidified understanding of the laws of nature as the laws of God. Since scientific method was thought to be the sole procedure for accessing truth, knowledge of God also needed to play by these rules and remain subject to their demonstration. In response to the modern liberal tendency to call all things that aren't "science" into question, many theologians began to claim that all of Scripture was scientific historical fact, and that this could be proved if we just looked hard enough. As a result, the doctrine of the inerrancy of Scripture (and even the use of this term belies its indebtedness to scientific method) soon emerged.

What we have sometimes failed to realize, however, is the extent to which the regime of scientific method dominates what we find in the text of the Bible. Through the lens of scientific method, the biblical narrative becomes a series of provable historical facts, and the critical issues of faith become the fight for creationism against evolution or the discovery of the remains of Sodom and Gomorrah. Giving science too much control over our reading soon places us in a real crisis: the text must now live up to scientific criteria which were—in part—developed as a prejudice against it. A Christian reading the text ends up with only one of two options here: (1) to pull Christianity out of the arena of true scientific knowledge by making it a set of inward, personal, and non-public beliefs, or (2) to force Christianity to fit into the mold of science, by claiming that God must fit the criteria of demonstrable fact. Either way it seems that much of the text is lost.

The Lens of "Rights" and "Causes"

We live in a rights-crazy culture. Solidified within the way we view reality is the notion that each of us has the right to freedom, self-expression, speech, religion, and action. To be human is to be a bundle of rights. As Stanley Hauerwas and Will Willimon observe, "It has thus become our [culture's] unquestioned assumption that every person has the 'right' to develop his or her own potential to the greatest possible extent, limited only to the parallel of rights of others."[2] In fact, we believe in this basic cultural tenet so much that we have become determined to find it in the pages of Scripture despite the fact that Scripture never speaks of humans in this way. The danger is that often this may lead us to reading the Bible in such a way as to rob it of its challenges, as if the text is merely meant to affirm and ordain my way of life and the causes I stand for. In this way we attempt to read rights language into every sentence of the Bible in order to justify our lives so we never have to face the call to repentance. Defending our rights, we can reduce the Scriptures to a list of human entitlements enforced and established by a God who loves us—meaning a God who does what we want and would never call us to change.

Yet despite our best attempts, the Bible just does not boil down to a treatise on human rights. One would be hard pressed to interpret the narrative of Abraham's near sacrifice of Isaac in Genesis 22 in terms of human rights. Similarly, it would be hard to read Paul's concern over promiscuity (or even marriage for that matter) if one began with the assumption of sexual experiences as entitlements. When our reading of Scripture gets taken hostage by this powerful force, the text becomes more about us than about God. We begin to read the story as "my" story, superimposing ourselves over the true subject, God. We must remember that in terms of liberation, Scripture only knows freedom as the freedom to serve God.

Activism, though altruistic and clearly less self-serving, can function in a similar manner to the protection of our rights. The passion we hold for our "causes" can become our starting point with the text, requiring the text to affirm not only our causes but also our particular understanding of those causes. In a memorable episode of *Seinfeld*, Elaine, perpetually disappointed by romance, finally meets the perfect guy. He is kind, attractive, and completely "into her." But in casual conversation, he mentions offhand that he is "pro-life." Elaine is devastated, declaring with a stiff upper lip that she could never date a guy who wasn't "pro-choice." Eventually, she finds that she has to say good-bye to the man she has probably been searching for her whole life. Our relationship with the text can easily echo Elaine's path when we demand that it conform to our causes.

Without a doubt, the roots of ecological activism can be found in the biblical doctrine of creation, a call to social justice proceeds from both the theocratic demands of Israel's economy and Jesus' haunting words in the Sermon on the Mount, and an unassailable demand for racial reconciliation leaps off the page in the expectation of Israel's treatment of aliens and Paul's doctrine of a church where there was neither Jew nor Greek. We believe that the Bible, read honestly and openly, should propel us into lives of committed and relentless activism. But when we begin with our causes or are insensitive to the power they have over our perspectives, the likely outcome is a reduction of the biblical text to a manifesto for our causes and a referendum for our specific policies related to these causes.

A recently published critical commentary on the administration of President George W. Bush was entitled *Dead Certain*, an obvious allusion to the strength of President Bush's convictions, a potential absence of dialogue with other perspectives, and the deadly implications of his policies.[3] Particularly in the passionate realms of rights and causes, we tend to open our Bibles already "dead certain." We do so to the detriment of a text that should confront us beyond all our certainties.

The Lens of "Success" and "Growth"

The interpretative lens of "success" and "growth" is a close cousin to the "rights and causes" lens and is a ubiquitous prejudice in reading Scripture, particularly in our American culture. Like a Starbucks on every urban corner, the promise that a commitment to Christ and commitment to a defined Christian lifestyle will lead to improvement in the quality of our lives, growth in our bottom line, and the provision of a variety of other "benefits" can quickly become part of the landscape of a contemporary reading of Scripture.

One of the first conversations Dan and I had came in the parking lot of a church we both attended at the time. We quickly realized that we had a similar critique about a guest preacher's sermon on the rich young ruler (Matt. 19:16–30; Luke 18:18–30), a New Testament encounter where a rich, devout young man asks Jesus what he needs to do to have eternal life. Jesus matter-of-factly tells him to sell all of his possessions and give the proceeds to the poor! The sermon that day began with this strenuously delivered disclaimer by the speaker: "Now, we know that God does not really call us to give all of our money away." His sermon, however, left us asking, are we so sure that God doesn't call at least some of us to give away our assets? Really? Is this always a passage that speaks to spiritual priorities rather than an all-out rejection of materialism?

The lens of success and growth is such a common and welcome guest in our interpretation that it frequently yields a range of apologies and explanations of Jesus' teachings. In our culture, there is a huge temptation to manipulate the text to justify our lifestyles. While it may be well known that the Bible speaks about money more than any other issue, many of us have no idea what it says about money. We just know what we would like it to say and we are content to argue away the tension.

Peter Waldo, a Frenchman from Lyon and a wealthy merchant who lived at the end of the twelfth century, clearly felt that the text offered some different possibilities. After hearing the moving story of a young man named Alexis, who was faced with losing everything his Roman parents would bequeath to him because of his choice to follow Christ, Waldo went to his priest to ask what he needed to do to be like Christ. The priest instructed him to follow Jesus' words to the rich young ruler in Matthew: "If you want to be perfect, go, sell your possessions and give to the poor, and you will have treasure in heaven. Then come, follow me" (Matt. 19:21). In response, Waldo set up an account to provide for his wife, put his daughters in a cloister, and gave the rest of his money to the poor. Then, throwing his coins into the street, he addressed his fellow townspeople with these words: "Friends, fellow townsmen, I am not out of my mind, as you may think. Rather, I am avenging myself upon these enemies of my life who enslave me, so that I cared more for gold pieces than for God and served the creature more than the Creator."[4]

Waldo's actions do not fit with the laws of our economics. His interpretation does not seem to be one that we would entertain for the slightest moment. In a world of free market economics, a reading of this text from Matthew would often lead us to assuage the wealthy man, telling him that he will be able to help many more people if he will just act in his own interest. Taking our cue from Adam Smith's well-known statement in *The Wealth of Nations*, we would look fondly on Waldo's attempt at Christian charity but we would remind him that: "It is not from the benevolence of the butcher, the brewer, or the baker, that we expect our dinner, but from their regard to their own interest. We address ourselves, not to their humanity but to their self-love, and never talk to them of their own necessities but of their advantages."[5] Reading the text in any other way is just too naive. Yet serious problems inevitably arise when we read the Bible through the lens of Adam Smith, for it seems that at times we have not really read the text at all.

We minister in a young congregation that is saturated with people who have been disillusioned and even broken by the dishonesties of a Christianity shaped by reading the Bible through the lens of growth and success. Too often the message of the church is that embracing Christianity will heighten every avenue of life—marriage, sex, business, friendship, and significance. But the way of Jesus might push us to downwardly mobile lives. Faithful Christians are laid off, rejected, and ignored just as often as those who do not proclaim our faith—maybe more!

By no means do we mean to imply that the Bible does not make economic promises; it would be hard to read the Old Testament without a strong economic emphasis. But to the extent that we import into these economic promises the lifestyles we see on E! Television or MTV's *Cribs*, we miss the communal nature of Hebrew and Christian economic success. Blessing, financial or otherwise, was always a blessing upon the whole people of God, not an individual blessing where one person of the community is given a wealth one hundred times that of his brother or sister. We must be careful when we begin to read our own success too deeply into the Scripture, for the Bible has always been a book about God and God's people, not individual success stories.

The Lens of Nationalism and Sentimentality

On the first anniversary of the World Trade Center bombings, President Bush made a speech in New York commemorating the horrific events of that dreadful day. His speech, however, was rife with some troubling allusions and biblical echoes. In his speech, the president claimed that the "ideal of America is the hope of all mankind." The president would push the syncretism of America and the kingdom of God even further, saying, "That hope [which is America] still lights our way. And the light shines in the darkness. And the darkness has not overcome it." Jim Wallis was quick to notice the fact that these sentences of the speech are lifted from the first chapter of the Gospel of John and to consequently point out the danger of the president's nationalistic interpretation of Scripture in his "Dangerous Religion."[6]

Similarly, the Presidential Prayer Team along with Church World Direct, Inc., sent out an e-mail offer in the weeks prior to the national

Patriot Day, a day of commemoration on September 11, promoting
its "Patriot Day Preacher's Package." Among the items included in
this package was the "moving 'Great Is Thy Faithfulness' church
video," which included comforting words from the president himself
and a slide with the backdrop of an American flag emblazoned with
a script telling the viewers to put their hope in God. It also included
a series of PowerPoint graphics for use during the Sunday sermon,
and even a sermon manuscript bearing the title "A Hopeful Lesson
Learned" based on Lamentations 3:19–23. The words of these verses
from Lamentations read:

> The thought of my affliction and my homelessness
>   is wormwood and gall!
> My soul continually thinks of it
>   and is bowed down within me.
> But this I call to mind,
>   and therefore I have hope:
> The steadfast love of the Lord never ceases,
>   his mercies never come to an end;
> they are new every morning;
>   great is your faithfulness.
>
> NRSV

But these words of a destitute prophet uttered on behalf of a nation
on the verge of destruction and exile need a bit of stretching if they
are to find a home in promoting the nationalism of one of the most
powerful and wealthy political entities in existence.

These are striking examples of nationalism and biblical interpretation. But most of us occasionally fall prey to more subtle forms of
nationalism that make their way into our interpretation of Scripture,
quietly intermingling the biblical vision of God's kingdom with our
national pride and hopes. Yes, we ought to be thankful for the freedom
we have in our nation, and there's nothing wrong with taking pride
in our country, but our nationalistic affections can easily subsume
the meaning of the text.

There are many other national sentiments that guide our reading of
the Bible in similar ways. For example, we often remember America's
past as being much better than it was. Many times we allow a feeling

of nostalgia for what life used to be like to sneak into our interpretation and force a "good-ole-days" reading of the gospel. Although our personal and collective histories have moments of great triumph and joy, an honest study of the past reveals no season of utopia. The early days of the United States were not an evangelical camp meeting. Greed, crime, promiscuity, and racism were all well represented. Romantic views of a particular season in our social history are often just that—a naive telling of a past that obscures problems for the sake of story.

Sentimental views of the past can reduce the Bible's cosmic and transcendent narrative of redemption to a road map back to a "better time." National myths ("America is God's favored nation"), historical myths ("Remember when people used to fear God?"), and familial myths ("Our family always finds a way through every circumstance because of God's blessing") not only trivialize our theologies, they also threaten to render trite the transformative voice of the Scriptures.

The Lens of Moralism and Heroism

In Nick Hornby's novel *How to Be Good*, Katie Carr—a good person, a physician, a mother, a wife, and a liberal thinker—wrestles with what it means to "be good." At one point in the novel, she engages the vicar of the local church concerning the issues she is having in her marriage. Of course the vicar is hesitant to answer. "It's not much to ask," Katie says. "Stay or go, that's all I want. God, why are you people so timid? It's no wonder the churches are empty, when you can't answer even the simplest questions. Don't you get it? That's what we want. Answers. If we wanted woolly-minded nonsense we'd stay at home."[7]

Katie speaks for many of us. After all, most of the time we do want answers. We want to know how to live our lives and we want to know right now. That's why often we attempt to approach Scripture as a blueprint or manual for life, wherein the characters of the stories illustrate simple morals of life, teaching us what and what not to do.

The problem with this type of reading is simply that the text does not read this way. Many of us have experienced the frustration and

confusion that attempting to live out the morals of the Bible has created for us. As an exasperated Ned Flanders once said on an episode
of *The Simpsons*, "I've done everything the Bible says—even the stuff
that contradicts the other stuff!" As pastors, however, it seems to
us that the instinct of Hornby's vicar is the right one: hesitate. The
vicar's faith and his own struggles with the text cause him to resist an
appeal to provide simple moralistic answers because the Bible refuses
to be forced into a compilation of moral teachings. The Scripture is
instead more like a narrative, whose subject is God and not necessarily human action. The tendency to moralize the text may distort
the action of God in the drama of the pages and persuade us to put
more emphasis than is warranted on the actions of the characters
and ourselves.

In a sermon aimed at young people, a well-known Christian speaker
focused his talk on the courtship and marriage of Rebekah and Isaac
in Genesis 24. In this sermon he analyzed the steps Isaac took to
prepare himself for marriage and the actions he and Rebekah made
together to ensure their healthy marriage, pointing out to the young
adult listeners the importance of doing the same. Listening with an
ever-increasing sense of aggravation, we were distraught by this por-
trayal of Christian dating based upon moralizing the actions of Isaac
and Rebekah. Our concern lay not in the points about dating that the
speaker made, but in the style of reading the Scripture he employed
in order to preach these points. Could there be a more dysfunctional
couple than these two? After all, are we to continue to view Isaac as
such a role model when he gives his wife over to King Abimelech two
chapters later in Genesis 26? In Genesis 27, Rebekah returns the favor
by cheating her beloved husband on behalf of Jacob, a son she favors
over her elder son, Esau. Some sacred romance!

Now, if the sermon series was "How to Create a Dysfunctional Family," then Isaac and Rebekah have done much to commend themselves
as "heroes." But idealizing the courtship and marriage of Isaac and
Rebekah betrays the reality of their relationship and its function in
the biblical narrative. Allowing ourselves to read the narrative *without*
a sense of moralism or heroism leads us to see that the marriage of
these two figures is never really a good one. Taking off the "moralism"
glasses helps us sense some significant theological implications in the

narrative to which we can be blinded when we are looking for some quick life application. The story behind the story is that God remains at work with real people and is perpetually faithful by redeeming failure after failure. Even more broadly, the narrative points out that God's great project of redemption is not thwarted by humanity's predisposition to greed, selfishness, and fear.

Everyone likes a hero. However, reading the Bible in an effort to find heroes and heroines of the faith inevitably leads to contortionist interpretations on the text. This can be especially true in children's, youth, and young adult ministries where our constituents are often less jaded (at least until they read the Bible!) in the search for a heroic role model. All of us have some predisposition to make the characters of the Bible into larger-than-life figures. We desperately need to remind ourselves that God is indeed the only hero of this narrative.

The Lens of Tribal Loyalty

In the Christian community, the loyalties we have as Protestants, Catholics, liberals, evangelicals, or any other tribal division are powerful forces that certainly operate as an interpretative fence that influences (and limits) the possibilities of meaning as we read Scripture. The examples of this reality are countless. In fact, this final lens on our list might be most restrictive in our reading of Scripture—or at least the most vindictive when scorned. It's said that "hell hath no fury like a woman scorned." We wonder if the author of that proverb ever met a Christian whose denomination or tradition was being dismissed or challenged.

Occasionally our tribal loyalties are obvious, marked by statements like, "We're Catholic, so we believe . . ." But affirmations of belief also presuppose or demand certain interpretations of Scripture. A teetotaler Baptist might think "non-fermented juice" when they see "wine" in the text associated with the actions of Jesus, even though that interpretation is very difficult to sustain (like in John 2:1–11 where Jesus turns water into wine at a wedding in Cana). Wesleyans and Pentecostals are likely to see their perspectives on "holiness" throughout the Bible. Theological arguments like the one that arises

from the Romans 7 passage become battlegrounds of tribal territo-
rialism as various traditions seek to defend their system of theology
or their essential beliefs.

We have already used the terms *liberal/mainline* and *conservative/
evangelical* and will continue to do so often. The church is gradually
emerging from a century where Protestants have been sharply divided
by a theological civil war (though Catholics and other traditions have
not been immune to the issues involved). Sociologists and church
historians have strongly asserted that the fundamentalist/modernist
controversy at the beginning of the twentieth century eventually forged
a virtual two-denomination church landscape of evangelicals/conser-
vatives (the heirs of the "fundamentalist" movement) and mainliners/
liberals (the progeny of the "modernists"). These original terms have
become either linguistically discredited (we now typically use the
term *fundamentalist* to denote political or dangerous radicals) or
nonsensical (in an era of burgeoning postmodernism, to claim to be a
"modernist" could be construed as a rejection of progressive thought
and the opposite of the original intent of this label).

Though the monikers have changed, the controversy and sharp
division largely remains. Very broadly, historically evangelicals/con-
servatives tend toward more literal readings of an error-free Bible
(emphasizing the divine origin of the Scriptures). The evangelical
gospel centers on a broken relationship between God and humanity (sin), personal salvation offered to all but only received by some
(particularism) by faith in the sacrifice of Jesus Christ as a payment
for that sin (substitutionary atonement), and the promise of a future
reign of God (a focus on the future and eternity as the true kingdom
of God). The evangelicals' innate particularism and hopes in eternity
catalyze programs oriented toward personal evangelism.

Again broadly, historically liberals/mainliners have also valued the
Bible but do not assume it to be without error. They have interpreted
the text by scientific and critical methods (highlighting the human
component in the writing and compilation of the Bible and challenging
the supernatural elements of the text). The liberal gospel often trades
the sinfulness of humanity for an emphasis on the innate goodness
of creation, which in turn universalizes the benefits of salvation and
moralizes the work of Christ. Corresponding to these shifts is a pref-

erence for a message of the present reign of God and the universality of faith in the here and now. This encourages programs for education and social justice rather than evangelism.

These are vast generalizations and both movements have transitioned in message and tone as our culture has moved into postmodernity. But for our argument, this long division filled with accusation and mistrust has created two warring tribes that have subsumed even traditional denominational loyalties. In the last part of the twentieth century, someone leaving the church family and looking for another would not necessarily search for a church in the same denomination. But if she were an evangelical, she would definitely look for another "Bible-teaching," "fundamental," "evangelizing" church. If she were a liberal, she would seek another "open-minded," "progressive," "justice-oriented" fellowship. These idioms reveal both the values of the tribe and the thinly veiled critiques of the other side.

We share this overview here for two reasons. First, as you read on, if you're looking to place us squarely in one camp or the other, you're likely to be frustrated. The mainline/evangelical divide has been forged in an era dominated by individualism. The hermeneutic we recommend challenges many of the social and philosophical roots of this individualism. It also liberates the text from some of the excesses of modernity and finds new spaces of meaning often precluded by the firmly defended borders of both liberalism and evangelicalism. The second reason is that so many students of the Bible are in interpretative bondage due to tribalism—either out of fear of straying from their tradition or of overreaction to the faults of their heritage.

I (Tim) have experienced the fury of a scorned tribalism many times in my professional life. My ordination council came off like a dark gothic novel partly because I did not accept the label "literalist" (which was a mandatory evangelical code word for one of my examiners even though my conservative seminary also eschewed this term), and I defended the ordination of women. So many seminarians graduating from Duke Divinity School (where several congregants in Emmaus Way are students or alums) or Mars Hill Graduate School (where I'm a board member) tell me similar horror stories from their job searches about the inflexible and punitive demands of tribalism. I have joked often in public forums that the residuals of this religious civil war are often so harsh that young leaders have to decide which group they will have to lie to in order to be employed or get ordained.

These are but a few of the boundaries, biases, and fence lines that motivate, shape, and even exercise authority over our reading of the Bible. In addition to these seven common lenses, regionalism, language, education, personal experiences, key relationships, and so many other factors shape, confine, and inspire our interpretative acts. We believe this is a critical question of self, community, and cultural reflection. Our contexts matter greatly.

As we conclude this partial list of boundaries and biases, we want to quickly assert that there is no "pure" reading of the Bible. Our interpretation of these texts never exists as some abstract, objective, culture-free reading. Hence our goal going forward will not be to search for a pure reading. Our posture is just the opposite. Acknowledging our biases can lead us to practices of interpretation that free the Bible to take us to transformative, redemptive, and even unimagined places.

As we begin this journey, our next step will be to consider an immensely significant theme—our understanding of the very nature of the Bible. This presupposition is a lens of interpretation with dramatic consequences on the outcomes of our interpretative energies.

→ 2

Recovering the Word in the Bible

A Living Word

We have a friend who does some organizing work for a not-for-profit journal based in Seattle. Every year, the journal conducts a film series focused on faith and justice issues. They invite scholars in the field of theology to discuss Christianity as it relates to everything from poverty to human trafficking. In an attempt to solicit money to support the film series, this friend contacted a man he had come to know while serving in an outreach program to Seattle's homeless youth. It seemed a natural connection: the film series was to focus on poverty, and this man was using his substantial financial resources to help the area's impoverished youth population. Our friend called his contact and left a message with the details of the event, the topics for discussion, and the films on the docket.

A few days later, he was shocked to receive a scathing phone call from this individual. The man was livid that our friend would ask him to participate in these "activist causes." Caught off guard and not knowing exactly how to respond (since they were already partners in an activist cause), our friend asked if they could meet for lunch to discuss the man's concerns about the invitation. During lunch, it became apparent that this individual had read a few of the articles on the journal's website, and had detected an unexpected critique of capitalism and our economic market system. For him, our market system was clearly supported by the teachings of Scripture. Any contradiction of this point was unbiblical and hence offensive and even dangerous.

He explained politely, yet firmly, to our friend that he wanted no association with organizations that devalued the Bible. Our friend tried to open a conversation about some of the biblical tensions surrounding economics and defend his journal's interest in this conversation. But the man wasn't biting. He finished the dialogue before it began by unequivocally assuring our friend that "Scripture interprets itself!" and that when it does so, it "conclusively comes down on the side of market economies!"

We have great respect for this man's dedication to the text of Scripture and his willingness to let it form his life of faith. Yet many Christians—ourselves included—have developed a reflexive response to the "Scripture interprets itself" ideology, recoiling in anticipation of being smacked in the head with a thirty-pound, red-letter edition KJV. Too often we have seen the Sword that pierces the soul turned into a baseball bat swung upside the head of those who disagree with particular economic, political, or sexual mores. "Scripture interprets itself" is little more than an idiom for a personal interpretation of the text that is not to be questioned. It is the interpretative twin of trying to get God on your side in an argument.

Simply put, dialogue about *the text* has become highly controversial in our culture. Even an innocent conversation about the meaning of the Bible can evoke a whole host of fears for many Christians. For some, those fears are born of the implications involved in allowing an unfettered reading of Scripture. For others, it's the fetters themselves that become worrisome.

It is, then, with literal fear and trembling that we set out to discuss one of the central questions of this book, namely, "What is Scripture?" As we engage this question, we will consider the dominant views of Scripture through modernity, discuss the nature of the text as "text," and attempt to expand our vision of Scripture to argue that reading it as the Word of God means listening to and reading more than just the words on the page.

How Firm a Foundation?

To begin the conversation on the nature and identity of the Scriptures, we return to the ascent of Protestant liberalism in the late 1800s and early 1900s and its growing separation from conservative thought. In this high point of modernity, the scientific method of objective analysis, experimentation, and the replication of experimental results reigned as the supreme arbiter of truth. Scientific methods such as higher criticism (which suggested that the Bible was filled with human errors and prejudices) and Darwinism (which appeared to directly contest the veracity of the biblical narrative) had seemingly devastating implications for the Bible and hence Christianity as a whole. Liberals and conservatives alike saw their sacred text embroiled in a gunfight with modern science with only a knife in hand.[1]

Protestant liberals responded by shifting the basis of their faith from the embattled Scriptures to a far less vulnerable foundation—universal religious experience. From the vantage point of this new platform, the Bible's primary mission was to testify to the yearning for God and the faith-driven impulses found in the soul of every human being. The Bible might be filled with "errors" as deemed by science, but its beautiful declarations and demonstrations of a universal spiritual yearning and the value of human experience could not be so easily dismissed or removed when the methods of science were applied to the Bible. In their own eyes, the liberals maintained the vibrancy of Christianity while simultaneously keeping it safe from the ravages of modernity.

Even as triumphant Protestant liberalism began to march toward prominence in our country during the 1920s and 1930s, conservative Christian leaders responded in kind to both the threat of science and what they perceived to be a shameful marginalization of the Bible by liberals. A series of Princeton scholars, sensing the inevitable vapidity of liberal thinking, began to mount a riposte to these currents of higher biblical criticism, modernism, humanism, and reductionism. One of these scholars, John Gresham Machen, the founder of Westminster Theological Seminary and the Orthodox Presbyterian Church, became renowned for his opposition to the burgeoning liberalism of this time. His arguments against liberalism centered on one issue in particular, the Bible. With this theological move toward a literal interpretation of the Scriptures, Machen and others sowed the seed for the "foundation war" that rested at the heart of the fundamentalist/modernist controversy.

At the onset of this struggle, Machen penned words that would become the heart and soul of the faith of so many evangelicals in our century: "Let us not deceive ourselves. The Bible is at the foundation of the Church. Undermine that foundation and the Church will fall."[2] He concluded his argument with a telling twist on the sentiments of St. Paul, stating, "The *Bible* is despised—to the Jews a stumbling-block; to the Greeks foolishness—but the Bible is right."[3] Whereas the liberal coalition clung to the ubiquity of religious experience and its developing brand of humanism in the face of modernity, the burgeoning fundamentalist—and eventually evangelical—movements would take shape around the Bible. What would become clear for conservative evangelicals over the next half century was that they had nothing if they did not have the Bible. It became the foundation, the truth, the way, and the life.

"No creed but the Bible!" became a defining battle cry. Many of us were nurtured in the passions and epithets of this battle. A frequent Vacation Bible School song said, "The B-I-B-L-E, yes, that's the book for me. I stand alone on the Word of God. The B-I-B-L-E. Bible!" Later this produced pithy aphorisms of our faith like, "The Bible says it. I believe it. And that settles it."

The biblical foundationalism of fundamentalists and evangelicals was only galvanized and empowered further by the tenets of modernism that ordained truth to be the province of objective, personal observation. An interest in apologetics—the rational defense of the faith and its sacred texts—rose to great heights during this time as the tools of science were employed defensively. With those simple songs and sayings from that era, the next generation was taught to assume that armed with a simple, commonsense reading of the Word of God, a person could not only come to a saving knowledge of God but also largely discern the essential truths of God's physical, created world. All truth was God's truth. Since the Bible was truth, all we needed was the Bible. In the hands of the evangelicals, the Bible began to reflect the very science that had assailed it so devastatingly.

Adamantly committed to foundationalism in their constructions of truth, both liberals and conservatives confronted the onslaught of modernity and modern science with different plans: liberals abdicated the text as their foundation and evangelicals used the tools of science to reestablish the Scriptures as their foundation. Our point is neither to argue for or against liberalism nor to argue for or against evangelical fundamentalism. As we implied earlier, in a world that has moved beyond many of the dominant presumptions of modernity, we want to argue for a textual hermeneutic that moves beyond the trench lines and polarizations of the mainline/evangelical cold war.

With that stated, we do want to offer some specific cautions to evangelicals in this chapter on the Bible as we attempt to construct what we believe to be a better hermeneutic. We're not playing favorites or picking enemies. The liberals have already paid a harsh price for their brand of foundationalism, their communities frightfully waning as the result of a diminished vision of the Scriptures. In marginalizing the text, the Christian left has in effect abdicated the field of religious dialogue, replacing this discipline with the poor proxies of humanism and cultural sensitivity.

At the same time, a foundationalist view of Scripture has come to dominate the evangelical understanding of the Word of God. The Bible has become the sole foundation of the faith upon which everything else stands. Foundations such as this, however, are weak, for when truth is erected like a tower on a base of non-negotiable essentials, it only takes a little tinkering with the base, in this case the Bible, for the whole thing to come crashing down.

The bigger issue for us is that there is a lack of recognition that this kind of foundationalism is not a long-standing Christian tradition but rather a response to the disillusionment with the Bible found in Protestant liberalism. Furthermore, there is a failure among evangelicals to see that their appeal to the Bible as a foundation stems from the same modern view of the world that led to this disillusionment in liberals.

It is becoming increasingly clear that we are watching the last gasps of modernity. Einstein's theory of relativity and the development of quantum physics, deconstructionism in literature, and postmodern philosophy have all come together to undermine the hegemony of the scientific method, commonsense realism, and foundationalist constructions of truth. We are at the end of an era. And with the ending of the modern era, the church must ask itself if we are clinging to a conception of the Bible that was born of the modern ethos and must therefore end with it as well.

Returning to Machen's words, however, what we find at the end of the age of Protestant liberalism and evangelical fundamentalism is that many of us (not just evangelicals) have, like Machen, substituted the Bible—not the paper and ink but the understanding of the Bible as a compendium of universal, objective, and static God-given truth—for the crucified Christ, the living Word of God. If you think this is an overstatement, remember that Machen states that the Bible is the stumbling block to the Jews and foolishness to the Greeks, whereas Paul states in 1 Corinthians 1:23 that it is the proclamation of the crucified Christ. In making the Bible our one foundation, we have failed to see that this foundation is at best a lesser substitute for the crucified Christ it proclaims, and at worst a starting point for egregious manipulations of Jesus' gospel.

We realize that this might sound like an extremely controversial statement to some. We are not saying the Bible is handicapped or deficient. We adamantly proclaim that the Bible tells God's great and unparalleled story of creating, redeeming, and sustaining love. But what we *are* saying is that when we elevate the words of the Bible in an abstract, propositional form to the level of the "sure" foundation of our faith, when we assume they can stand *un*-interpreted and *dis*-embodied, we as a church are left with serious problems in the structural sustainability of our faith and our communities. The dangerous temptation is a biblio-idolatry that constructs faith on our reverence for the Bible rather than on the person, message, and work of Jesus Christ.

There are many horrifying examples of biblio-idolatry, stories of a revered and idolized Bible being used as an impetus or support for a message that is entirely contrary to that of Jesus. The city we live in provides an example of such a deviation.

In *The Best of Enemies*, Osha Gray Davidson tells the remarkable story of how a local leader of the KKK (C. P. Ellis) and a black activist (Ann Atwater) miraculously developed a thriving friendship after working to reform the public school system in Durham, North

Carolina, in 1970. Ellis had learned the racial hatred and bigotry that pressed him to join the KKK as a young man. As Davidson tells it, when C. P. attended his first Klan rally, he was enthralled with the excitement of the event. He recalled that while standing at the rally, he felt that finally here was an energetic, God-fearing, and passionate group of people, a church he could be a part of. It was, he believed, a cause grounded in biblical truth, stemming the tide against the ever-encroaching world of evil. From his recollection this message was loud and clear, as at one point during the rally "One man, a minister, shouted that God himself had created segregation back in Genesis when he made night and day. 'Hadn't God separated the black from the white?' he cried, and the crowd yelled back, 'Yes, Yes!' 'Wasn't God, then, the first segregationist?' he roared, waving his right hand above his head, one finger extended toward heaven." This minister concluded his remarks, saying, "'We, the Klan, are following God's laws.' . . . Therefore, the Klan's work was God's work."[4]

This interpretation of the Bible is repugnant—not only to us but also to the biblical foundationalists we know. But it also gives us strong pause, because it displays the way in which a foundationalistic reading of the Bible can so quickly and easily become drastically distorted. A love and reverence for the divine origin, authority, and beauty of the Scriptures is not enough. Even a healthy dose of respect for the Scriptures can be manipulated into an offensive argument that falls short of the gospel. When the book becomes the location of propositional and abstract truths, without giving precedence to its primary message, the living Christ, it can be used as a foundation to make any argument—even those that seem unconscionable to most of us. In this way, the Bible can easily become a mascot to the worst of humanity.

Again, the Bible in the sacred abstract, if you will—revered, read propositionally, uninterpreted, and disembodied—is neither the heart nor lifeblood of our faith. It was not intended to be so. Instead, it is the testimony to the lifeblood, Jesus Christ. We realize that this is a fine distinction, but we believe it is of great importance.

As we read the testimony to God's work in the world, we must always do so with respect to the life, death, and resurrection of Jesus Christ. We must always invite it into our lives and let it form us. This process of interpretation takes us far beyond simply looking to the Bible for divine instruction. It demands that we be actively involved with the good news it proclaims.

In response to the ideology that we simply listen to what the Scripture says about an issue, Dale Martin, a professor of New Testament at Yale, comments:

> The text cannot interpret itself. I sometimes illustrate my point when asked to speak about "what the Bible says about homosexuality." I put the Bible in the middle of the room or on the speaker's podium, step back, and say "Okay, let's see what it says. Listen!" After a few seconds of uncomfortable silence and some snickers, I say, "Apparently, the Bible can't talk." This is not the frivolous gimmick it may initially seem. Our language about "what texts say" tends to make us forget that the expression is a metaphor. Texts don't "say" anything: they must be read. And even in the reading process, interpretation has already begun. And if we want to move on from reading the text out loud, say, to paraphrasing it or commenting upon what it "means," we have simply moved further into human interpretation.[5]

Martin affirms the point that reading the Bible as the Word of God is never as simple or as straightforward as looking at words on a page. Instead of viewing Scripture as a flat collection of words that provide a secure foundation from which to build our theologies and worldviews, we have to understand that we must interpret those words. And we believe that this interpretation happens best when the body of Christ, the church, discerns the Word of God together.

The Bible as the Living Word of God

Sifting through the aftermath of the modern age's foundation wars leaves us with both a dire warning and a sharp caution. From the battered, diminished liberal camp—who shifted their flag from the Bible to a foundation of human experience—we see the peril of marginalizing the Bible by equating divine revelation with human faculties. Liberals are still picking up the pieces, gradually discovering that the reaction was ultimately more devastating than the threat.

From the evangelical camp, filled with new converts and many of the spoils of victory, we see the seeds of vulnerability and even decay. The stratagem, rooted in reverence, to buttress the Bible as the foundation of their faith now leaves them exposed and standing on treacherous ground. The Bible, though it testifies to Jesus' gospel, now rivals its source as the locus of our worship. A corollary and naive insistence that the Bible is simply read—apart from the diligent participation of an interpreting, practicing, and Spirit-led community—threatens to relegate its revelation to inert abstraction or the whims of unchecked individual agendas.

Since we have not embraced "liberal" or "conservative" as self-descriptive (though both of us have evangelical backgrounds) and are advocating a hermeneutic that moves past the specific historical interests and practices of these two movements, it will be helpful for you to know exactly what we *do* believe about the Bible. So here it is: We believe the text manifests God's living Word, a message lived out in the person of Jesus Christ. We believe it is the great narrative of God's redemption of humanity and creation, provocative and persuasive in its invitation to join this work, and that it is formative for the community of believers. We believe the Bible does not function as a foundation for individual belief and spirituality but rather functions as a central and essential community text. We hope that this project is received as a heartfelt testimony to the work of God's Spirit in communities that seek to read, follow, and embody the gospel of Jesus Christ. And we hope it is an invitation to a series of practices of interpretation that we believe are both responsive to the invitations of God's Spirit and formative as they teach us to hear the voice of God more clearly in the text.

Our view of the Bible comes from the historic testimony of the church as well as our experiences of prayer and the practice of our Christian faith within a variety of wonderful communities. It also comes from one other strange place—the churning wake of postmodern philosophy. Though postmodern thought brings a variety of threats and baggage to the gospel, it also offers a liberating exit from the ruts of foundationalism. Certainly, there are many writers and scholars who think of postmodernism as a fad or even an incoherent collection of thoughts—and they might be right in many instances.

Yet we believe its anti-foundational impulses provide a welcome opportunity to recover the living Word of God.

While postmodernism often retains the labels of "new" or "faddish" from the casually interested, the philosophical discussions at its root have been occurring from at least the mid to late 1950s. Many would even trace these roots as far back as World War II or to the end of World War I and figures such as Karl Barth, Ludwig Wittgenstein, Franz Rosenzweig, and Martin Heidegger (to name a few), each of whom wrestled with the ideas of context, intention, and interpretation.

One key element in postmodern philosophy has been a change in the understanding of how knowledge and language work. While modernity (modern science, epistemology, and linguistics) typically thought that the way we acquired knowledge was by starting with a foundation and building from the ground up, postmodernism tends to think of the way we acquire knowledge, and even the way we use language itself, as a web. .

Instead of thinking of our storehouse of knowledge as being built upon one or two indubitable ideas or concepts (a secure foundation), postmodern philosophy purports that we build an intricate web of knowledge, where no single concept stands as the foundation but where each of our concepts relies upon the others in order to provide it with support and stability. Hence, we don't work from fundamentals, or foundational elements; we weave concepts across one another in order to form a web of knowledge.

Furthermore, this web of knowledge or language is ineluctably connected to a tradition. That is to say, knowledge and language are not universal, but are specific to historical communities and peoples who live together and interact with one another. They are local—more like dialects or accents—which suggests that a shared history, a hidden script of daily actions and conversations, helps to determine what is known and how it is communicated. From the postmodern perspective, truth and text reside within specific local contexts rather than being transcendent propositions arranged in a hierarchy from the most important (the true foundations) to the least significant. Hence, truth and language (used to convey truth) function in a more local manner with greater subjectivity. Truth is the truth lived out in a community of people as we, through language and action, make it intelligible to each other. The perspectives of others become essential for making the truth and what we know intelligible. Our knowledge depends on our community, as does our language and understanding of ourselves.[6]

One clear example of this is the realization that language is by nature a communal habit. For instance, when we first learn to speak, we do so through listening to those who are talking to us and not by studying a dictionary. When the first questions are posed to us, such as, "Where's Mommy?" we not only begin to gain some understanding of the meaning of the term *mommy*, but we also begin to learn how to ask questions and the role of questions in verbal communication. We learn intonation, sentence syntax, and even grammar (poorly, we might add, for those of us who grew up in the South). Through continual practice, all the while continuing to listen to the conversations going on around us, we learn to speak. Our language and the knowledge that we build upon it is formed layer-by-layer, strand-by-strand within a thick web of communal communication and interaction. We speak because we have been formed in the communal habits of doing so. And we form our understanding of truth within this local, relational matrix.

This portrait of truth, though certainly not perfect, does at least have some powerful biblical recommendations. Our minds quickly turn to some of the critical texts of Genesis. The creation story demonstrates that God is the origin of life, and that compared to the limits inherent in creation, God is infinite and unlimited. The first great lesson given to the created humans includes the idea of embracing their finitude (they were to be servants and stewards of the creation rather than authors and owners, and hence, were worshipers of God) and acknowledging their relational dependency (they will need each other to fulfill the tasks of stewardship and worship). The sin that destroys the peace of Eden is the rejection of these limits—it is the insidious desire *to know like God*. The first painful consequence of this world-altering rejection of God's plan is that humans will now find themselves divided from God and, as happens with the killing of Abel by his brother, Cain, divided against one another. In so many ways, the descent of humanity at this point of the narrative looks like the modern project of knowledge—humans seeking to find the ultimate principles or formulas of life without a dependency on or respect for the differing experiences of the community.

The story of Babel in Genesis 11, which ends this long section on origins, picks up many of the same themes. The plan of the humans, now cooperating with each other but cooperating against God, is to build a tower to the heavens in order to see the world and truth from on high. Throwing off the idea that as creatures they are limited in their knowledge and, therefore, dependent on God and one another, they set out to conquer the instability of the world by trying to gain the perspective of the gods. They deny their nature as creatures limited by their finite perspective and dependent on God's revelation to know and understand the truth of their created purpose. We can again turn to the story as a challenge to the premises of modernity—they search for truth in the heights far above the complexities and differing perspectives of the human condition. (Isn't it interesting that God resolved the human condition with an incarnation, God embodied in the mess and muck of the human condition, rather than building a tower the right way?)

God's response to their project is severe. The tower is destroyed, the humans at Babel are scattered, and they are made culturally divergent by different races and languages. God is not threatened but offended by this tower doomed to failure. Truth will not be found on high. Only in their diversity, now enhanced by God's gracious scattering of humanity, will they learn their role in creation and the extreme importance of human dependency, listening now to a myriad of local stories and perspectives, in discerning ultimate truth.

Postmodernity radically impacts and enhances the way we read the Scriptures. Though some undoubtedly will fear change, needless over-complication, or a descent down the slippery slope into relativism, the interpretative and missional possibilities of this shift are remarkable and profoundly liberating for those who seek to read the Bible as inspired text. The Bible is freed to be the inspired stories of peoples whose threads come together to form a coherent web, a tradition of human beings dedicated to the specific story of God's work in the world. Rather than being a universal treatise of unprejudiced facts about humans, or a collection of wise sayings and general observations, the Bible functions as the central text of the story of the people of God.

This journey through history and philosophy reminds us that the Bible is the living, active Word of God rather than an abstract, impersonal message set down centuries ago from on high. It is a tradition that is all about God's revelation, supremely God's revelation in Christ. When speaking of the Bible, we must note that it is not, in its essence, words on a page. Instead, it is truly a living Word—inspired by a living God, penned by living authors limited and challenged by the confines of their contexts, and received by a living church motivated not to pause in reverence or admiration but to embody the story and message in a mutually dependent worshiping community.

There is little wonder that Jesus, God incarnate, the one the writer of Hebrews calls "the radiance of God's glory and the exact representation of his being" (Heb. 1:3), takes the title of the "Word of God" (John 1:14). Both Martin Luther and Karl Barth help us with this distinction of God's Word as a living text. As Luther says, "Christ is completely wrapped in Scripture as the body [of the baby Jesus] in the swaddling clothes."[7] The distinction we are trying to make here is slight but critical to regaining an understanding of how Scripture is the Word of God. Karl Barth, the twentieth-century theologian, helped us to begin to recognize how we might understand Scripture as the Word of God apart from the potential abstractions of foundationalism when he said, "The Bible is God's Word as it really bears witness to [Jesus Christ]. . . . The Bible is not in itself and as such God's past revelation."[8] In short, Barth's claim is that the Bible itself becomes the Word of God insofar as it attests to the revelation of God in Jesus Christ and stands as God's abiding witness to this event.

Following this line of thinking, we can see that to claim the Bible to be the Word of God, which is what we in fact do, is to claim something much more rich and complex than the belief that there is a literal, timeless reading of each and every word in the Bible. Instead, we have to read the text as text, that is, as the central witness of the tradition that attests to God's work in the world. Such a discipline does not imply an unchecked subjectivity (we'll have much more to say about this in chapter 3) or any less regard for the Scripture. But it does imply that we will need many voices in the process of interpretation, for only a collective people can make up a tradition.

We recognize that the big concern in reading the biblical text alongside others is that it will quickly descend into chaos—that every idea and opinion will have equal weight and that there will be no hope of reaching definitive conclusions. Aside from our belief that this is not an altogether bad result, we also believe that a collective reading and response to the Bible allows us to tap into three essential aspects of our Christian tradition that are much more difficult to access as individuals: canon, catholicity, and community. Each is not only an inalienable component of our tradition, it is a vital act of communal interpretation.

While we will speak to each of these aspects separately, we are aware that they often operate at the same time and on overlapping levels. Together, they help us to interpret the text of Scripture as the living Word of God and to let its story of revelation shape our lives.

Canon, Catholicity, and Community

Canon

Canon, literally "rod" or "rule," is the term Christians have historically used to refer to the whole of the Bible, the texts collected and affirmed by the church as God's revealed Word and the guiding rule of our faith. This process of collection and affirmation occurred over a couple of centuries and was not without dispute and controversy. Our faith compels us to trust that this process was guided by God's Spirit both in spite of and because of the agendas, biases, and prejudices of those involved. In fact, the story of the canon's collection and blessing is a powerful historical example of our thesis on community interpretation. Respect for the canon also implies a significant interpretative trajectory of allowing every genre—Gospels and letters, poems and songs, histories and apocalyptic visions, regardless of whether we find these texts to be obscure, obvious, or offensive—to speak to the church as a chorus of authoritative voices.

One of the central, and misleading, presuppositions of the "Scripture interprets itself" ideology is the notion that the books of the Bible fit together like a neatly crafted puzzle, each piece coming together perfectly, leaving no tension, no inconsistency, and no contesting points of view. Any serious reader of the Scripture, however, cannot commit to this point of view without ignoring significant pieces of the Bible: The violence of the book of Joshua versus the pacifism of the Sermon on the Mount, Jesus' view of marriage in Matthew versus the words of Song of Songs, or Paul's view of faith and works versus James's understanding. The Bible is rife with tension and stories that do not fit neatly and perfectly together. This is not to say that they are incongruous or that the Scripture is incoherent and unhelpful. In fact, many Christians have found quite the opposite to be true. Life is often filled with tension and discord. The pieces of our own stories rarely fit into neat blueprints. It can be greatly comforting to know that the story of God's people is filled with messy lives and unanswered questions.

One of the main problems with a foundational model of understanding Scripture is that it inevitably leads to a flat reading of the text. Richard Lischer, homiletics professor at Duke Divinity School, explains this phenomenon, noting that "The flat reading approaches every text in a verse-by-verse fashion on the unspoken assumption that the content of each verse is as important and helpful as every other verse in the text."[9] Flat readings remove the texture of the Bible by leveling its words, rendering equal every component of the text, and often "telescoping" our interpretation by zooming into specific verses and sound bites and effectively detaching them from their contexts while ignoring the inherent tensions with other texts. While the attraction in this way of reading is the illusion that it leads to what feels like a more objective hearing of the Word of God—taking every word as straight from the mouth of God as a command—it misses the point of reading the Scripture as a whole, allowing the tensions within it to guide our reading and open the text up for us. Accepting the Bible as the canon for the church allows us to read it complete with the rhetorical devices, biases, ironies, theological perspectives, and themes of the writers as the many threads that come together to compose the fabric of the text.

Reading the text in this way means we will have to continue to read it repetitively, paying attention to the tensions and consistent themes of the Scriptures in order to learn to read them better. Just as one does not learn the spirit of a great novel by reading it one time, so one does not obtain the timeless spirit of the Bible by obtaining some objective principle from each verse. Reading the Scripture as canon means that we have to live with the text and read its themes over and over again. It makes it impossible for us to treat the Bible as something that can be easily learned and applied. Instead, recognizing the Bible as canon makes us take it even more seriously.

We must also be mindful of the nature of these letters, Gospels, narratives, and hymns. For instance, the New Testament was not written in a godly language; it was written in the vernacular of Koine Greek, the popular spoken language of the people of first-century Palestine. It was written by ordinary men (and possibly women) who were finite beings with limited perspectives on what had happened with the advent, death, and resurrection of Jesus, the Christ. This is not to say that the texts are flawed and need to be viewed with suspicion or demeaned, but it is to say that they attest to the incarnate Christ in a very fleshly way. They are attestations written by human authors who, under the inspiration of the Spirit, were convinced that Jesus was the risen Messiah and were moved to recount and proclaim this fact to those around them. They did so in the language and concepts they had at hand.

The books are firsthand accounts of the revelation of God. At the same time, it's a mistake to assume that the Spirit took over the bodies and minds of the writers. To deny the human role in the creation of the text is to deny the whole event of revelation upon which our Christian faith is founded. Our faith is shaped by an Immanuel belief and hope—God among us, God truly incarnate in human flesh as "God's Word," and an eventual resurrection of the body. Such an affirmation precludes any belief that the God who became flesh in Christ would eradicate the human element in the writing of the texts that testify to this event.

Using the whole canon as an interpretative tool also challenges and limits the inevitable impulse of all Bible readers to create a "canon within the canon." When confronted with complexities and apparent contradictions in the text, all of us inevitably turn to the passages and books we know best or to which we assign greater significance. The common result is preachers with redundant sermon texts and repetitive messages that often exclude portions of the biblical narrative or significant theological possibilities and, as a result, often fail to speak to the whole gamut of our lives.

Every theological tradition faces this challenge. Esteemed New Testament professor Gordon Fee used to quip in his lectures at Gordon-Conwell that he would often preach texts from Paul and the epistles at mainline churches and texts from the Gospels at evangelical churches because both decisions would engage unfamiliar ground for each tradition! Coming from evangelical backgrounds, we've seen this phenomenon many times, sermons that began in the Old Testament or the Gospels where the stated text was used as a mere springboard into Romans or Galatians where "things are really explained."

A holistic reading of the Bible opens us to seeing the richness of its perspectives as well as allowing us to understand that any given text may have more than one faithful interpretation. While both historical criticism (as an attempt to get to the world behind the text and beneath its layers) and biblical foundationalism aim toward finding a singular meaning for a text, understanding that the text is polyvalent explains why different preachers can faithfully approach the same text and yet end up crafting very different sermons. Because the text is incarnational, because it contains tensions and complexities, and because we must always engage in reading any text within the whole and vast canon, we must read it in a way that allows for a variety of faithful interpretations. That variety pushes all of us into a deeper connection with the text. As Walter Brueggemann has so eloquently noted, "The claim of polyvalence is an invitation for Christians to relearn from Jewish interpretive tradition."[10] Engaging the Bible as canon allows us to *midrash*—the Jewish practice of arguing over how to interpret the text (a point we will return to later in our discussion of the role of community).

I (Dan) was recently asked to assist with a preaching class for the Divinity School at Duke University. As the final assignment for the class, the students were to write a sermon for the graveside service of a stillborn child. While the students were not given a particular text to use, a few of them ended up choosing the same one—Jesus' blessing of the little children in Matthew 19:13–15. What was surprising, however, was that even though these students had been given a specific context and were working from the same passage, their sermons drew off of variant interpretations and ran in different trajectories. Yet it was nearly impossible to label some sermons as having missed the true meaning of the text, while rewarding others for having unearthed the "real" treasure of the text's meaning.

The canon itself never assumes biblical passages to have one meaning or that the Bible fits together without internal tensions. Jesus often quotes the ancient prophets, reinterpreting their words for his listeners and pushing them into deeper levels of understanding. A faithful reading of the Bible involves reading it as a collective whole, allowing the tensions to stand while continually returning to these texts and refusing to close them with a single interpretation.

Catholicity

We use the term *catholicity* to refer to the history, tradition, and expansiveness of the body of Christ. It is the testimony of what the author of Hebrews calls the "great cloud of witnesses"—those who have lived the Christian life before us, have read and interpreted the Scriptures, and have written to and instructed those coming after them. Catholicity is the heritage of the Scripture stretched along the line of faithful Christians who have been reading it for nearly two millennia. Catholicity is a second act of community in the interpretation of the Bible.

Recently, I (Dan) was engaged in a conversation with a friend who has been trying to compose a memoir. For the most part, he has enjoyed a productive writing process. But he's noticed how difficult it is to remember his childhood years. They seem so long ago and so distant. On a recent trip back to his hometown, however, he realized that the problem wasn't really his memory; it was his location. When he was surrounded by all of the landmarks, smells, sounds, and people that had played key roles in his experiences as a child, he found himself painfully aware of how removed he had become from the person he once was. If he had stayed in his hometown, remained embedded in its story and in the lives of its people, perhaps his childhood memories would be much closer to the surface.

As people caught in a world of global capitalism, we are increasingly finding ourselves to be an unrooted people. Cell phones, cars, job transfers, frequent-flier miles, and the Internet have changed our lives in the last fifty years more than most of us realize. Few of us live in the same town where our grandparents are buried. And even fewer of us have any knowledge of our family history. Hence, many of us have a hard time remembering who we are.

In the face of the dislocation in our culture, many people live their lives by constantly reinventing themselves. In a world of virtual personalities, success depends on the ability to present the right self at the right time. In this climate, the challenge of listening to the way the Bible has been read through many generations and ages becomes exceedingly difficult and even more necessary. Indeed, reading these texts faithfully means, in part, recognizing that we are not the first people to read them. We must learn to lean on the history of their interpretation to help us determine what they are saying to the church today. Catholicity calls us to read the text within the walls of the church, within the bounds of the cloud of witnesses that is our tradition. It means understanding that we often need to be reminded of who we are and that we don't get to make everything up for ourselves on the spot in some form of online, virtual Christian personality. To be faithful to the Scriptures and to read them as the Word of God means reading what the church fathers, the scholastics, the mystics, the Reformers, the liberation theologians, the monastics, and our grandparents had to say about these texts.

Frankly, this interpretative challenge keeps us honest, humble, and often up late at night. For more than twenty years, I (Tim) have interpreted the Bible in a manner that leads to a strong egalitarian conviction that argues for the full participation of women in every pastoral office and role in the life of the church. That may feel like old news for many Christian traditions, but that's not the case in the traditions Dan and I grew up in. I served for two decades in two churches—one in a well-educated, high-tech community and the other in a college town—that defended their complementarian position on gender (a position that does not allow women to hold some offices) with well-thought-out exegesis. One of their strongest arguments in the dialogue over this issue was catholicity—that the church through the ages had consistently read certain New Testament texts as prohibiting female headship in the church.

A commitment to catholicity forces me to take those arguments seriously even when I strongly disagree, even when they create missional frustrations for me. Catholicity in interpretation challenges me to not only respect the Scriptures as God's living Word (they were inspired for God's agenda rather than my own comfort or sensitivity) but to remember that I don't get to just interpret and teach as I see fit. I am forced to wrestle in prayer and dialogue often when my interpretative convictions differ from the history of the church. I must ask a series of questions before I move in a new path, and even then I must tread lightly.

At the same time, catholicity asks us not to simply rest on the interpretations of the historical church but to contribute to that history ourselves. We do that by asking the questions the church has always asked: In what ways do our culture and our context differ from that of the original readers and the contexts of faithful readers of the past? What new possibilities do these differences create for the text? Are these changes significant enough that to be missionally faithful to the text requires different actions from the original or historical church? Catholicity demands we ask these questions even as it provides us with a deep sense of identity. Just as a commitment to canon brings the interpreter into the community of texts that make up our Bible, the commitment to catholicity brings us face-to-face with the vast community of historical biblical interpreters.

Community

Our reading and interpretations of the Scriptures are sculpted and informed by specific communities who faithfully attempt to practice and embody the message of the text. A foundationalism that holds the possibility of a sacred, abstract Bible—a Bible that can exist as God's Word apart from the people to whom it was revealed as a gift—is on shaky ground. The Bible, identified and received as a living Word, demands the presence of faithful community to interpret and embody the text.

Stanley Fish emphatically makes this connection between practice and meaning, asserting, "Texts only exist in a continuing web of interpretive practices."[11] For the Christian community and our Bible, this means that embodiments of the text such as prayer, hospitality, evangelism, engagement with the poor, sexual practices, and mission not only make it a living Word, but to a great extent shape how we read the Bible. Just as the words of Scripture give direction to our practices, choices, and rituals, so too all of these are acts of interpretation. This is how two communities reading the same texts can come to two very different conclusions.

Not only do community actions in general inform our reading of the Scripture, but the specific people with whom we read play a significant role in determining how we interpret passages. During the first year in the life of Emmaus Way, we experienced a powerful example of both practice and presence in the understanding of text. Two years earlier, my (Tim's) wife and kids formed a friendship with a homeless man they had met asking for change in downtown Chapel Hill. They picked him (and all of his possessions) up every Sunday, brought him to church, took him out to eat afterward, and gave him a bit of money to help him through the week. Over the years we walked with him through addiction, AIDS, homelessness, and life. Slowly, he began to become part of our community.

Our meeting space for Emmaus Way was near this man's "home," so when we began to meet, he attended regularly. The community was extremely compassionate and gracious to him even when his behavior was an affront to our suburban sensibilities (like asking for financial help during the Eucharist or wanting to sing impromptu songs in the middle of our worship gatherings). Someone from the community would always drive him home after church, usually with a stop by the grocery store to get him some supplies for the week.

The practices involved in this relationship certainly enhanced our understanding of biblical texts on compassion, generosity, and the breadth of diversity among those who call Jesus "Lord." But his presence—and the occasional presence of his friends from the street—proved to have a vivid impact on our community's interaction with the Bible.

When our sermon conversations were about poverty, prison, or shame, he would often speak up with personal illustrations that were far outside the experiences of everyone else in our community. For most churches like ours, the social status of a "prostitute" is a casual abstraction. But a female friend of this man, a woman who supported her drug addiction through prostitution, was also a frequent worship companion, so texts that involved Jesus' compassion for prostitutes stepped off of the page for us. We only had to look across the room to see what the call to love the least of these (Matthew 25:31–46) actually means.

The living community shapes the way we read and understand the Scriptures. As we practice the faith together in baptism, communion, preaching, serving, suffering in the way of the cross, praying, and pursuing peace, we are engaging in an embodiment of the Scriptures. It makes sense, then, that this list of Christian practices ought to include the practice of talking about—and even arguing about—what we read and discover in the text. As the community of God, as the body of Christ, the living church should be engaged in active conversation over the meaning of Scripture, engaging one another's interpretation.

This is the midrash tradition we mentioned earlier. The living, acting community engaged in deep discussion of the Scripture allows us to read it as the Word of God. As Richard Lischer notes, "The Bible is best interpreted on location by those who consider themselves active players in its drama."[12]

We have pointed out that reading the Bible as the Word of God requires interpretation, and in fact it requires that we engage the text communally. We have tried to organize this form of interpretation under the categories of canon, catholicity, and community, but none of these categories is sufficient to stand alone and each of them should always be overlapping and operating at the same time as the others. While the premise of this book is "reading the Bible in community," you will find the threads of canon and catholicity woven all through our discussion of community. We think this is what it takes to engage the Bible seriously, to read it as the life-giving Word of God for our church.

Having identified the nature of God's Word and some categories for community engagement, we turn next to address some of the fears that are natural to community interpretation and offer not only strong justification for the role of community in biblical interpretation, but also specific practices of community that catalyze our sensitivity to God's Spirit and the process of faithful interpretation.

3

Let the Chaos Begin
The Hermeneutics of Peoplehood

We concluded the last chapter by stressing the utter importance of reading the text together as a practicing community in order to read it as the Word of God. And while most people seem to like the concept of reading in community, we find that when they take a moment to think about their actual communities, they wonder if it's such a good idea. Even when we acknowledge the incarnational essence of the Scriptures (which implies that the Scriptures are inseparably tied to human languages, historical and cultural contexts, and the inspired agendas of the authors) and even when we believe that the context of the community engaging the text is intimately connected to how we read and understand it, there is real concern that the intersection between Scripture and community will have less-than-amicable results. And we fully admit that reading the text in community could be a catastrophe. Some of these fears of giving the text to the community are well founded. Because Christians believe the Bible to be sacred Scripture and central to the life of the church, it has real power. And this in turn means that whoever has control over its reading and interpretation claims the lion's share of power in the community. The power of the text, while inevitable and promising, can also be twisted and misused—something we all know too well.

Over the past two decades, Dan and I have heard numerous pleas for help from small group members whose weekly meetings have turned into theological/political/cultural wrestling matches between outspoken, adamant, and often uninformed alpha dogs. The familiar chorus of those caught in the crosshairs of these struggles is "please step in!" They want someone—the pastor—to give an authoritative word on an issue or a rebuke to end the bickering.

We've also encountered more than our share of small group evangelists who were self-appointed orthodoxy guardians. They had seen it as their responsibility to intentionally join or lead these small groups they perceived were drifting from the straight and narrow of "right theology" toward the abyss of _____ (insert: "fundamentalism," "liberalism," "Catholicism," "Calvinism," "Arminianism," or any other "ism" that would inspire some members of your community to terror and intervention!) in order to abate what they perceived to be the deluge of encroaching chaos. Little did they realize, however, that their hostile takeover was merely perpetuating a less-than-helpful approach to the text.

The point we made in chapter 1—that communities and individuals often find "exactly what they are looking for" in the Scriptures—appears to argue strongly for a limited role of community in Scripture interpretation.

Truly, we are all selfish and biased when it comes to our needs. Recently, we listened to a pastor friend lament a personal attack (on biblical grounds!) by a congregant who lambasted his "abdication of authority and biblical integrity" because of his egalitarian position on gender and church leadership. This pastor added with a grim chuckle, "That same guy loved my hermeneutics when my same logic offered him the freedom to remarry after a painful divorce years earlier!" Stories like this one, of self-interest operating as the final arbiter in our interpretation of Scripture, abound in our churches and Christian communities. We gulp and admit that we are a selfish lot—the whole of us. No one is exempt. In the last chapter, we asserted the strong connection between community practice and interpretation. The combination of selfish intent, the deeply ingrained sense that we need to put what we read into practice, and the power that comes with authority can literally be lethal. For in this way our desires can hijack the text, taking it hostage and leading to situations where the most persuasive or strongest among us get to read it and enforce it the way they want.

This fear is well founded—we have seen its terrible consequences. In the summer of 2005, Anglican archbishop Emmanuel Kollini from Rwanda stood before a small group of students and faculty from Duke who had recently embarked upon a pilgrimage of pain and hope to this land ravaged by genocide in the 1990s and asked the question, "How do we train Christians to say 'No' to killing?"[1] Here in the United States, we might think that's an odd question. But he asked the question in a land where Christians had taken the lives of fellow Christians and churches had at times become tombs for those seeking safety inside away from the chaos and killing. The Bible had been used to support the atrocities in this community (as it has been used to support so many other atrocities throughout human history). How would they make sure it didn't happen again?

The bishop's question strikes at the heart of how we read and understand the Bible in community. Prophetic voices have at times called our attention to the disaster created when a demagogue or ruthless majority starts to use the text for their own exploitive purposes. In 1845, with the "peculiar institution" of slavery reigning strong in the Southern states, Frederick Douglass penned these powerful words challenging the faith of Southern slaveholders. Douglass inveighs, "I assert most unhesitatingly, that the religion of the south is a mere covering for the most horrid crimes,—a justifier of the most appalling barbarity,—a sanctifier of the most hateful frauds,—and a dark shelter under which the darkest, foulest, grossest, and most infernal deeds of slaveholders find the strongest protection."[2] Douglass then concludes his vituperative with the comment, "Between the Christianity of this land, and the Christianity of Christ, I recognize the widest possible difference. . . . We have men-stealers for ministers, women-whippers for missionaries, and cradle-plunderers for church members."[3] What Douglass harshly critiques is not the sorcery of an evil group of people set on the destruction of God's creation, but—and this is the scariest thing—the actions of those Southern Christians who thought they were being faithful in their reading of the text.

What is perhaps most unsettling about the history of slavery in our country is not only its brutality and its complete racism, but quite simply the church's role in fortifying this atrocity. Good, intelligent, even faithful people participated in this collective sin. Pastors ordained to preach the good news of Jesus publicly proclaimed the goodness of slavery and the virtue of the system, the very actions that led Douglass to openly challenge their view of the Christian faith.

These Southern Christians were able to read the text in such a way so as to provide theological grounding for the egregious institution of slavery. In part, they were able to do so because their actions helped determine the meaning of what they read in the pages of the Bible; they read it the way they wanted to and used that power to lord it over an entire group of people. They are a vivid example of how we can make the text subservient to our own cultural, social, or personal desires.

Our history remains filled with Jonestowns, Wacos, and other communities that have taken God's Word to unthinkable extremes. Even in less dramatic circumstances, the Word of God is hijacked as the ever-present justification in even the most inflammatory or most banal of church struggles. Whether we are fighting about pacifism, the ordination of women, the inclusion of homosexuals in the church, or the appropriate time to conclude the morning worship service to allow congregants to see the opening kick-off or be first at the country club buffet, there always seems to be a scriptural "word from the Lord" to hide behind or reinforce the certainty of our arguments.

So, while the Bible remains the most widely published and purchased book in the world, it also frequently remains the foundation for some of the most heinous acts and frivolous assertions of our time, most often when it has been appropriated to serve the interests of the most powerful person reading it. Reading Scripture is dangerous business, and it's this danger that prompted one of our favorite theologians, Stanley Hauerwas, to quip, "We need to get Bibles out of the hands of the public."[4]

The Search for Utopian Authorities

Despite the premise of this book, we often find ourselves in avid solidarity with Hauerwas's sentiment. On bad days, we arrogantly imagine Stanley with us, a three-person biblical censorship commission, going door-to-door collecting Bibles and commentaries from the ignorant and unworthy. There is a temptation to find an ultimate authority to end these horror stories of scriptural infighting, blind devotion, and selfish dissection of the Word of God. Of course the obvious flaw in this plea for a benevolent, utopian, interpretative authority is deciding what authority that would be. But that flaw doesn't stop Christians of all stripes from seeking that ultimate authority.

Sometimes our search for authorities and our devotion to these authorities leads us to outlandish conclusions. We were recently mediating some wounded feelings between a congregant and one of his childhood friends in regard to this congregant's imminent divorce. The conflict naturally centered on the appropriateness of the separation and the choices that led to this painful situation. This friend of our congregant subscribed to a theological system that had a very literal and precise definition of when divorce was allowed. This definition was so precise that in the middle of one meeting, the friend blurted out, "Sometimes I just wish you had an affair so that this divorce would be biblical and permissible."

We have already pointed out that our theological constructs function as powerful boundary-makers when reflecting on Scripture. In this case, the person's sincere (and misguided) adherence to a respectable authority produced a wild hope that contradicted the very goal of that same authority in regard to marriage. This friend represents the tension that is created when we place all hope and security in whatever or whoever we see as the final authority in our reading of Scripture. Without the tempering effect of other voices and the expanded view of authority they bring with them, we can dismiss the conflicts that come when faith and life collide far too easily. Instead of wrestling with the text and seeking God in our circumstances, we can fall back on an "accepted" view of the Scripture and ignore the deeper places to which the Spirit might be pulling us.

We should immediately add here that we're not arguing for the absence of *any* authority in scriptural interpretation. In fact, by the end of this chapter we want to suggest the wealth of power that can emerge from the community reading together. But we do want to adamantly state that there is no ultimate authority. There is no benevolent, utopian prophet/preacher/guide out there short of God. And of course, we're all struggling to understand that same gracious and sovereign God!

In the Free Church tradition (read: Low Church) and many congregational polities, we often replace the dictates of denomination, confession, or highly defined theological systems with the integrity, charisma, and vision of gifted and dominant leaders. For many, the model of an authoritative teacher or preacher expounding the meaning of God's Word is the most normative and sacred form of biblical exposition. Sometimes we even feel the need to beam this teacher or preacher in via satellite in order to provide more people with the chance to listen to his—and yes, it usually is a "his"—powerful message of authority. Obviously this too has its limits and perils.

I (Tim) had the good fortune of learning this in my first pastoral position. While still a twenty-four-year-old seminarian, I landed a job with an extraordinarily talented church staff. In addition to being mentored by some of the best leaders around, I also learned very quickly that this staff of "the famous" and "soon-to-be-famous" fought for pulpit time, argued over office sizes and locations, and formed competitive cliques around ministry visions and philosophies. This early tutorial in the frailties of even highly regarded leaders was dramatically augmented years later by the experience of observing the exits of three extraordinary pastors due to some form of moral failure. Truthfully, those failures did nothing to invalidate the ministry of those leaders. They only reaffirmed their humanity and the ubiquitous nature of sin. (Remember, there are only certain sins for which we terminate pastors and lay leaders—greed, racism, arrogance, and stubbornness, among others, seem to get a free pass when they aren't intentionally applauded!) But in these sad situations, we are again reminded that we cannot put all of our interpretative chips and hopes in gifted, authoritative individuals.

We are a mess. And we will remain a mess. We are biased and prejudiced by our loyalties and limited experiences. But this irrefutable reality and the inadequacies of our authorities do not mean that our reading and interpretation of the Bible is hopeless. Nor does it mean that we should somehow strive to eliminate the human element from the reading of the Scriptures. We cannot forget our understanding of the nature of Scripture from chapter 2. The fact that the Bible must be read by finite and frail humans if it is going to be Scripture for anyone is one of the main reasons why we believe in its divine and authoritative nature. The inspiration and transformation of flawed communicators and the expression of transcendent truths despite the limits of human language are unmistakable markers of a divine presence. To steal a word from comedian Stephen Colbert, the "truthiness" of the Bible (meaning its aura of truthfulness due to its long history of encouragement and edification of those who seek God's presence)— despite its diverse authors, contexts, and characters—not only makes it compelling but also commends it to us as God's Word.

Community as Cure

The messiness of our humanity does indeed influence our use of the Bible. Yet there is no need to fear the human component of scriptural interpretation or make a futile attempt to eradicate its presence. We believe that it is humanity itself that can save us from the challenges inherent in putting the Bible in the hands of the "public." At the risk of reaching new heights of counterintuitive logic, we submit that the "antidote" for our prejudices, biases, limits, and the human tendency to misuse power is a *more* extensive inclusion of community in the process of reading and understanding Scripture.

There is a powerful biblical precedent to support this point. In 1 Peter 4:8, Peter encourages his readers to "love each other deeply, because love covers over a multitude of sins." This oft-quoted directive falls in a larger paragraph (1 Peter 4:7–11) that focuses directly on the attributes of Christian community (other directives include a self-controlled life, prayer, hospitality, and appropriate use of our gifts and abilities in service). This expansive exhortation on community

comes on the heels of a long narrative. Peter has worked hard to affirm
a staggeringly bold identity for the neophyte and persecuted church. As
a "chosen people" and a "royal priesthood" (1 Peter 2:9–10), they are
heirs of Yahweh's great historical narrative of forming a worshiping
people. This identity brings a huge mantle of mission. As "aliens and
strangers," they are to live with an essential and obvious goodness such
that those who persecute them will be moved to faith (1 Peter 2:11–12).
For Peter, one of the greatest opportunities to live and embody this
mission comes under oppression and suffering. Hence, he speaks very
directly and particularly to Christian citizens in a suffocating empire,
slaves in an oppressive economic system, and wives in the midst of
a harsh patriarchy, urging them to follow the example of Christ in
persecution and to utilize the backdrop of flawed human systems as
an opportunity for mission.

The words of 1 Peter 4:7–11, then, are a culminating summary to
this missional exhortation in regard to suffering and social reality.
The directive to "love each other deeply, because love covers over a
multitude of sins" does not come to us as a trite, pithy biblical truism
that is deeply anesthetized to the harsh and banal realities of humanity.
Instead, it stands in clear acknowledgment that, to use our previous
words, we are a mess.

So what does this memorable text mean? The word that Peter
chooses for "cover" is a root of our word for "apocalypse" (*kaluptei*).
He is not talking about sweeping a little dirt under the rug. He believes that the exercise of love creates an apocalyptic or obliterating
impact of the sinful realities of human life. Not that evil, sin, or even
our selfish prejudices will disappear. No one could accuse Peter of
that kind of naiveté. Peter is writing to a marginalized and suffering
people and knows full well the severity of wounds that result from
human fear, hatred, and injustice. But he believes the profound love
ensconced within community can overwhelm and destroy the legacy
of these horrors! Peter believes fully in the redemptive capability of
human community that is shaped by God's Spirit and directed by
the values of God's kingdom.[5] Community represents possibility.
It offers a path and possibility for us to overcome, or perhaps more
accurately "overwhelm," our damages and liabilities in every act of
humanity as well as in the reading of the good news of the biblical

text.[6] In other words, we do not have to interpret the text through the often-catastrophic bondage to our biases. The presence of God's Spirit and our submission to the call of the Spirit to love each other can transform our humanity into a missional asset in the reading of Scripture.

Community as Necessity

Community can confront the biases and selfish intentions we bring to the text and to life. It can instead place us in the center of God's redemptive purposes. The letter of 1 Peter gives us some clue as to the nature of community as it functions in this manner (we'll return to the quality of community a bit later). But this description of community is more than a beautiful possibility; it is an *intended* necessity.

The language of intention drives us to the biblical story of origins, God's creating work in Genesis. These stories of creation assert the absolute necessity of community for humanity to live in God's purposes. The story of creation begins with a sharp distinction between the Creator and the created. The Creator is pre-existent and not contingent on the activities or purposes of any other. The creation originates from a state of non-existence described as void and chaos. Order and purpose in the creation come solely from the intent and activities of the Creator. Despite this dramatic contrast of origins, the author tells of a surprising and remarkably intimate connection between the Creator and the created, most particularly humanity.

Humanity is lovingly grafted into an already ordered universe (rather than chaos). We are spoken into being, formed out of the very breath of God. Finally, a significant missional purpose is bestowed to humanity, to be worshipers of the Creator and to proclaim this posture of worship by accepting the mantle of stewardship over God's creation.

Unexpectedly, humanity is created with an essential diversity represented first in gender—male and female, spiritually equal yet remarkably different. This diversity is forged from the greatest of intimacies. We are told that the first woman was created from the body of the first man. Perhaps uniformity would have simplified the tasks of worship and stewardship, but that was clearly not God's intention. It is our differences that decisively mark us as worshipers. In our differences, we are constantly reminded that our personal experiences and perspectives are not universal, that we are finite. The diversity of creation hardwires into created humanity a relational appetite and the inescapable need for mutuality and appropriate dependence. The story's shared-rib explanation of the origin of humanity emphasizes that we are literally a part of each other. We simply cannot know God to the fullest as solitary worshipers.

Community serves as a necessity for us to live in God's created, intended purpose. The Genesis words "it is not good for the man to be alone" (Gen. 2:18) reside in the text like a beacon. As we come to our sacred texts, revealed by God to direct us in our mission as stewards and worshipers, we must come as the community of the created, fully aware that we cannot interpret and contextualize these narratives and directives *alone*.

Of course, "the community of the created" brings with it just a few, shall we say, logistical issues. We don't ever gather as a whole race. Post-Babel humanity is divided by time, language, ethnicity, experiences, and all the consequences of our post-Eden brokenness. Gathering as specific communities in specific contexts, huge questions loom: How do we gather in smaller groupings and not ruin the whole process? If bias is present in every individual reader, are these biases not exponentially empowered and compounded in our imperfect communities?

The Hermeneutics of Peoplehood

The entirely accurate catechetical answer to this question is a determined expectation of the role of God's Spirit in our communities, our interpretative dialogues, and our missional responses. But we must insist on more exploration of this question. How do we as communities read the Bible in God's Spirit?

Somewhere beyond the idea that the text must be interpreted only by the "experts" who then pass its message on to the masses, and the idea that each individual bears the responsibility for reading Scripture on his or her own, facilitating all kinds of spiritualized prejudices and maligned theologies, there is another alternative. This third alternative is what theologian John Howard Yoder calls "the hermeneutics of peoplehood."

Yoder introduces this phrase in the opening chapter of his book *The Priestly Kingdom*.[7] He begins by tracing the long history of the practice of dialogue and open community interpretation of text, particularly in the ethical mission of the church. His explanation also offers a rationale for why this practice has waned to the point that it has to be remembered and justified among contemporary Christians.

Yoder next explains that Western thought has "been a pendulum swinging between the collective and the individual."[8] The far points on this pendulum represent our greatest interpretative fears, collective authoritarianism and individualistic anarchy. Drawing from his own tradition of the Radical Reformation, Yoder asserts that there is another path. He writes:

> It is the testimony of radical Protestantism that there does exist a third option, which is not merely a mixture of elements of the other two. Communities which are genuinely voluntary can affirm individual dignity . . . without enshrining individualism. They can likewise realize community without authorizing lordship or establishment.[9]

The distinctive elements of this third option are free association (which precludes the tyranny and coercion of authoritarianism) and covenant (which insists on a coherence that prevents anarchy—that is to say, it is our basic agreements that make our disagreements interesting, appropriate, and formative).

The challenge in Yoder's model is to find a way for these expressions of free association and covenant to coalesce into appropriate acts of interpretation. This brings us squarely to the quality of the communities we form. Communities differ radically in scope, goals, and values. Without defining some universal measure, we likely would agree that all communities are not equal. For example, a white supremacist group or a criminal association might theoretically be characterized by free association and a shared covenant. But they certainly don't fit

Yoder's idea of "affirming individual dignity . . . without enshrining individualism."

Yoder guides this conversation on the quality of community by directing us to the only Gospel where we find the word *ekklesia* (literally "assembly"), which later morphs into our word for "church." In Matthew 18:15–20, we find a remarkable promise to the early followers of Jesus who will later become the church. They are told "to bind" and "to loose" and promised that their acts of binding and loosing will be ratified in heaven. If this is one of the primary gospel statements about the community that will form after Jesus' ascension, then, as we might say in the South, "It's a doozy!"

Yoder writes more expansively on this idea of binding and loosing in *Body Politics: Five Practices of Christian Community*.[10] In the community dialogue of *binding*, we arrive at moral obligations. This is the community antecedent to being able to assert in a specific context that "one should or even must." In *loosing*, a community absolves moral obligations. In this act, the community functions as priest and makes assertions such as, "You are free to live in liberation from and forgiveness for the pain you have caused others by your selfishness or sin."

The key to binding and loosing is not even the ethical values that demand binding, but the commitment to live in forgiveness and reconciliation. The proper and persistent application of binding and loosing should result in a community's increased experience of reconciliation and forgiveness—the love that covers a multitude of sins. In this expectation, we find, once again, evidence of the need for the guiding presence of God's Spirit to direct the interaction of text and community.

Reading as a community requires much faith, for truly God's Spirit is the source and author of our desire to be reconciled and forgiven. Continuing our aggressive desire to press the "hows" of the Scripture/community intersection, we are curious about the nature of responsiveness to God's Spirit. How do communities receive and reflect a commitment to live in reconciliation? How do they gather to seek the kingdom of God and how do they gather in a posture of humility and generosity since no community fully represents the diversity of God's people? These are enormous questions because reconciliation seems to be the essential ingredient in the birth of free association and covenant necessary for reading the Bible.

Reconciliation is obviously hard. Most of us yearn to live reconciled with our friends, family, and colleagues, yet so often fall short of this hope. In order to experience reconciliation more often, we need to move this idea from a theoretical hope to specific practices. We would assert that the impulse for reconciliation lives in the free space created by the practice of hospitality as a pervasive spiritual discipline and as a defining practice of community. We believe that a biblical practice of hospitality is, in its essence, an act of binding and loosing, that demands and assures the reconciliation that both invites us to freely associate and compels us to firmly adhere to the covenant shaped by the contours of Jesus' kingdom.

Acts of hospitality directly inform how we interpret the text by defining who we allow to sit in the circle and read with us. Hospitality is the dual act of receptivity (a wide-reaching receptivity to the perspectives, ideas, and needs of others) and honesty (meeting others with an honest and appropriate presence in regard to our own perspectives, values, and needs).[11] The hospitality that we are describing finds its power (and the basis for its honesty) when it is anchored in a set of values and commitments of Jesus' kingdom. Jesus' redemptive kingdom and our hopes in this kingdom that we call "gospel" (or literally "good news") give breadth and breath to our hospitality.

So when we ask, "What kind of community reads the text?" our immediate answer to this query is that it's the hope-filled, other-cheek-turning, extra-mile-walking kind of community. It's the kind of community that is actively engaged in the practices of loving our enemies to the point of friendship; of being utterly dependent on God rather than our own ingenuity; of walking humbly because we realize that we're all victims of our own lusts; of eschewing earthly treasures; of asking, seeking, and knocking. It's the kind of community described in Jesus' Sermon on the Mount (Matthew 5–7).

This is the kind of crazy association where meekness, poverty of spirit, peacemaking, purity, and showing mercy when you don't have to are assets rather than liabilities. It is the type of hospitality that creates a context for our engagement with the text. Putting this in

Yoder's language, we would suggest that the practice of hospitality is the source of our free association (the origin of a Spirit-led interpreting community) and a commitment to the values of Jesus' kingdom is the basis of our covenant-making (the coherence a Spirit-led interpreting community) because the formation of a community of God's people is the whole goal.

As pastors, nothing is more delightful than seeing examples of communities who are practicing the ethics of the kingdom encountering the biblical texts. In these moments, commitments are made and vulnerabilities expressed that remind us of the presence of God's Spirit in the community and the surety of the hope we confess. In my (Tim's) former church, I saw this happen on several occasions related to an arena of life where all bets are usually off in regard to hospitality and reconciliation—finances!

I should have known something "strange" was afoot based on my first year of ministry in this community. I had previously worked in a very large church where I had a full-time administrator who booked events, signed contracts, and managed the finances. Now having to do these tasks for the first time, I planned a weekend event and grossly miscalculated the costs to the extent that I overspent the annual budget in the *second* month of the fiscal year. I went hat in hand to our financial leadership expecting to be fired or at least severely critiqued. Instead, I found grace and mercy. Offering forgiveness to me that evening, they even went so far as to make a commitment to add sufficient funds to our budget that year so that we could operate according to plan.

A few years later, in the midst of a building program that was severely challenging the operating budget, our leadership team was approached by a fine organization asking about the possibility of partnering with us on the building project. The offer involved the potential of more than a million dollars. There were four of us on the board that strongly felt that this collaboration would change the tone and ethos of our community. Others felt that the offer was a miraculous intervention and a sign of God's mercy to us. This was one of the rare times on this elder board when we divided according to political values—the social liberals opposing the offer and the political conservatives eager to proceed.

This leadership team had always read the texts on God's provision with a radical faith perspective. On the evening of that discussion, we read and prayed through Matthew 6:25–34: "Therefore I tell you, do not worry about your life, what you will eat or drink; or about your body, what you will wear. Is not life more important than food, and the body more important than clothes? Look at the birds of the air; they do not sow or reap or store away in barns, and yet your heavenly Father feeds them. Are you not much more valuable than they?" (vv. 25–26). To the dismay of the board majority, this group of four, including me, vetoed the offer. (We used a consensus style of decision making, so one veto would have been enough.) One would imagine that post-meeting conversations would have been filled with challenge, frustration, and perhaps even accusation, but there was never another word said, formally or informally, about the veto (the only veto in my fifteen years on this board). This leadership community not only made room for a radical reading of texts on money, they also had an extremely hospitable view of friendship.

The denouement to this story was equally exciting. Our potential partner moved to another plan for expansion that worked out far better for them. And just a couple years later, during the very week we signed papers to authorize construction of a new facility, our modest community received a three-million-dollar gift from a former attendee whom no one on the current staff even knew. Even better, following our legacy of reading the text, the leadership team decided to give away about a quarter of the gift to other churches and organizations. Eventually, one of the largest beneficiaries was the community Dan and I help lead today, Emmaus Way, when yet another leadership team decided it was missionally important to extend hospitality to a church start-up that would differ from them in practice, vision, and even doctrine.

When the spiritual practice of hospitality combines with the biblical text, the possibilities of mission, repentance, and transformation are truly limitless. This is a dramatic story, but we see these collisions every day as friends open their homes to others, share and sacrifice beyond the limits of comfort and convenience, repent from entitlements and selfish plans, and commit to love enemies to the brink of friendship.

The Text/Community Intersection: Coming Full Circle

The hermeneutics of peoplehood are embedded with practices of reconciliation, forgiveness, and hospitality shaped by the values of Jesus' kingdom. Acts of association and covenant based on these practices shape a community hermeneutic that liberates the biblical text from our worst biases. Even more so, the Scriptures literally become the Word of God for us as they live, breathe, and speak within the very fabric of our communities. The intersection of text and community is truly a space of possibility where some of God's created intentions for community are fulfilled.

We want to affirm this possibility in two examples that we will lay out in the next two sections of the book. First, we want to take you inside a series of text conversations. These conversations are generated out of our small community, one that is fully committed to being an interpreting community. This means we are committed to facing our limits and the many biases we bring to the text. We are also committed to honoring the texts as God's inspired Word to the church and living the challenging paths of community we have described in this chapter. We are a community that intentionally seeks to put itself within the hermeneutical circle of Christian practice and reading the Bible. Of course, we regularly fall short of these high standards. But we continue on this path and have found the Scriptures to be powerfully transformative to our lives together in worship and mission. We hope to share a bit of that transformation in part 2 of the book.

This chapter has been formed around the bold assertion that a series of community practices are intimately woven into our interpretation of the text. Interpretation and community practices of the gospel cannot be separated. In part 3, we will come back to this and specifically address practices we believe form the full circumference of the circle that forms a community hermeneutic. These practices are wide-ranging and, we believe, draw us to the text with a passion to read, discuss, struggle, and contextualize it in such a way that it becomes transformative and salvific.

Part 2

Turning to the Text

→ 4

An Interpreting Community

The Bible is intentionally and relentlessly communal. Emanating from the triune divine community, the text truly becomes the living Word of God as it is received as such by specific human communities. We have suggested that interpreting the Scriptures is the collaborative effort of multiple communities, the full community of inspired authors and compilers of the text (the canon), the historical community of those who have read these words as sacred text (the catholicity of the text), and specific practicing communities. From our perspective, drawing on the rich theological language of John Howard Yoder, the communities that best rise to this challenge are those who follow the Spirit's leading by forming or associating based on the discipline of hospitality and those that organize or cohere on the basis of Jesus' kingdom teachings. In this section, we want to demonstrate these realities, honestly and to the best of our ability, with the humble cooperation of our worshiping community, Emmaus Way.

Authenticity is not the only reason we have chosen to illustrate the above points in our own community. We have enlisted our community because it is simultaneously unremarkable in many attributes while also being at times extraordinary (in our biased opinion) according to Yoder's constructs of community. The unremarkable nature of our community is essential to this book's thesis. We believe we are advocating a community hermeneutic that is entirely replicable in any other worshiping community.

We have also wanted to go much farther than just saying, "You can do it!" We want to say in the strongest possible terms, "You should do it!" This is where the strengths and special qualities of our community do come in. If this were a book on church planting, we could fill the pages with frustrations, mistakes we've made, missed opportunities, and miscalculations. But we truly love this community and find many unique gifts and blessings in both its vision and its people. We believe many of the special attributes of the community are direct results of our commitment to be an interpreting community and the practices we faithfully employ toward this end. (The third and final section of this book will be dedicated to some of the transformations.)

Understanding ourselves as an "interpreting community" pushes us toward texts that we as individuals avoid, breathes life into texts that we have become weary of through too much attention, utilizes and overwhelms our personal prejudices, expands the range of our interpretation, and most importantly presses the text into our local community as the incarnate Word of God.

At first glance, the mantle of "interpreting community" appears to be a bit of a battlefield promotion for our small church. Living and gathering at the doorstep of Duke University and still quite near the University of North Carolina, we can be overeducated and overly ideological. It takes no imagination for both of us to hear the adjectives and qualifiers that our rural, blue-collar kin would apply to the people of Emmaus Way. We like to joke that our community maintains two social classes—"the pre-affluent" and "the educated poor." Higher education is certainly our norm and where we are most vulnerable to critiques on the absence of diversity.

Despite this, we do have a good bit of social and lifestyle differences. Our politics are mixed, though we have a few more liberals than conservatives, and our theologies are quite diverse, though many in our original community hail from the evangelical tradition. In our racially divided home community of Durham, North Carolina, we wish our church had much more racial and ethnic diversity. We are also a small community in number (less than one hundred). We are either very traditional or very eccentric, depending on who is talking about us. We have visitors who claim we are one of the most non-traditional churches they've ever attended, while other guests claim we are the most traditional church in which they've stepped foot.

We are not so creative that we claim to be on a cutting edge that others have not found, and we are certainly not perfect. We suspect that many of the pastors and leaders in other communities who visit our worship gatherings expecting something really unique go away a little disappointed. There is music. The Eucharist is celebrated. (Some have even accused our festival style of celebrating the sacrament to be "snacks after church"!) Though a lot of people talk, one person does tend to talk more than the others. Though we gather in the round and eschew any form of stage, it is pretty clear where the focus is and who is directing the service. In short, it is a church. We do, even when the forms differ somewhat, the activities one typically associates with "church," and we find these activities to be essential for our life together following Christ.

Where we are unique (especially in our geographic location) is the rationale for some of our practices and the expectations that have emerged in the community from our vision. One special quality is that we have developed a passion for the intersection of word and community as well as our distinct willingness to hear each other's voices. This is not an innate skill. It is a learned practice we've worked hard to cultivate. The community expects to be asked to interpret text. They would now be profoundly disappointed if this responsibility were taken away. Though most have admired the Bible and have respected it as God's Word all of their lives and some have expertise in the tools of exegesis, the community passionately believes in the challenge and privilege to interpret. They greatly value the diversities in our community and are open to hearing divergent voices. We believe that many of the strengths of our community are due to this commitment to a community hermeneutic.

Process

Three of the four chapters that follow offer a window into a typical text dialogue for our community. (The fourth will include a dialogue within our worship gathering.) If "interpreting community" sounds a bit lofty for our small church, then "interpretative dialogue" is certainly far too dignified for this exercise of engaged banter, passionate comments, constant interruptions, sacrilegious outbursts, life-shortening snacks, and good drinks. But, honestly, we think something sacred happens in these events. The value of the product for our community is inarguable. Our text conversations widen our understanding of the scope of the possible interpretations of Scripture, challenging us to embrace and embody meanings of text that offend our sensibilities, upset our sense of comfort, and force us beyond what we are usually willing to serve and believe.

To demonstrate this process, we invited our pub group to join us for this series of conversations. (You will hear more about this group later.) The pub group seemed very appropriate for this task. The group meets weekly for honest and comfortable dialogues while also remaining quite fluid (no pun intended), meaning anyone can drop in—which is often what happens. They have some strong ideological differences but are also lacking certain aspects of diversity. In other words, the group has many of the attributes and limitations of a typical church small group or a neighborhood book club.

We also opened each of the conversations that follow to the whole church. The only preparation for the conversations included announcing a genre of Scripture (see page 88) and a specific text. Some came having read the text and others had not. Everyone was informed that the conversations would be recorded as a podcast (which is normal for our Sunday worship dialogues). We were very intentional in *not* recruiting specific persons—be they "experts" or those who represent voids in our community's demographics—in order to remove any objection that we were uniquely prepared for such a conversation. We share these descriptions to remind you that a community of interpreters and listeners exists in your circle of friends or fellowship. Your group would have diversities that we lack and would certainly lack some that we have. But this process is entirely replicable in your community.

For the purpose of podcast quality and uninterrupted dialogue, we parted from our usual pub for these three evenings to meet in our regular worship space. We settled in, once again embracing our identity as a Scripture-interpreting community, and plunged into a series of texts.

Our desire is that the texts themselves be the star of these conversations, so we'll dispense with any long introductions of the participants. Instead, we'll introduce our friends as we go along. We've also chosen, rather than to give you a battery of quotes, to concentrate on the broad themes and movements of our conversations. All of our friends were willing to be identified by name when we do quote them or summarize their thoughts. It has been our tradition to do text dialogue in an accountable manner, speaking vulnerably in public domains. The group, which differed each week, was more than willing to continue this value and share it with you.

One final note about our group. We live in a university community where criticism is part native tongue and part community sport. In the academic world, critique is the oldest and most common form of praise because only that which matters merits the critique of others. Our group, then, is well versed in the art of criticism. As you join in on our conversation, you might find yourself refreshed at the honesty of our thoughts or you might be stunned at our irreverence. This is who we are, but that doesn't mean every conversation—or every group—will look like this one.

You might be drinking good wine instead of our "three-buck chuck" or not drinking at all. The tone of your conversation might delete some of our finely honed university backwash sarcasm. Authenticity to context is the key to tone and location. Be who you are. The real issues are the questions and the genuine freedom to ask those questions and respond without impunity. As we proceed, you'll see that our text conversation involved just as much construction and interpretation as its deconstructive elements. But don't miss this point—it is good to let it out! The questions and concerns we asked (and more that we didn't ask) are there whether we like them or not. Sometimes the difference between being prophetically true and simply trite are the questions we tolerate before we get to the truisms.

A Word on Texts and Genres

We thought long and hard about text selection. This seemed a place where we could cheat and ruin the whole exercise. This concern pushed us to be sensitive to the traditional genres of the Scriptures (the Law, historical narratives, the Poets and Prophets, Gospels, Epistles, Apocalypses) while also generating our own genres that effectively separate the Scriptures, and to demonstrate the breadth of a community hermeneutic. The genres we settled upon are as follows: the obscure, the emotive, the familiar, and the controversial. Not only do these fabricated genres accentuate the reader's—or interpreter's—range of relationship to the text, but also one could fairly state that most, if not all, of the Scriptures fit within these designations.

These divisions in some measure predict what texts we avoid or choose to engage. As we have said previously, all readers of the Bible have a tendency to create a canon within the canon. Fellowships and teachers that have religiously avoided the obscure can navigate through the traditional genres of the Bible while still neglecting a whole collection of texts. Churches that migrate to the controversial can find text to fuel acrimony in every genre. We believe our non-traditional genres go a great distance in subjecting community interpretation to the whole of the Scriptures.

→ 5

The Word in the Obscure

Genesis 34: The Rape of Dinah

In a scene that will become familiar as you read this section of the book, about ten people from our community gathered in Emmaus Way's worship space. This space is an urban storefront (hardwood floors, high metal ceilings, warm lights) with comfortable sofas. We brought plenty of snacks, a cooler of beer and sodas, and a few bottles of wine. We talked long into the night (which is often our custom on pub nights). The conversation continued long after the podcast had been stopped.

The length and energy of the conversation was not a surprise to us. We were most confident in addressing the obscure genre of Scripture. By the time they are writing dissertations, graduate students tend to become experts on very precise, specific, and sometimes unheard-of arenas within their greater discipline. Hence, our university subculture seems to set us up for a good discussion of an obscure text. The biblically literate in our community are quick to toss out jokes about Eglon (the Moabite king whose huge girth swallowed the sword of the Israelite judge, Ehud

[Judges 3]), the horrors of the sin of Peor (Num. 25:3; Josh. 22:17), and incomprehensible texts like Genesis 6:2 (when "the sons of God" desired "the daughters of men"). Those in our community who are unfamiliar with the Bible seem to relish these stories and particularly the honest confusion about them from those who grew up in the church or who are more familiar with the Bible. Given our environment, we admittedly felt that we had a bit of a home-court advantage in this genre. Because of this we also decided to add a twist, choosing a text that was not only obscure but also hard to render neat and safe.

We were also not surprised because Scripture dialogue has become a practice that our church has found extremely fruitful and one we have continued to employ each week both in preparation and in our sermon dialogues. In doing so, we have found that imaginations are liberated, hearts are heard and encouraged, lives are challenged and convicted, and the Scriptures are opened to us in ways we could never have imagined. Furthermore, and more importantly, engaging the text together forces us to actually *enter* it, often allowing it to turn us upside down and inside out, and then place us in unfamiliar territory. The strange world of the Bible became strange for us again as we listened to each other wrestle with it and articulate it to each other. And we saw again that our community seems to crave these conversations.

We were not disappointed during the evening. We were mysteriously formed when we sat down together to square up with this obscure text. Encountering this unsafe and perplexing episode of Genesis, however, we found something powerfully meaningful and life changing—like a treasure one stumbles upon in a field. This would prove to be the case time and time again. We soon found that obscure (even obscene) texts can be strangely liberating. After a brief retelling of this story, we'll share in broad strokes some of the themes of our dialogue.

The Story

The rape of Dinah, the daughter of Jacob, occurs in Genesis 34. Jacob, with his large family and extensive flocks, has faced the brother he cheated, Esau, and has bought land near a Canaanite city. When Dinah goes out to visit the women of the land, she encounters Shechem, the son of the local ruler, Hamor the Hivite. Filled with desire, Shechem rapes her. This unthinkable act sets in motion a bizarre and unpalatable narrative. Shechem has a great affection for Dinah and begs his father to do whatever is necessary to make it right by securing Dinah as his wife. Hamor does just this, offering to Jacob's clan the prospects of further intermarriage and, thus, a profitable economic alliance. Shechem adds that no magnitude of a bride price would be refused.

In response, Dinah's offended brothers brew up an unholy and clever plan. They demand that all the men of the city be circumcised to erase this offensive breach of ethnic purity violently tainted by Shechem's sexual appetite. The men of the land, with visions of wealth and property, agree to the plan. But while they are still nursing their wounds, Dinah's brothers Simeon and Levi kill all the men of the city, including Hamor and Shechem. They remove Dinah from Shechem's house and their brothers loot the city, presumably gaining an enormous profit. In a later text, Jacob "rebukes" (if indeed it is a rebuke rather than self-serving worry) his sons' actions, while they counter his curse with the moral equivalent of shrugged shoulders, coyly asking, "Should he have treated our sister like a prostitute?" (Gen. 34:31).

Blessedly Inappropriate

Our community has developed a great sensitivity about contexts. When reading the Scriptures, we are eager to grasp a whole range of contextual issues—the historical context of the passage's content, the environment and provocations of the writer, the literary arrangement of the text by the writer, the long historical context of the church's reading of the passage, and our context as readers and people of faith. One of the challenges of this passage is that the pursuit of context is treacherous. This quest unearths a veritable pit of sensitive, often highly inappropriate questions—the kind of questions we regularly avoid in public interpretation. We ran headlong into some of those questions.

Travis, the husband of a Duke Divinity student, works for an organization that specializes in capital punishment opposition. He shoved us immediately at the rather large elephant in the room by asking whether this was rape, by our contemporary definitions, or some form of "consensual, defiling sex." Bill spoke next (and thank goodness it was Bill!). All the following adjectives and descriptions apply to him—compassionate, sensitive, and thoroughly loved in our community, especially by those who have suffered or have been marginalized in organized Christianity. To complete this picture, he is in his fifties, has a twenty-five-year résumé as a senior pastor in a variety of US and international settings, and also has a doctorate in psychology. At the time, Bill had traded his pulpit for the ownership of a café in a neighboring community. With a little grace we were all happy to give him, beloved Bill took the really narrow path on this one by asking whether Dinah made herself fair game in that environment by going out in the land as a young woman alone. Bill phrased it as "going out to meet the girls." Bill pressed the idea that Dinah was knowingly in the wrong place and that she surely had accomplices. As a daughter of the clan leader, she would have been a protected woman, most likely with servants who attended to her needs.

This suggestion of Dinah's culpability drew the loving ire of Brandy and Amy. Amy is an ordained Methodist pastor who is currently back in graduate school preparing for a career in public health and non-profit management. Brandy is a first-year Duke Divinity student. We had little doubt that they were more than sufficient to the task of holding up the feminist end of the night's dialogue. They were both very quick to remind us that our reading of the text on this evening was not to follow the common path of a male perspective tacitly affirmed by women who do not speak. (Much of Brandy and Amy's advocacy for a feminine perspective are offered in the next section.) After the guys finished verbally torturing Bill (and sucking up to Amy and Brandy), the whole group knew that it was quite significant to explore the nature of this shameful sexual act.

With the help of biblegateway.com and a few other online services, we quickly recognized that the translations are consistent in referring to Shechem's sexual exploit as an act of violence by employing English words such as "seize" and "rape." Nonetheless, Travis and Bill took us to an awkward but necessary place. The present nature of and practices related to relationships, marriage, and sex are radically different from those espoused in the ancient Near East hundreds of years before Jesus. And the disparity between our modern view of relationships and that of the ancient world was only accentuated by the fact that even in our small discussion group there was a significant diversity of opinions on sexual matters.

The actions of this narrative and its unspoken assumptions of sexual politics are foreign, uncomfortable, and even mysterious to our culture of volitional marriage and volitional sexual expression under the banners of varying ethical standards. For example, in cultures of nomadic patriarchy where daughters are safeguarded possessions often used as barter for the political and economic goals of their clans, what really was the nature of this sexual wrong? In cultures such as these, do women even have the power of sexual consent? Is the primary offense in the story the economic loss (the marring of property), the shame (as expressed by Dinah's brothers in the story), the breaching of a social code of hospitality, or the sexual violence against Dinah?

Bill, who was really on a roll that night, nudged us down another perilous path when he asked about the role of beauty. Shechem's desire for Dinah is said to be "great," encouraging the possible assumption that Dinah was a beautiful woman. Bill pointed out a bit of speculative irony, reminding us that Dinah's mother (Leah) was not considered "cute" by Jacob, but her daughter sure appeared to be so. As Bill put it, "I don't think boys have changed much." But have they? Is this about beauty? And for that matter, what is beauty? Brandy quickly reminded us that if we are going to employ modern assumptions to interpret this event, then we should at least remember that most rape crisis agencies teach that violent sex is more about the exercise of power rather than sexual motives or the desire of someone deemed beautiful.

The link between beauty, power, and sex is very real, unsettling, transcultural, and persistent over time. Contemporary studies reveal that there is a strong correlation between male wealth and perceived feminine beauty.[1] The writers of the Hebrew Scriptures would certainly agree. Their writings teem with portraits of the full harems of kings, the instant sexual selection of women of renowned beauty by men of power, and ridiculous-seeming family dynamics exacerbated by beauty. (I'm thinking of Abraham's and Isaac's foiled "plans" to disguise their "beautiful" wives as sisters in foreign lands [Gen. 20; 26:1–11], and Jacob's indignity when he found that he hadn't married the beautiful sister [Gen. 29:15–30].) At our text party, Bill quipped as if from personal experience, "Beauty always complicates matters." When we asked him if he "considered himself a wealthy and powerful man" filled with the sexual innuendo of the discussion thread, his grown son began to complain bitterly that it appeared we had not bought enough beer! The conversation had reached its low point, meaning we had finally approximated the level of this text.

The interpretative path of this Hebrew story runs with little or no pause through the nature of the sexual offense to the account of the human responses to this egregious act. Like any sexual violation, the consequences are social, corporate, and broad reaching. Because we now live in a diverse, mobile, pluralistic culture our sensitivities, experiences, boundaries, and expectations related to sexuality vary greatly. This diversity collides with these biblical texts that affirm some of our sexual assumptions (like the link between sex and power) and yet move far outside the range of any of our norms (and we've yet to even broach the issue of corporate, voluntary, adult circumcision in the text!). An open, honest, occasionally inappropriate, confrontational community conversation clearly brought us closer to the interpretative issues of this text than any of us would have been able to go alone.

Gender Wars

This will come as no surprise to you, but as our conversation ensued, it often erupted into a series of emotions, perspectives, and challenges surrounding the issue of gender. We live in a world rife with the realities of differing genders, differing sexual orientations, and differing sexual narratives based partly on these differences. The simple binaries (male/ female; straight/gay; slut/virgin; married/unmarried) break down in our sexual landscape. We need terms like *transgender*, *formerly married*, *sexually experienced virgins*, *biological parent*, and *baby mama*, to name a few, to simply begin to sort out the vast nuances of sexual roles in our culture. Listening to the voice of God's Spirit in our very diverse experiences seems essential and unavoidable if we hope to unravel narratives that strike such varying chords based on our differences.

Brandy and Amy were quick to challenge any blanket assumptions of responsibility on Dinah's part by the guys at our discussion. But our gender differences were even greater. Some of the guys (including Dan and me) kept pushing like barn-shy horses toward forms of abstract speculation (given the culture, was this really a rape, and if so, what would that mean?) and macro-analysis of the story (why is this narrative in the Bible?). Admittedly, reading this story in Durham, North Carolina, in the wake of the infamous Duke lacrosse sex scandal and subsequent disbarment of our district attorney due to willful mismanagement of the case, creates an incredibly unique local context, an impetus to reflect on the societal impact of sex crimes and accusations.

Dan did just this, offering his personal disgust with rape yet also reminding us that we live in a town that had been torn apart by a rape accusation. As proof-positive that context means everything, the accusations against these affluent, white, male athletes—while untrue—did not seem so outlandish given the history of our city. It was this context that led many in our city and even at the university to call down the wrath of God on these young men. And yet, despite all appearances, our ire at these young men had been misplaced at least to the extent that we wanted to see them face the full extent of the law for actions they had not committed. (Consequently, probably the worst thing about the rush to judgment against these young men is not how they have been supposedly victimized by an overaggressive DA, but the simple fact that the young men who were at that Duke lacrosse party have never since been asked to repent for their mistreatment of women and the racial epithets that were uttered. As it turns out, if you can prove yourself a victim of some sort, you can do nothing wrong.) Important generalizations spring from this biblical text and our own local story of sexual shame.

Bill continued this tack of speculating about this crime in the abstract. In a deliberate understatement, he reminded us that the sons of Jacob were also a group of very "rowdy boys" possibly looking to take advantage of the situation for their own purposes. Their severe reaction to their sister's rape, the murder and looting of a city, seems to be driven by a whole range of selfish and insidious motives. As Bill put it, "perhaps the boys doth protest too much." These are fantastic and necessary trajectories of exploration because they lead us into a discussion of truthfulness.

But leave it to the women to see the most obvious component of the narrative that the men were quickly glossing over! Brandy and

Amy were insistent and persuasive that we not marginalize the personal element of sexual violence committed against this one woman. Social research reveals a shameful amount of sexual victimization of women in our culture (18 percent in one study).[2] These statistics drop sharply for men. As a result, as men we remain limited by our gender perspective and are typically blind or insensitive to the rape element of the saga. We can say with some conviction that none of the guys glossed over the circumcision component of the narrative! There were plenty of moans, exclamations, and sets of crossed legs when we got to this commitment by the men of Shechem's city!

The women in our group also immediately recognized the absolute silence of Dinah—this in a story about Dinah! The men, whether playing the role of villains, perpetrators, negotiators, or casually interested bystanders, seem to have their say. But Dinah's voice is not heard. This is not an unfamiliar situation (male violence and female silence) for us today. Brandy, making reference to a recent work entitled *Texts of Terror*, offered a strong personal testimony to how passages like this can operate like terrorizing texts to women.[3] This story is an obvious example of how gender limits our ability to interpret the Bible and yet how gender diversity opens the door to new facets and territories in the text that often remain undiscovered.

Blaming God

Many of us raised in various Christian subcultures of America have gained the reflex of, after having made a sacrilegious comment, looking frighteningly to the sky in fearful anticipation of a well-aimed lightning bolt. This simple jest by those of us who respectfully affirm the presence of God in our universe communicates the lack of confidence we share in criticizing or directing anger toward God. Some of us, however, are learning to move past this fear. In our discussion of Dinah, God took a few hits but no lightning bolts were spotted. In fact, this part of the conversation accelerated our interpretative work.

Almost all of us remarked that we had never heard any minister preach on this text. Brandy quipped that none of the "Psalty" praise tapes she listened to as a little girl mentioned it. This text is largely obscure because our churches intentionally avoid it, certainly for the delicate and complex sexual matters included. But perhaps another reason for its obscurity is that God doesn't fare so well in this portion of Jacob's story. Gone are visions of stairways to heaven filled with angelic presences (Genesis 28), the allusions of perpetual economic blessing (Genesis 30), and the bestower of personal blessings (Genesis 32). In their stead, we find potentially a provincial deity who allows favored sons to foster a deceitful plan that facilitates the murder and plunder of an entire city. This shorter vignette comes as a portion of a greater story where God "loves" and "hates," choosing some and seemingly neglecting others. Jacob is "loved." Esau is "hated." Jacob cheats and is repetitively blessed. His uncle Laban cheats, and, well, thanks for playing and good luck next time. Wives are favored over other wives. Sons are favored over other sons.

Someone in our group asked, "Who likes these stories about choosing and hating?" Mark, whose tenure as a Presbyterian elder almost ended in excommunication over his divorce, was quick on the draw, saying, "Presbyterians, that's who!" The subsequent cleaning up of a couple of spilled drinks and retrieving of a few expectorated M&M's gave us a chance to take a breath on this one. As we've said often in this book, our pains and our experiences are never far from the conversation when the Bible is involved.

This whole story reeks of human selfishness, petty rivalries, murderous competition, and spiritual infidelity. And where is God? Though Dinah's silence is disappointing and painful, God's silence in the text is remarkable and even shocking. In our discussion, I (Tim) had remarked that I had once spoken on this text at a large campus ministry event. I assigned the key roles in the story to various students, asking them to come on stage and speak out their lines from the text. I made quite an ordeal in offering the role of God, via popular acclaim, to someone who had a strong speaking voice and significant social respect in the audience. Of course the big show was just a set-up to demonstrate the silence of God in this text of horrors.

In our conversation, we kept returning to this silence. Mark may have said it the most boldly when he noted, "The conspicuous character who doesn't show up is God. God doesn't start something . . . stop something . . . crap, where is God?" Dan recalled Al Pacino's rant while playing Satan in *Devil's Advocate* that God was just a game player and a watcher. He likes to set things in motion and sit back.

On top of this, Bill added to the idea of God's absence that "it seems if you're a member of the family, you can do no wrong." Our group had enough Old Testament savvy to cite the truism that the characters of the narratives are rarely heroes or ethically pure even when they aren't acting in morally repugnant ways. The only real hero in the Bible's "immorality plays" is God. But Brandy's response was sobering: "What do you do when the hero isn't acting heroic?"

Travis helped us to get past our personal potshots and sharp questions for God (slanted certainly by many dark nights of theological wrestling by our small community). Directing us back to the choosing, hating, and loving, Travis reminded us that God's "love" and "choice" isn't always a good thing and that not being chosen for the team can actually work out quite well. As he put it, "Being loved can mean some bad stuff!" Being loved often involves such activities as "taking up a cross" and being persecuted and reviled by those who do not love God. Like every community, we bear our own scars from pains incurred in the faith. Much of our sharp tone comes from this very reality, caring for others so much that it hurts, following callings that are fraught with criticism and risk, and having the courage—or foolishness—of speaking aloud questions that others hold in silence while bearing the scorn of those who believe this to be blasphemy.

There seems to be a variety of components necessary for the affirmation of God's gracious intervention in the morass of our world. First one must be able to assess the reality of humanity and creation in need of grace and intervention. A second often forgotten or forbidden element is the freedom to direct strong questions, even painful indictments, to our God, as is modeled so often in the Psalms. This portion of the conversation ran headlong down this narrow, less-traveled path. We would strongly assert that our embrace of the goodness of God and the value of this text as God's Word to us at the night's end (see the end of this chapter) was directly related to our freedom to raise these questions of concern, fear, and disappointment.

Enlisting the Academy

As we have discussed the concept of this book in seminaries and in our network of friendships, one concern has tended to emerge often and usually quickly: what about scholarship and the academy? We are often asked if we are neglecting the work of the experts and the traditions of the church and replacing them with the "whims" of our local community. This issue came up in our text conversation as well—we'll get to that in a moment. But it deserves a bit more explanation before we proceed.

In our small church, disproportionately filled with graduate students, many make their meager incomes as servants and pledges of the academy. While it might be the case that some communities pay too little attention to scholarly voices, we tend to be plagued by the opposite problem—people in our congregation sometimes say we are too academic in our discussions of the text. While we certainly do recognize the value of academic discussions, many times we feel overly influenced by them. Hence, the question could be reframed as it is directed specifically to our context: Is our community practice with text some form of rebellion to the master many of us serve? Is it an attempt to break free from academic domination?

It is a question we should—and do—ask ourselves. But demythologizing the academy quickly allays these concerns. First and foremost, the academy itself is a dialogue, albeit at times a grumpy, pretentious, and obscure dialogue filled with symbols and language that many of us are not trained to understand. Despite this obscurity, and hence the limited population who understands the conversation, a dialogue remains.

Laypersons and the uninitiated can easily miss this dialogue, especially in regard to the Bible because the Scriptures are so often presented to us in absolute terms. We read the commentaries and books of scholars and pastors who sound absolutely convinced by their interpretations and opinions. So many sermons are presented in strong, unwavering tones of surety as "messages" from God (and who is to argue with God?). In some preaching circles, a lack of certainty is a mark of weak leadership and vision. Even with those who are more vulnerable in personality, the interpretative decisions and scholarly forks in the road are typically trumped by the urgencies and expectations of the twenty- or thirty-minute sermon (and I would be willing to bet that many of those who preach much longer would fit in the category of being utterly convinced in their opinions). One lesson we learned from many great scholars is there is often a direct correlation between the adamancy of tone ("certainly the way to read this text is . . .") and the volume of disagreement over its meaning.

At Emmaus Way, we just finished a series of sermon dialogues on the book of Romans. If there ever was a portion of the Bible that has prompted inflexible and adamant interpretations, it's Romans. In truth, though, academic opinions on Romans are as varied as the number and type of scholars working in the field, chasing differing trajectories of interpretation based on systematic theologies and the national, cultural, historical, and epistemological differences of the interpreters. Perhaps ad nauseam, we spent portions of every evening exposing the differences of interpretation to our community.

Now some may want to retort by saying, "There are a lot of people who are wrong about Romans! But the real Christians [or the real evangelicals, or the real Lutherans, or the real whomever] see the clear message of the book as _____ [fill in the blank]." The following story should be some deterrent to this line of thinking.

Jeff McSwain, the former Young Life area director in Chapel Hill/ Durham, received national attention this year when he and several local YL staff resigned or lost their jobs as a consequence of a doctrinal dis- agreement.[4] While forming a new ministry to urban teens and develop- mentally challenged teens, Jeff was asked to discuss these doctrinal issues with a small group of prominent evangelical pastors whose churches were Young Life supporters. A couple times the conversation got a little uncomfortable and contentious. Then a wise pastor offered the follow- ing point that we'll paraphrase: "We are all united under an evangelical ethos and perhaps even in our discomfort with some of Jeff's thoughts, but we need to remember that when we leave this room we'll still be in disagreement over issues of baptism, the language of salvation, and the proper governance of the church (no small matters indeed!)."

Our point is that there is far less consensus, even among leaders and scholars in the same traditions, than you would imagine over biblical interpretation, even on matters that can hardly be called peripheral. A preacher might be adamant about his or her message during that 11:00 hour, but the equally respected pastor on the next corner is likely to be disagreeing during the very same hour. Even hiding behind denominational or theological labels does not entirely remove this reality. In regard to the academy, it just brings its own highly informed dialogue to the text.

In our text conversation, the academy made a significant mark. A couple of us had heard Jo-Ann Badley, professor of biblical studies at Mars Hill Graduate School, teach on the Dinah passage and inserted her thoughts into our conversation. Badley's teaching offered some insight into the greater structure of this story and significant perspective into both the obscurities and offenses of this text.[5]

I (Tim) have reflected on this teaching for several years and thus offered the group on that evening a synthesis of Badley's teaching and my own reflection. The Jacob story appears to revolve around two remarkably parallel narrative structures that frame Jacob's departure (a journey literally away from home and metaphorically away from God's graces and reiterated promises of blessing) and Jacob's return home. The story is framed by two genealogies of two "rejected" (or not chosen) brothers from different generations—Ishmael and Esau— and turns on the directionality of Jacob's travels. Given this analysis, the story could be diagrammed in the following manner:

The Flight Narrative	The Return Narrative
Ishmael Genealogy (25:12–18)	Esau Genealogy (36:1–43)
A Beginnings (25:19–34)	A* Endings (35:1–29)
B Isaac and the Philistines (26:1–35)	B* Jacob's sons and the Shechemites (33:18–34:31)
C Blessing (27:1–40)	C* Blessing (33:1–17)
D Jacob's Flight from Esau (27:41–28:9)	D* Jacob's Approach to Esau (32:2–32)
E Encounters Angels (28:10–22)	E* Encounters Angels (32:1–2)
F Arrival in Haran (29:1–30)	F* Departure from Haran (31:1–55)
G Children (29:31–30:24)	G* Flocks (30:25–43)
Jacob's Return to Canaan	

In this narrative structure, the shameful episode of Dinah's rape and the dealings of the Israelites with the Shechemites stands in parallel to Isaac's dubious and faithless encounter with Abimelech, the

king of the Philistines. In this segment of the story, God commands
Isaac (along with his sons, Esau and Jacob) to stay in the land of the
Philistines despite the potential of respite from a drought by fleeing
to Egypt. Great promises of wealth, blessing, and favor from God are
made in this story to Isaac, just like those that will be made later to
Jacob. Isaac obeys God by staying in Abimelech's city, Gerar, but he
faithlessly doubts God's promises of safety by proffering a shameful
lie that Rebekah, his beautiful wife, is his sister. When Abimelech
sees Isaac caressing Rebekah, he is incensed. Bringing Isaac in for an
audience, he furiously speculates about the potential consequences
of this deliberate deception. What if one of the men of his land has
slept with Rebekah and brought guilt upon the whole land? (This
conjecture offers some perspective on the sexual dynamic of Shechem
and Dinah.) Isaac is ordered out of the land. Despite Isaac's faithlessness, God's faithfulness to him is revealed in his clan's perpetual
ability to find water (always an urgency in the nomadic life but even
more so during a drought) and Abimelech's eventual plea for a treaty
with Isaac and his clan.

As we look at this parallel event as well as the whole narrative
structure, several themes jump off the page. Location, directionality, and the proximity to God's blessing of Israel are all related and
extremely important. Isaac is to stay in Gerar. When he is forced to
leave, God blesses his destinations with the provision of water. Certain
locations are off-limits in the narrative and would presumably lead
to hardship (like Egypt in this case). When Jacob (like his father due
to his own deceit) is forced to flee Esau, he is told to go to his relative
Laban's land, which will assure that Jacob marries within the tribe
(another important ethical imperative that sheds light on the episode
with Dinah). When circumstances dictate that he must leave Laban's
land, his journey is presumably home and eventually to Bethel.

The location of Bethel is extremely significant. Bethel was the
place where Jacob saw the vision of a stairway to heaven but sadly
remarked that "surely the LORD is in this place and I was not aware
of it" (Gen. 28:16). In Jacob's flight from home, he is not aware of
God's presence and apparently does not believe in the inevitability of
God's blessing (which is reiterated all through the narrative). On his
journey home, he finally receives God's blessing in the aftermath of

his wrestling with a divine visitor (Gen. 32:22–32) and experiences it tangibly in Esau's forgiveness of his deceit (Genesis 33). The whole journey ends in Bethel, this time with clear awareness of God's presence in blessing. He is commanded by God to settle there and build an altar (Gen. 35:1), which he does in full awareness of God's blessing and the significance of Jacob's being in this place (Gen. 35:7). At Bethel, Jacob is once again given the name "Israel," which becomes the name of God's people and the primary symbol of their being chosen by God for blessing and the blessing of the world.

Reflection upon the structure of this series of stories produces an obvious question: "What in the heck was Jacob doing settling near the city of Shechem along the way!?" The issue of marital purity by avoiding intermarriage with the Canaanites is clearly significant to the story. God has constantly reminded the tribe that their spiritual blessing would be marked by economic prosperity (Gen. 25:23; 26:3–4; 27:28–29; 28:1–4; 28:13–15 at Bethel; 32:28–29). They do not need to go to extraordinary lengths to find wealth. When they needed water, God provided it. God had provided a huge family (an economic asset in those times) and huge flocks to Jacob (the essence of wealth) despite Laban's protestations. But as they settle at Shechem, one detects once again the scent of greed (coming close to a prosperous city) and the faithlessness that has plagued this story (acting as if they need to find and secure their own wealth). This stop in the journey puts the tribe in a place of spiritual threat (namely, intermarriage and idolatry) and military threat (which was always present in a nomadic world of limited resources when different families and nations came in proximity to each other).

Jacob has willfully set up shop in the wrong place in a story where location and proximity are paramount. Dinah *is* in the wrong place. Shameful sexual violence takes place (even if it was an expected norm—remember Abimelech's fears). One now sees that Jacob's tribe got what they wanted in the first place, greater wealth and power, in the most shameful and faithless manner, at a great cost for their sister and by means of committing a horrific tragedy upon an entire people!

This story is a macabre example of human stubbornness and shame in a metanarrative of grace and blessing—an interruption in the movement of the narrative that reveals what God is working with in his attempt to redeem humanity and, as an intended corollary, the magnitude of his graciousness and forgiveness in the end.

Community and Scholarship in Tandem

Badley's scholarship applied to this long narrative is significant and insightful. Her work on the narrative ordering is obviously the product of long reflection and scholastic experience with Old Testament narratives. There are elements to her reconstruction of the Jacob story and some of my own synthesis that we could have never gotten in one group conversation. This simple reality points to the significance of intersecting the scholarly dialogue over the text with our own conversations.

But it is equally important to see how dramatically our community's thoughts resonated with these insights from the academy. Luke Timothy Johnson explains:

> Too often, we begin Bible study by showing them all the ways in which they can't read. "You don't know archaeology, you don't know history, you don't know what's going on, so let me instruct you on what you're supposed to find in the text." Whereas, I am convinced that if you take any 10 people off the street, bring them into a room, have them read a passage of Scripture together, and work with them as you're reading, within an hour they will come up with every solution to the text that's ever been invented in the history of scholarship.[6]

We were very careful not to interject Badley's observations until the very end of our dialogue. Nonetheless, we smiled often as the group drew ever closer to these points. We enjoyed vilifying the much-loved Bill during our evening together. But Bill had sensed the significance of location and proximity in the story. He didn't make any statement about complicity but said Dinah was in the wrong place because her father, Jacob, was in the wrong place. The writer of Genesis added that bit of detail (the visit to the women of the land) to draw our attention to both location and motivation. And Bill was quite prophetic when he quipped that "the boys (Simeon, Levi, and the rest of the brothers) doth protest a bit too much." Our group was persistent in sensing and exposing the greedy heartbeat of this story that drew the tribe of Jacob toward a location fraught with the dangerous possibilities of forbidden intermarriage, blasphemous idolatry, inappropriate economics, and physical threat.

Even the delicate conversation about the role of beauty was affirmed by much of the scholarly conversation on the passage. Like it or not, women during this time were economic assets, a form of property, that required protection and demanded respect in this culture of nomadic patriarchy. Our conversation did an excellent job of balancing our contemporary sensitivities about sexuality with the strange and offensive (to us) sexual politics of Jacob's world.

This sexual code, much of it recorded in Deuteronomy 22 (proofs of virginity, capital punishment for sexual offenses, financial gifts to fathers of sexually slandered daughters, the difference between rape in the country and the city where a girl is required to call out for help to be innocent), exists far outside our sensitivities. It reveals how much our notions of marriage and sexuality have changed over time. Travis was quite astute in raising the question of what kind of sexual offense was involved. Our group did an excellent job of exploring these great cultural differences, honoring the context of the Scriptures while demanding that those texts speak into our contemporary wounds and interests. The diversity of our group allowed us to forge ahead for larger interpretive issues without glossing over the violence done on an individual level (particularly to Dinah).

This first example of text conversation in community strongly affirms our assertion that the intersection of text and community does not require the marginalization or the negation of the academic community. We would say the opposite, that this process creates space for the work of scholarship.

The Hard Work of Hermeneutics

One of our pet peeves is that the task of hermeneutics can be so easily forced into a flat reduction or outright ignored in many settings. The preacher so often applies the text only to the world that he or she knows or can imagine. Those chained to various degrees of literalism can utterly miss the tensions and dramatic differences between the world of the Scriptures and the context of the current reader.

There is something about a diverse group of friends on the road of discipleship coming together over a challenging text that drives the conversation to hermeneutics. Reading a text devotionally while alone in our favorite chair or proclaiming the lesson of a text from the authority of our pulpits can lead us to rest in the comfort of a static interpretation. But static interpretations are fleeting fantasies in the open conversation of a diverse community. We bring too many differing life experiences to the table to allow for an overflowing level of certainty. Our interpretative methodology drives us to demand that the text function as Scripture for and in the whole of the practicing community. An abstract meaning disembodied from the questions, needs, and context of the community, even if attainable, is not permitted or desirable. The community demands that the text truly live as inspired Word, breathing life into our wounds and hopes.

Amy was the first to ask the critical question, "Why does this story exist in the first place?" Amy is well aware of the function of historical narratives. She understands that our expectations as readers of Scripture and the intent of the biblical writers is to discover and compose historical stories with both declared and implicit theological metanarratives, ethical lessons, and spiritual motivations. Amy was particularly concerned about the potential "collateral damage" with a text like this that drives us to search for goals of the text and intersections with our lives. By collateral damage, she means not only the horrors in the lives of the participants of this passage but also a history of misuse in the church (offering heroic justification for the choices of Jacob's sons, ignoring the feminine perspective of this story, affirming the silence and disengagement of Jacob since he has become a "converted" patriarch at this point in his story, and more.)

As our group began to engage Amy's question, we were quick to affirm the previous point that there was something special about taking on a text like this in community. Bringing this text into our community as Scripture required levels of courage in questioning and exclamations of outrage that are frequently hard to summon alone, or if they are experienced, remain largely unarticulated in order to avoid the shame often associated with "questioning" God or God's Word.

For our community, this text began to take on the guise of a larger-than-life morality tale. We received this text much like a Quentin Tarantino movie such as *Pulp Fiction* (and Dinah's story certainly merits the genre of "pulp fiction"). In one scene, two ruthless, hired assassins (played by John Travolta and Samuel L. Jackson) drift into an inane conversation about burger names in Europe that sounds a lot like the banter that occurs every week in our pub group. Though they are killers for hire, they sound a lot like us.

One of the artistic movements of *Pulp Fiction* is to confront the imaginary "goodness" of polite society by demonstrating their similarities to those they rightly consider "evil." This is the power of a morality tale. In embracing this similarity, we recognize that we, at a certain time and place, are fully capable of the horrors we abhor in the film. In the same manner, one of the functions of Dinah's story in the Scriptures is that of a morality tale. The narrative takes us to a frightening, realistic space where we see our own greed, violence, and willingness to live outside of God's redemptive work and goals of mercy. This journey is especially dark and meaningful for those of us who may claim to be God's tribe, just as Jacob's family would have been prone to do.

Another of our takes on the Dinah story as inspired Word is its demonstration of a point that we previously dismissed, the gracious and redemptive character of God. After a conversational journey through our frustrations with the silence of God, this point rests more comfortably in our consciousness. Whenever we look carefully at the failures of humanity on a grand scale and vulnerably own those failures more personally, we develop a vision for the breadth and depth of God's love for us and the extent of God's intervention into the morass of our lives.

Of course, it is important to never lose sight of the reality that our tawdry, "pulp fiction-esque" story is part of a much larger narrative where God is not silent and operates incarnationally in the worst of human history. Like so much of life, timing is everything. As we've said before, the difference between trite affirmations and life-changing truisms is a function of timing and place in a conversation. Our earlier challenges to God allowed us to boldly offer these conclusions about the redemption and goodness of God to each other.

Finally, and perhaps oddly, the very nature of this story as a portrait of failure affirms the value of Scripture to people in our community, who are admittedly prone to encounter the Scriptures with some combination of expectations, doubt, and suspicion.

The writer of Genesis does not wrap this narrative in a pleasant bow. Instead, it ends with a morally deflective question by Simeon and Levi, the perpetrators of great violence: "Should he have treated our sister like a prostitute?" The only conclusion to this outrage comes in Genesis 49:5–7 as Jacob speaks his final words of prophetic blessing over his sons:

> Simeon and Levi are brothers—their swords are weapons of violence. Let me not enter their council, let me not join their assembly, for they have killed men in their anger and hamstrung oxen as they pleased. Cursed be their anger, so fierce, and their fury, so cruel! I will scatter them in Jacob and disperse them in Israel.

The evening's participants all affirmed that one of the reasons we receive the Bible as inspired Word and text for the church today and beyond is the presence of texts such as the rape of Dinah. As Jacob's final words indicate, the Scriptures are not silent on the failure of humanity. These are not the edited words of humans standing in self-affirmation and only gentle reproach for our sins. Tales such as this brim with cultural honesty about the necessity of our redemption, and yet, at the same time, they shimmer with the promise of that coming mercy even as they speak of the ongoing graceful presence of God.

→ 6

The Word in Pain and Joy

Psalm 22: The Cry of Dereliction and a Song of Deliverance

Psalm 22 is probably one of the most well-known psalms in the whole of the Psalter. Even those who don't know the whole thing are somewhat familiar with the first line, "My God, my God, why have you forsaken me?" This desperate plea continues for the first twenty verses of the psalm as the psalmist cries out to God for deliverance from suffering and impending hostility. God remains holy and enthroned but unnervingly distant as bulls and dogs circle the lowly, lonely, and broken poet. Yet, the text takes an unforeseen turn at its loudest moment in verses 19–21 amidst the screams of the writer. Help arrives and God comes near, splitting verse 21 in half. Shouts of joy burst forth as a rowdy worship celebration breaks out and the world is made right by God. Horror turns to gladness, dystopia becomes peace, as God's salvation springs upon the scene from nowhere. It is an enigmatic text to say the least.

Most of us will recognize verse 1 as the disturbing shout offered by Jesus just before his last breath on the cross (Matt. 27:46; Mark 15:34). It's a line that has been the cause of much comfort for those in trouble and needing to take solace in the humanity of Jesus. It is also a line that creates much consternation for the concerned theologian who maintains the necessity of defending the impassibility of God. The opening words of this psalm have echoed over the centuries, communicating the unspeakable, horrific, and majestic mystery of the death of the Son of God that lies at the center of our faith.

Preaching (and simply reading) from the book of Psalms is, no doubt, a difficult task. We have to say that on more than one occasion when given the choice on what to preach we have quickly bypassed Psalms in order to preach the Gospels, Paul, an Old Testament narrative, or even the prophets. While a poem may be a nice way to conclude a sermon, most of us find it extremely difficult to base a sermon upon something as elusive and emotional as a psalm. Without a quick and easy theological "truth" to run to, we as pastors have tried to steer clear of that unavoidable writer's block one experiences when sitting down to construct a sermon from these texts.

Perhaps with no surprise at all, our dialogue began with silence. We were all struck by the fact that after reading Psalm 22 together we initially had nothing to say. There we sat gazing at the pages of the text and each other, speechless. We all seemed to be reliving those awkward days of high school English, when the teacher would ask for comments on Shakespeare or Poe, and we'd all shrink back in our seats hoping she would not ask us to comment on the meaning of the poem that eluded quick understanding.

Needless to say, we quickly found ourselves wondering why we had thought to pick this psalm as a text in our "emotive genre," because, when read aloud, it all of a sudden seemed to be too emotive for our cultured public discourse. With this realization, it seemed only natural to begin with the question: well, what type of psalm is this? How did the Israelites sing it? Was the tune upbeat and rock-a-billy, or was it morose and melancholy? In what part of the worship service (assuming the ancient Hebrews had something like a worship service) did it occur?

"Well, of course, it's to the nice, tranquil tune of 'The Doe of the Morning,'" Mark, one of our resident musicians and producers, laughingly commented, pointing to the textual note of introduction. We have to admit that reading the lines of this psalm against the backdrop of the tune of "As the deer pants for the water, so my soul longs after you" was a little too much even for our strong sense of sarcasm. The raw emotion of the text did not quite seem to fit with our contemporary aural familiarities, leaving us to chuckle at the thought of how these Fiona Apple–style lyrics would be received in a modern-day praise-and-worship gathering. What a party-pooper this psalm must have been for the worship team. Just imagine the band plugging in, only to see this ancient Debbie Downer of a song enter the room. Whamp, Whamp, Whaaaaaaaamp . . .

Getting Real

Communities are comprised of many stories. There are several individuals in our community whose painful past experiences have left deep scars on them. We are a people who don't always come to church with our hearts full of praise, ready to celebrate the holiness of God while trying to ignore the pain wreaking havoc in our lives. Amy, the former pastor you met in chapter 5 who has recently battled her own share of demons, pointed out that while initially Psalm 22 does not appear to be very uplifting, it may be just the words that those experiencing pain need to speak in worship. The cry of dereliction at the beginning of this psalm, and which echoes throughout the first half of it, speaks authentically to the lives of many personal stories. It speaks to real life in a way that some genres of worship music consistently miss. The psalm is raw and exceedingly honest.

So why do we have such a hard time reading this text? Why do we always want to run to the comfortable end before sitting with the first twenty verses? As pastors we are all too aware of the fact that our church bears a strong internal divide between the "haves" and the "have-nots." During our discussion, Tim pointed out that there is more than an economic divide buried in that separation. It is a divide between those who have known real pain in their lives and those who have not. While engaging with people on varying sides of this divide, we have also come to see that much of the time the gospel seems to have more meaning for those who have encountered suffering in their lives. And as a result, a worship service, small group, or prayer life that has no place for pain seems to lack a depth of engagement with the gospel.

Those on the suffering side of this divide, those who are living the hell we so often try to pretend does not exist, find a Christianity dominated by those who have not known pain to be extremely superficial. "So often I've found the modern church full of clichés," Amy intoned. "People say all kinds of things in order to avoid really interacting with pain. They say, 'Oh, you know this isn't God's plan,' or, 'All things work together for good.' All those things you really don't want to hear when you're in trouble. It doesn't seem to give people permission to simply sit with those who are in pain," she continued.

"Yeah, I mean, when have you walked into a worship service and found yourself singing along with a tune like this?" asked Mark with more than a hint of pain-informed sarcasm. Their comments pointed to the tendency to shrink the text to such a small size that we discover our faith incapable of speaking to the broad range of human experience, especially the human experience of intense suffering and pain.

Suffering Together

Many recent books have been written critiquing the hyper-individualized character of our culture. We believe the modern infatuation with the individual has been such a dominant narrative that it continues to taint our read of nearly the whole of the Bible, and this is a point worth stressing again and again. In the contemporary cult of the individual, few portions of the Scriptures have been as bastardized as the Psalms. This corpus of prayers, songs, and poems composed to be vocalized by the whole people of God, that is, by collective communities, has been turned into thousands of individual, God-given promises of wealth, health, deliverance, a great new job, and a Porsche in the driveway. As Amy adamantly pointed out, "The poetic attestation to Israel's (remember that this name means 'to struggle with God') relation to Yahweh can so easily be turned into a compilation of pocket prayers, each as a quarter to be placed in the giant gumball machine in the sky."

When we simply take as a starting point the individual and her Bible, it may be too easy to twist Psalm 22 in ways that miss much of how it was meant to be heard. As Mark pointed out, "Given the fact that much of ancient Hebrew culture was not literate, how would it affect the interpretation of the passage to recognize that it would not have been engaged by the single individual, alone in her study, but by the whole people in song together amidst the various practices of worship in the tabernacle or temple?" Simply hearing this text with others as a passage for the whole community and not for the individual seems to refuse an overly materialistic or overly spiritualized reading. More importantly, it doesn't let us run past the pain of the text because it forces us to see that pain in the faces of those gathered with us.

Our group shared a laugh at how the strong juxtaposition of verse 1 ("My God, my God, why have you forsaken me?") to verse 3 ("You are holy") might sound in a modern worship service sung as an echo where the women begin with, "I'm miserable," and the men return, "But you are holy." Our sardonic imaginations flooded with pictures of Ned Flanders of *The Simpsons*, his house collapsed around him, singing about the goodness of God. Reading this psalm together, we realized that we could not let each other run quickly to the words of consolation at the end, and as a result were forced to wrestle together with the strong tension and uneasiness this psalm began to evoke.

Reading the Old Testament, our community has been consistently shocked by the number of times God seems to be conspicuously absent from the picture. Here again in the first half of Psalm 22, God seems to be in God's normal place—missing from the scene. It is a scenario that was probably all too familiar to the Hebrews. And yet it is in this situation, as Dan pointed out, that they seemed, over and over again from Exodus to Malachi, to remember how God worked for their ancestors. They recalled the stories of Abraham, Isaac, and Jacob. They spoke again of the days of God's delivering them from the hands of Pharaoh when they cried out to an absent God in Egypt. Though God was missing from the scene, together they continued to speak of this God who acted in their history in such a decisive way. Through dark days, their collective memory reminded them of the fact that they were not alone, that they were Yahweh's people and that, contrary to all appearance, Yahweh was not dead. But while the memories of God's deliverance were strong, their experience of the pains of Egypt and God's long silences were equally so.

Living in Durham provides our community with a somewhat unique, and possibly jaded, perspective on our culture. While technically Durham is one of the three cities surrounding an area known as Research Triangle Park (often called the Silicon Valley of the East Coast), which encompasses some of the most affluent zip codes in the Southeast, if not the entire country, people in the Triangle area typically think of Durham as the unwanted stepchild. To our Chapel Hill and Raleigh neighbors, our city is usually thought to be a place of random and intense violence, gangs, drugs, prostitution, and the like. Yet many of us living in Durham know it to be something quite the opposite. In fact, we find it to be a community of respite from the crazy, all-out competition for material goods that seems to have engulfed our successful region. Hence, many in our community have a heightened sensitivity to the consumer culture of our nation and the ways in which this insidious virus has infected the church.

In a world where we seem to be able to select our gods just as we do our morning cereal, our shaving cream, and our brand of toothpaste, interacting with a God who is often silent seems to be a waste of time and, quite frankly, a bad economic decision. Why wrestle with a God who doesn't jump to fulfill every desire and impulse before you even know you have it? Why struggle with a God who lacks attractive and foolproof packaging to guarantee the best possible product? If enemies are encircling like ravenous dogs, why call out to the God who seems to be hiding in the trees when you can purchase a Smith & Wesson 45 ACP 4½-inch automatic pistol for $597.80 (a great deal even for the 1-percent-a-year tither) and have it delivered same-day air guaranteed? As Joel, a person in our community who grew up in close proximity to one of these extremely affluent zip codes and who has some strong theological convictions regarding what it means to live faithfully in a culture of unrestrained consumption, pointed out, "The relational toil implied by Psalm 22 is so new to us lazy American consumers. We don't want to put forth any effort; we don't want to struggle; we don't want to work!"

In contradiction to our trained instincts to choose independence, individualism, and a god who will best fulfill our immediate needs, we began to think together of what it might mean to suffer in a community, looking together for a God who has not yet arrived. Our group began to consider the fact that this psalm, while written in first-person-singular language, is actually communicating more of a communal (first-person-plural) experience. This was an insight reaffirmed in our research of the scholarship on this passage. Richard J. Clifford informs us, "The singer is not a private individual but the king himself" speaking as a representative of the people of Yahweh.[1] In contrast to our first inclinations to read the cry of dereliction as an expression of individual despair and frustration, together we began to surmise what the psalm might communicate if we were to read it as a corporate plea.

One of us noted that as the psalmist pleads his (or their) case to the Lord, he does so by turning God's attention to the Exodus. "To [God] they cried [in Egypt], and were saved" (v. 5 NRSV). It was when they were in the hands of Pharaoh that, "In [God their] ancestors trusted; they trusted, and [he] delivered them" (v. 4 NRSV). Rescuing the people from Egypt, guiding them out through the divided waters of the Red Sea, God gave birth to the Israelite people and claimed them as his people. And it is God's people, God's possession, and God's own reputation that are at stake here. This Creator God, the God who spoke to Abraham, the God who brought forth Isaac from a barren womb, the God who blessed Jacob and who brought the Israelites up out of Egypt, is entirely bound to the fate of this people. Their future is Yahweh's future. They were born out of pain and suffering, and these ancient communal stories of God's work in similar times become the loci of hope. Hence it is God's action with the people—even many years ago—that seems to bring solace.

The Hope without Explanation

Any reader of this psalm cannot miss the drastic shift that it makes in verses 21–22, and our group was quick to jump on it. What had been a psalm of lament and despair all of a sudden in one verse unexpectedly becomes a psalm of hope and praise. As Tim mentioned, "This psalm takes one of those crazy-psalm turns. Completely unexpectedly, the poor will eat (v. 26), dominion belongs to the Lord (v. 28), spiritual redemption comes rushing in, but nothing up until this point looks like God has dominion. Are we missing something in the middle? How do we get from point A to point B? This hope seems hard to embrace because it is so abrupt!" It is hard to embrace, especially for intelligent, cause-and-effect trained readers. A solution might be nice, but it seems deeply unsatisfying when we can't see all of the steps. We want God to show some math in the margins! How will we know we can trust this hope with half the equation missing? How can we trust that God will put this broken and fractured world back together without sharing a few notes? We *need* to know how!

We live in a world that has an established method for solving problems. To reach a solution, you develop a hypothesis. You test that hypothesis. You test it again by reproducing your experiment. Then you have someone else test your hypothesis in order to get independent verification. Finally, you publish your results in a scholarly paper, and let the rest of your colleagues in the field run your experiment. If all goes as planned, you end up with a detailed theory, describing the cause of the problem and the solution you are offering. If you want your theory to be received and your solution to be accepted, then you must keep very specific notes describing your process closely so that others will know how to reproduce it and achieve the desired result. By placing such veridical emphasis on this approach to knowledge, we accept that anything that does not abide by this scientific method cannot be known.

This psalm refuses to play by our rules. No science, no method, no reproducible results, simply despair that turns to hope. It's a hope we could never expect and never anticipate. And it's just the way God loves to arrive on the scene. As Tim pointed out, "God comes out of nowhere!"

One person in the group continued this line, profoundly noting, "Hope without explanation is something that makes me uneasy. It seems farcical, fictitious, and out of touch with reality. I tend to have little appreciation for a God who appears out of nowhere and gives no definite description of God's intentions and methods. And I have a feeling that I'm not the only one." For more than two thousand years,

Christians have worshiped a Messiah who came to his own and was not received because his people could not believe that this poor beggar was the one who would deliver them. And we still have a hard time with the idea that God would come to deliver us in a way that we are not able to anticipate or categorize. And, yet, when the Gospel writers placed these words in the mouth of the dying Jesus, they were making a ludicrous statement: "This poor, wandering Jew, dying the death of a criminal, is God's Messiah." This cry of dereliction, which looks like the last curse of a dying peasant, is the annunciation of God's redemption. Here the promise to Abraham, the promise to Israel, the promise to redeem this world is fulfilled. Gotcha!

If this point seems to trouble you as a reader, we assure you that you are not alone. It made our group uneasy as well. The obvious, big problem here is, as Joel pointed out: "I just don't see how that can be called fulfillment. Because when I think of fulfillment, I think of the whole plan of restoration having come to fruition." As we continued to wrestle with the psalm, we began to see that hope is the key. Hope is both fulfillment and yet not fulfillment. It is to find yourself in what many New Testament scholars and preachers have termed "the already/not yet." We continued to wrestle with this tension between the first and second part of Psalm 22.

Within this tension, Dan began to reflect on why this psalm must have captured the imagination of Jesus' disciples and the Gospel writers. "Having had their eyes opened to see God's unexpected and unpredictable work in Jesus," he began, "the early Christians must have been driven to reinterpret their reality. While suffering immense persecution and the delayed return of their Lord, I think they also continued to see their world through the eyes of hope. Jesus had brought the beginning of a new age, re-creation was happening, but it had not (and has not) yet come to fulfillment." Because redemption emerged from where they did not expect it, they continued to hope that it would soon emerge in full. And as we anxiously await the completion of God's age of dominion, we are called to live as if it were already here. Dan continued, "We are participants in the new age as an act of hope that its full completion is just around the corner. This is not to say that we are the Messiah, but we are his followers—those who have embraced his life and have begun to live it as his disciples."

Worship: Getting Real Again and Cultivating Patience

This whole discussion of hope, however, remains bittersweet. As one member of our group pointed out, "Why then do we identify more with the first part of the psalm rather than the last part? That is, if we are living in the time of the process of redemption and the age of fulfillment, why doesn't it look or feel like it?" It's a tough and very real question. It's the ultimate question of hope. And it's the question that brought us back, in the end, to an encounter with this psalm that led us into a time of heartfelt confession and honesty.

Joel offered his own confession in reading this psalm. "The form of Christianity that I was marketed looks more like a product, a product you really need—and you should feel very anxious about having it. 'My God, my God' is a sinner's prayer. It needs to be spoken by all those who are not saved, and its answer comes at a reasonable price. But once you consume it, that's it. Jesus died for your sins, a state that coincides with the first part of the psalm, but one only need return to this psalm to preach on Jesus absorbing God's wrath over sin for us or to rededicate one's life through fear-stained repentance. No one ever read the back end of this psalm. . . . There was never any talk of communal hope. No one ever talked of caring for the widow or the orphan, no talk of justice or any of these huge themes of the Old Testament." This comment prompted Tim to remark that he'd often seen this form of the Christian message as "kind of God's version of sub-prime lending!"

Dan then made his own confession to the group, submitting the ironic admission of how his involvement with missions and his deep study of the faith had completely ruined his prayer life:

> One thing that I've found very hard since traveling on various mission trips abroad to Mexico, North Africa, Honduras, and places in South America is that it's become extremely hard for me to pray. It just doesn't seem to fit anymore. I mean, I'm asking for things like, "God, please let me into a doctoral program, or let me find the woman of my dreams, or please let Y2K happen so that my student debt will disappear," while there are people around the world praying that their children will be able to eat. Encountering the type of suffering that I have seen in various places completely destroyed my sense that God ought to

be interested in my greatly charmed life. It made me feel guilty, even when I was offering my most altruistic prayers for those out there in need. Yet, I found myself struggling through some very intense spiritual battles of my own and wanting to ask for God's deliverance. And this would always point me to the tough question here: what is the legitimate "My God, my God, why have you forsaken me?" Is it all right for me to pray for something I have really dreamed of doing— something tied directly to my vocation in the faith? Is it okay to pray for my family and my future, when the fact that even if these things did not work out, I'd still have lived already a life that is vastly better in comparison to others in Darfur or El Salvador? Is it okay for me to speak this prayer, or is it only for those in dire situations where their kids need to eat?

Brandy, one of our first-year divinity students with a passion for caring for outsiders, chimed in with her own confession: "Yes, and that even brings up the question of, what should I do? Should I be in divinity school or in Honduras?" If we are in the business of proclaiming hope in a troubled world, is it not extremely important for us Christians to locate ourselves in those places of trouble? What are we supposed to do? Is hope just a clever way of saying that it's okay to sit on the sidelines while nothing really changes? Is the proclamation of hope just another way of putting a religious stamp on our satisfaction with the kingdom of God not coming?

Amy responded to this concern by saying, "I'm with you in my own struggle, but in terms of the pastoral mindset, how do we relate to the various types of people who are hurting in our churches? Does God only care about people starving? So if you're wealthy, then you are on your own? Not sure . . ."

Adding to these thoughts, Tim offered his own confession not so much as a response but in reflection on his own journey through a similar period:

Somewhere in 1995 or 1996 was when I began to learn to pray again. It seemed like my paradigm of talking to God ran out of steam when I was in my early thirties. Many of my professional friends found themselves in similar situations, running spiritually on giftedness until their stamina ran out or honest observation about the mysteries and inequities of life overwhelmed their formulas. The odd thing was that when I quit looking at prayer as something I had to *create*—which is very American—and when texts and liturgies like this could become my prayers, then I began to find my voice again with God! Prayer became an ongoing litany of horror or joy, desperation or fulfillment of the historical Christian community that I could join with my own voice and my own experiences. I didn't need to be paralyzed by my sense of loss (as compared to perhaps those who had lost much more) or my shame (compared to those who have seen horrors I can hardly imagine). The voice and hope of this psalm and texts like it could be my hope and plea.

Reading and interpreting this psalm together, walking with each other through it, listening to what each other heard in it, we began to let the psalm take on a voice of its own. It was beginning to become a prayer for all of us, something that incorporated all of our voices and offered a form of speech with God that we began to understand was requiring us to enter into each other's stories. As a people crying out to the Lord, using words we had not crafted on our own, we were drawn to encounter one another's hopes and frustrations, which prompted us to look even beyond our own experiences, confessing our own inadequate readings and looking toward how this psalm might be lived out in the real pain of our world.

Of course, this seemed to work against the grain of spirituality with which a few of us had become accustomed. Many of us had been taught that recited prayers smacked of "religion," not relationship, an element atop the list of works of righteousness we had learned to criticize in other expressions of Christianity. Anything but extemporaneous prayer could not be authentic, and therefore, inevitably had to be merely empty ritual and habit.

But what we soon realized from reading this psalm is that maybe we don't always know how to be authentic. We don't know what authenticity is, because the truth might be deeper than what we are used to saying. It might be—and probably is—deeper than our initial desires, while our spontaneous attempts at honesty and authenticity never get down to the deep hopes of who we are as a people. Maybe reading, interpreting, and praying this psalm together forces us to pray things we would not normally say by joining us in a larger and historically longer expression of pain. And it is from this expression that a larger, unforeseen, and deeper sense of hope resounds.

In a church culture that seems to have stage-time only for stories of victory and success, this psalm gave to us the words to speak a new language of faith. It carved out a space for the stories of hurt and pain in our congregation, stories of confession and lack of faith, stories of failure and the dire need for deliverance. And it told us that this could be worship! In this way the psalm seemed to nudge its own way into our community, by demanding that if we intended to read it as Holy Scripture, then we would have to let this psalm actually be a prayer of our community. We would have to give room for someone to tell this story. It meant that we were going to have to make space in worship for honesty and confession, while refusing the impulse to try to answer every problem or question. It meant that we would have to learn to be a church that comes closer to people who hurt, people we can't do anything for, and live close to them.

Only here can we begin to speak of the hope that we find in the testimony of Israel and that Christians believe is present in Christ. Only here do we find ourselves joined to a longer, deeper, and more cosmic voice of those crying out for deliverance that can grant us a new vision of hope. It's not sexy at all. It's a hope that takes two steps forward and one step back, requiring that we live in patient expectancy. But it's the type of hope we found in the text, and it's the type of hope that brings change—even if in small doses.

→ 7

The Word in the Familiar

The Gossman Passion: An Artistic Engagement

Every preacher and teacher becomes, at some level, a sworn enemy of the familiar. Opening the lectionary to find texts that have been preached many times before and can be recited by even the marginally biblically literate leaves the preacher feeling she has nothing to say and, frankly, bored with her own redundant message.

Preachers in traditions that do not use the lectionary face the same challenge. Even in the excitement of Advent and Easter, they can often find themselves struggling to write a sermon from these texts that have been worn dull with repetitive use. The Hallmark holidays can be even worse. Mother's Day and Father's Day—don't we feel like we have said it all, all too often? Don't get us started on national holidays, where the preacher may have to land a triple axel by preaching the familiar while also potentially compromising the integrity of his or her theology due to the political tolerances of the community.

Sadly, even in the congregations of the greatest orators, the most spiritually engaged congregant often has some of the same emotions about familiar and common texts, albeit without the same investiture or vulnerability of the preacher. If comic strip text bubbles appeared over the heads of many in our fellowships, utterances like "Yeah, I know that we are all prodigals," "Right, his only begotten son," "Who did I start on my fantasy football team today?" and "I hope I turned the Crock-Pot on and the coffee maker off before I left!" would pop up for all to see.

The familiar is a formidable foe for every preacher and teacher. These texts that have become cultural idioms, like "the good Samaritan," would also seem to be the least likely to be impacted favorably by community interpretation. A community reading of the familiar seems as if it would only lead to compounded statements of the obvious, reiterations of banal sentimentalities, and long, uncomfortable silences. But, we have found this simply to be not true. In fact, what we have seen is that the familiar is often made so because we have bound it up with the limited experiences, low motivation, inflexibility, or static reflexes (to say the same thing that once may have been refreshing and remarkable) of the solitary interpreter.

The Gossman Passion

One Palm Sunday, our community had a profound and unique (for us) experience in engaging a familiar text that illustrates the potential of community interpretation even for extremely pedestrian texts.

Mike Garrigan, one of our community's musicians, was challenged a few years ago by a local priest to take a passion text from the Roman Catholic lectionary and set it to music. The result was *The Gossman Passion*, a thoughtful musical interaction with biblical narrative named in honor of a retiring priest Mike had known for some time. We first met Mike when he was finishing this project. We were instantly intrigued and enthused by the concept of a synthesis of biblical text, musical composition, and imagination. After having heard him perform the piece on several occasions, we were eager to bring this work to Emmaus Way.

Mike is familiar with musical challenges and successes. His post-collegiate, alternative rock band, Collapsis, was successful enough to draw the attention of Universal Records and an eventual contract with that label. He also played with a band called Athenaeum. He saw his share of significant venues, got some sustained radio time, and plenty of critical affirmation in the art weeklies during these two seasons of his career. But setting the passion to music was an entirely different challenge.

The result was a record that uses only the Matthean text of the passion from the Roman Catholic lectionary. He added no words and only omitted about ten words from the text to safeguard the flow of the piece. His *Gossman Passion* has six songs/movements. Mike serves as the "red-letter guy," meaning he sings the words of Jesus. It begins with "Take and Eat," a choral pop song that is more upbeat, appropriately repetitive, and easy to sing, which serves to quickly draw the congregation into the text. "Gethsemane" follows and marks the beginning of earnest lament in the presentation. "Caiaphas" is a somber, complex musical narration that takes the story from the garden through the trial and slander of Jesus. The music is marked by many key changes, tempo changes, and modulations that add a soulful texture to these harsh texts.

Wade Baynham, our music/arts pastor, sang the stark words of Judas, Peter in the midst of his denials, and Pontius Pilate. Wade is a gifted professional in his own right with the unique ability to carry alone the sharp syntax and painful content of these short quotes. His work humanized these tragic figures by placing them in a different voice and allowing them to rise prominently and emotively out of the long narrative.

The fourth movement, "Barabbas," takes the story to the cross where "Eli" places the audience squarely in the midst of Jesus' execution. "Eli" is another pop choral piece that essentially allows two memorable and highly accessible songs to bookend the complex laments in the center. This musical shift to a form that is highly accessible assures that the audience enters the cross scene and is able to contemplate it more fully. Mike has made sure that the choral aspect of this song is an honest platform rather than a censoring barrier to Jesus' words of isolation and agony. *The Gossman Passion* ends with "Tomb," a powerful requiem that leaves the narrative and audience with the dark consequence of Jesus' willing sacrifice: the burial of the Son of God in a tomb made by men.

In the dialogue and question-and-answer session that followed, the responses of our community to *The Gossman Passion* were very obvious. Several mentioned they had heard the passion again—for the first time! For many in our community, these very familiar words simply leapt off the page. Wade's vocals added a texture of humans in agony to the supposed "villains" (Judas, Peter, Pilate) of the story. Instead of residing as distant failures, these three men were brought in uncomfortable proximity to our community. So rich were their pleas and dismissal, that we all felt that these men were speaking our own faults and doubts. They betrayed, denied, and cried in our voices. We joined them in their agony and acknowledged our solidarity with those who put Jesus in the tomb.

Certainly as a community, we could not escape the reality of Jesus' tomb. The lectionary and Mike's music left us in this place, not without hope, but inescapably in the tomb with Jesus. Many in our community had only worshiped on Palm Sundays in joyful parades of waving palm branches to be joined the next week with the exultation of Easter with the tragedy of the passion inadvertently (or advertently) edited out. As Frederick Buechner so artfully teaches us, it is the tragedy of the gospel that creates the space for the comedy, the joy, of the gospel.[1] Experiencing the joy and surprise of Easter requires that we also walk through the valley of the shadow of death. Several in our community commented that was one of their first guided tours through this dark and necessary antecedent to the resurrection.

Interestingly and not remarkably, the open sharing in our community's Maundy Thursday worship gathering just days later was filled with vivid expressions of loss and pain, confessions of failure, and expressions of concern for the wounded in our lives. Mike's artistry had taken us into the heart of Jesus' passion, giving life to the familiar and painful story that is so central to the Gospel narrative.

As we interviewed Mike later, he quickly impressed on us that the impact on the artist was equally dramatic. He has faced many criticisms in his three years of performing *The Gossman Passion*. Some parishes objected to the role of Jesus being played by an "artist" rather than a priest, and others objected to the genres of music represented. Staunch traditionalists felt the text needed no *enhancements*! Mike, like so many artists who take on such a project of the heart, referred to *The Gossman Passion* as "one of my worst business decisions ever!"

Admittedly, his *Passion* project is hard to market. We love the CD, but it is truly a performance piece, crafted for a specific time and place in the church's calendar. And the star of the piece is not Mike or any of the other performers. The star is the text—talk about a marketing dilemma when the star is unable to facilitate blog posts, twitter updates, YouTube teasers, Facebook groups, and media interviews! But Mike is quick to point out that he was touched and spiritually transformed in both the writing and the performing of *The Gossman Passion*. The story of Jesus' sacrifice became embedded in his soul. He described performing this text like a bizarre game of darts in a darkened pub where, regardless of the angle or effort of the toss, one hits the bull's-eye every time. This is the power of this text. For Mike, this was nothing short of a life-changing and faith-changing project.[2]

Reintroducing Communities to the Familiar

Our point in describing this unique interaction of our community with the text is not to encourage replication in kind every time you face a familiar text. This would be a huge and unnecessary burden for us to place at your feet. *The Gossman Passion* took months to write and craft into its current state. The musicians in our community who performed it with Mike are experienced professionals. Despite their training, the piece required more rehearsal and preparation than our usual worship music. And it is still a work in progress. Mike has many new plans for its performance next year! But by reflecting on Mike's work, we can draw several lessons that will reintroduce your community to the most familiar texts of the Scriptures while allowing them to take you to unforeseen places of interpretation and meaning.

The first lesson we are learning in working with gifted artists like Mike is to give them freedom of voice and to let them lead. The unique gift they so often bring to the community strikes at the heart of the issue of this chapter—they give us new eyes for the mundane and the common. In their vision and craft, the ordinary begins to speak with extraordinary insight and prophetic power. The sad truth is that many artists we know have faced both trivial and humiliating acts of censure from the church in regard to their gift to enliven and upset the mundane. If you listen carefully to their stories, you will quickly find a common thread of their being confined to expectations of "setting the right tone," avoiding images and challenges that upset the status quo, and near sacramental investitures in the comfortable and expected rather than creative vision. You could hardly imagine some of the obstacles and insults Mike has faced in presenting this piece, even though it is composed solely of biblical text!

We have often used Bob Dylan's brilliant song "All Along the Watchtower" as both a confessional and a prophetic declaration of hope in our worship liturgy. This simple, brilliant, 160-word song employs only simplistic archetypes (the joker, the thief, princes, women, and servants) that describe both the barriers to creativity and an eschatological hope for new vision.

The joker, likely an autobiographical character, is a symbol of an artist who along with the thief approaches the fortress of tame, civilized society from the outside at "a cold distance." His lament of society's lack of vision is every artist's cry: "Businessmen they drink my wine oh, and the plowmen dig my earth. None of them along the line know what any of it's worth." In the inevitable collision, the citadel is breached and "the money safe" is taken by the thief. The last image—the safety of the fortress compromised—leaves us with a hopeful vision of a world liberated from its addictive illusions of comfort and safety and its ignorance of the gifts of the joker.[3] This has become our anthem for letting artists transform the familiar.

The second lesson for other communities is that we are all artists. (This is a lesson that the gifted often need to remember.) Even for those of us who dread creative demands and lack any skills in performance, we maintain an inalienable creative gift—our stories. Amy, the former Methodist pastor you met in earlier chapters, reminded us recently of the power of story both to recognize tragic and familiar realities many of us would like to deny, and to see visions of redemptive hope for the pains we share. Last June she led our Sunday conversation on the parable of the good Samaritan (Luke 10:25–37). In retelling this story, she took the vantage point of the wounded man on the roadside, and told a remarkable personal story of pain and redemption. Her journey as a wounded follower of Christ includes depression, despair, a debilitating illness that eluded diagnosis for over a decade, shameful prejudice and treatment as a woman in ministry, professional isolation, and constant misunderstanding. Yet, the hope of Christ found her in the place she least thought it would, while she still struggles to believe and trust it.

When she told her story, in a vulnerable dialogue setting no less, only a handful in our community knew any of her history. Her words of challenge to the Christian community in regard to its treatment of mental illnesses still echoes loudly in our midst. Amy placed herself in the story of the good Samaritan as the wounded traveler, watching the community of faith walk by afraid, distracted, or unconcerned. Ten minutes into her presentation, this text was alive, convicting us as well as demonstrating the path of hope.

There's only one Amy, and we are quite lucky to have her in our community. But it would be a grave mistake to think of the content or the dramatic nature of her story as solitary and unique. In fact, her very point was to challenge this notion. Every community, in our experience, teems and brims with stories like Amy's, begging to be told and fully capable of giving full breadth to even the most common biblical texts. In fact, one reason some of the texts of the Bible have been used so often is their relentless intersection with the norms of our lives.

There are many barriers that silence stories like Amy's—judgmental reflexes, ingrained self-righteousness, and the idolatry of "comfort" in our churches are among the most obvious. But we think it is often the preacher who remains the most prominent roadblock to personal storytelling in our fellowships. Whether it is a need for control or attention, or an expectation to be the community's spiritual hero, leaders often impede personal storytelling in the community by neglecting to give people space and time to do so.

Though we're sure we fall prey to these desires at times, we have found that the commitment to community hermeneutics is like oxygen to an open flame in regard to community storytelling. When communities are given the privilege and responsibility to interpret the Bible in an environment that is open to the realities of their lives, personal stories seem to flow from their lips, pens, and keyboards. In turn, the stories that are told constantly offer fresh perspective and new angles on the text. Amy taught us that things are never as they seem. There are hidden and powerful stories enmeshed in common façades—in her case, the pastor and leader many would assume not only has life figured out but also experiences some solace from the normal struggles of life because of her profession.

Our artistic leader and co-pastor, Wade, has written a musical exclamation point to this assertion of the importance of the familiar and the great possibilities for grace and growth ensconced in this realm for those who care to explore it. With two NFL football players in his immediate family and having once been married into another family with a sports celebrity at the head, Wade has been surrounded by lives that many would dream of and some would label as "extraordinary." His personal story and the irony he perceived in regard to the liturgical designation of the time roughly between Pentecost and Advent as "Ordinary Time," prompted him to write a song with his former band, The Basics, entitled "Ordinary Time."

The first verse of the song begins with a familiar lament of the ordinary life that might come from any voice when confronted with a culture or family ethos that exalts superstars:

> I've had a real hard time making sense of it all.
> I know what I want, it's not like before and I'm still here,
>   beating at the door.
> I don't think it's too much to ask to have some things go my
>   way.
> I'm sick of being ignored—I can do so much more, and I
>   could use a break.
> I don't want one day to just bleed into the next—I want to feel
>   my heart beat.
> I want to be extraordinary.

There was a time when Wade's career involved strong flirtations with major record labels and ready access to the cultural elite. But the song's ironic reversal highlights a paradigm shift toward grace and the embrace of the ordinary:

> Ordinary time, Hope Creek flows, the land erodes away
> Ordinary time, you take my hand and I can face the day
> Ordinary time, Hope River flows and finally jumps the bank
> Ordinary time, I'm not the same, and I have you to thank.

I'm not getting any younger, and the days they just fly by ...
I'm not getting any stronger, and I wouldn't call me wise
They always told me I had potential they couldn't wait to see
But there's a voice in my head, like a noose 'round my neck
Telling me you haven't done it yet
But I'll take the grace, the grace given me,
and I think I'll learn to embrace the ordinary[4]

With these lyrics, Wade rejects our cultural definitions of "extraordinary" and the burden this creates in our life. The song's invitation is to see the ordinary as anything but ordinary. The ordinary becomes fertile ground to experience the greatest riches of God's grace.

Every community needs the familiar—rituals, stories, and rites of passage that mark our identity and repetitively reinforce that identity. Though the lack of imagination and creativity can certainly calcify the familiar texts of any community, communities still crave familiarity on some level. But our familiar rituals, traditions, and idioms never have to be the dull version of the ordinary. Every community has the internal resources to give unique and enlivened voice to the familiar events of its life together.

Even the most homogenous communities bring a rich diversity of experience, need, and insight to the most familiar of stories and texts. Communities are never fully static—their context of needs, emotions, and perceptions is always changing. When communities engage familiar texts, there is always the possibility for interpreting them anew by applying them to the specific thread of their shared life. The possibilities abound for fresh and bold words of prophetic proclamation about the community or the culture that surrounds us, for the creation of new songs and poems that help us respond to the text. We all have the innate capability to explore the familiar with new eyes. Because our stories and experiences are inevitably diverse, the ordinary always contains the possibility for grace. The familiar becomes a gift, an entry point to the gospel for all who seek and knock.

→ 8

The Word in Controversy
Romans 1: Asking and Telling in the Church

In this section, we have tried to demonstrate how a single, small community, with all the limits inherent to being such a community, can model the practice of community interpretation. Our obvious goal is to inspire you by demonstrating that a commitment to this hermeneutic can yield some beautiful insights and transformative results.

Our dialogue on the obscure profoundly displayed that expanding the process of interpretation to include a community of readers offers many more entry points into such texts, allowing us to hear anew forgotten sections of the canon as God's Word for us. Our conversation on Psalm 22 offered a clear example of how community can liberate the deeply personal and poetic portions of the Bible from cold, propositional analysis or simply the limited emotions and experiences of a single interpreter. Gathered as friends around this artful expression, our sharing ushered us into a confession of personal vulnerabilities that continue to build intimacy in our community. In the previous chapter, we moved our depiction of community hermeneutics from an intimate gathering of friends to a corporate worship gathering and demonstrated how commitments to creativity, artistry on all levels, vulnerability, and storytelling give us new eyes to see well-known texts, bringing to life texts in our Bibles that have grown lifeless with familiarity.

Admittedly, however, we think our biggest test of modeling the community practice of reading Scripture and interpreting together requires that we step headlong into the controversial. An old axiom we learned in pastoral theology classes was that one's theology wasn't honest or robust unless it could hold up in the intensive care unit of a hospital or at the graveside of a lost child. Texts that engage challenging or controversial issues potentially pose the greatest threat to a community hermeneutic, for if anywhere, it is here that a definitive and authoritative voice seems necessary.

Yet, we wholeheartedly believe that Christian communities are in dire need of having controversial conversations. We will constantly point out the rewards to having these conversations (see particularly chapter 11 on hospitality). Though we may be open to scores of interpretations of the good Samaritan (Luke 10), most of us hold our opinions and theological turf much more tightly when it comes to controversial issues, the kind that can turn a community hermeneutic into open war or schism. As a result, more often than not we tend to avoid these difficult conversations, only broaching them with others who we know already agree with our opinions and theologies. In a move that is either thrillingly experimental or completely suicidal, we have hoped to train our community to do just the opposite. So here goes!

The Gap Between Text and Topic

Even the first step of selecting a topic and text was difficult. Several obvious topics like pacifism/just war, poverty and money, homosexuality, and abortion came quickly to mind, standing out as issues of intense cultural debate. While we believe from what we have seen that a discussion of war, pacifism, and military policy tend to provoke more ire on both sides, we did not think those issues would provoke a high level of diverse opinions in our specific community. So, with some honest trepidation, we decided to address the intersection of the Lesbian, Gay, Bisexual, and Transgender (LGBT) community with the church. This was a topic where we were sure that there would be huge diversity of opinion in our fellowship and potentially entrenched disagreement.

Controversy and division over these issues within the greater church can hardly be understated. Recently, we were chatting with a pastor friend who had just returned from the annual meeting of the large denomination in which she serves. This pastor offered an offhand, dismissive comment as if her observation was already a historical event, stating that her denomination would inevitably divide as a result of their internal LGBT debate. In her words, "I think both sides are simply eyeballing each other and trying to get in the best position to dictate the division of pension funds, like a grade school game of musical chairs. No one wants to be left outside the circle when the big split comes."

Jaded perhaps, but our friend's assessment of the magnitude of the "gay controversy" within the church can hardly be challenged. As emergent church planters, this issue sadly has been regularly put to us as the ultimate litmus test from churches in our community (from both sides of the debate) as a means of determining whether we can partner with them in ministry. We remember quite vividly the first time our community got this question. On the day we were commissioned from our supporting fellowship, we described a vision of radical hospitality. The first offhand question directed to us when the service ended was, "Does radical hospitality involve gay people?" With that kind of buildup, we were naturally drawn to this discussion—and suitably frightened.

There are other challenges with this discussion besides the anger and divisiveness it seems to evoke. As is the case with many challenging issues, the topic does not immediately direct us to one specific text. We believe this is one of the reasons for such intense acrimony in Christian communities, though the experience is not unfamiliar.

Much of the time when it comes to acerbic issues, there simply are not long teaching texts directed specifically to these passionate questions. (Haven't we all been looking tirelessly for that propositional chapter, with maybe an ancient PowerPoint study guide thrown in, on the origin of evil or why God seems to choose Jacob the trickster over his hardworking brother, Esau?) Even when some of these issues are overtly addressed in the Bible, these teachings can be obscure, demanding responses and ethics we do not fully understand or dictating clear prescriptions that are far outside of our accepted norms.

For example, Leviticus 20:13 proclaims, "If a man lies with a man as one lies with a woman, both of them have done what is detestable. They must be put to death." This clearly creates a cultural and interpretative challenge, but notice that this passage may not be as conclusive on the issue as it first appears. It does not appear to include lesbian sexuality or the complex situations arising from those who have been born with androgynous gender characteristics. Recalling our belief in the importance of reading the text with the whole of the canon, the best plan is to embrace the whole body of biblical teachings on the issue. While affirming that course of action, we also realize that the voluminous amount or the sheer absence of biblical material can still make interpretation difficult.

Hence, venturing into our community conversation on homosexuality, we decided to focus primarily on Romans 1:18–32 because of its prolonged and graphic discussion of this topic (also, it is the only passage in the whole of the canon that discusses female homosexual relations) within a longer theological argument. Our hope was to engage this passage while still keeping an eye on the rest of the Bible. Regardless, we felt a constant tension between text and topic throughout the evening. As you will see, the farther we explored the topic, the harder it was to stay within the primary interests of the text.

Getting Started—Slowly: The Conversation about the Conversation

A preliminary summary of the course of our conversation may provide some guidance and caution for your community as you take on issues and texts such as this.

Understandably, our usually talkative, bantering, witty, and humorous group got off to a slow start. After reading the text, admittedly a very sobering "sin" text on many ethical issues, we seemed to find ourselves with little or nothing to say. Our group was larger than usual, affirming a point we will make strongly in chapter 9—that our communities really want to be conversant on difficult and painful issues. In retrospect, we faced two challenges in getting the conversation started. First, our group really didn't know where others stood on this issue and neither did we know the full extent of each other's life experiences related to LGBT topics. As a result, everyone was looking for "safe ground" to start our interpretative conversation. Perhaps we all sensed the simple truth that there is no safe ground when it comes to opinions on a potentially explosive topic. Any comment seemed likely to collide with the experiences, wounds, or opinions of others in the dialogue.

Secondly, our group really wanted, as several expressed directly, "to do well" in the conversation. It was important for our community's self-image and pride in our identity as a conversing group that we *be able* to talk about any issue and maintain our friendships and shared mission. This passion for hospitality and dialogue, at least, led us to take a respectful tone. We employed questions before declarations, exercised self-examination, and affirmed a passion for community over and above persuasion.

Having articulated the importance of community and the value of hospitality, we finally crawled out of our "sensitivity quagmire" and into the text of Romans 1. A well-trained group, we began by looking to the context to give meaning to the passage. Bill, our much-loved friend, ordained Seventh Day Adventist pastor, and café owner, was quick to point out that the social fabric of the text involves a division of folks "who want to pursue God" and "those who simply don't want to deal with God at all." Joel, a passionate activist and an ardent student of the Bible, reminded us that the argument of Romans reaches a crescendo at the close of chapter 8 where we are reminded that there is no condemnation for those who are in Christ's embrace. We all were quick to note "idolatry" as superscript to this text, pointing out that these actions and attitudes according to Paul are the natural delineation of those who have moved away from an awareness of God's love and a participation in God's redemptive mission.

These quick forays into the bigger argument combined with the theological heritage of most people in the group to quickly lead us down a path of interpretation that assumed the sinfulness of homo-sexuality. These first statements were gentle in tone and very self-effacing, yet still on the trajectory of this implied conclusion. Dana, a third-year medical student also pursuing a master's in public health, was the first to be vulnerable, explaining how convicting this pas-sage is for any reader. As she put it, "As humans, we have perverted everything—caring for the poor, sexuality. It's just that some idols are more acceptable than others."

This brought a chorus of echoes about our living in the double bind of a sexually obsessed and a truly sexually confused culture. For instance, while our culture seems to be horrified by the implications of polygamy and potentially underage marriage in the compound of the Fundamentalist Church of Jesus Christ of Latter Day Saints recently raided in Texas, Hugh Hefner's Playboy Mansion has become a culturally revered icon of fun and excess and one of the most de-sired "photo ops" for the A-list. Several Christian churches we know are challenging their couples to take the 100-day challenge, where they commit to having sex for 100 days in a row. Both culture and church seem to be entangled in simultaneous obsessions with and revulsions of expressions of human sexuality—a merciless double bind of confusion.

Our group was eager to abstain from sexual self-righteousness, and hence no one was reaching to gather the first stone. Joel expanded on our fears of self-righteousness by reminding us that Christians have also tended to focus on certain arenas of sin (like sexuality) to avoid challenging reflection of their lives on other moral topics that are also of grave interest to the Scriptures. "It bothers me, how we ignore the green element [of the Bible]. We ignore the Old Testament social justice passages. We're comfortable with investing in the stock market and com-panies that are laying waste to the environment, but then we are ready to drop the hammer on homosexuals." We thoroughly agree with Joel. A little sexual condemnation is always a great diversion from our other idols, the church's version of a good old-fashioned "red scare" or Cold War politics that keeps the public's eye and attention off of internal or local issues. Several quickly echoed this sentiment, saying that we truly needed to embrace all of the idolatrous condemnations of the text if we were going to speak of homosexuality in this way as well.

Oddly perhaps, this self-critique introduced our first collision. Brandy offered a gentle challenge: "It sounds like we are including homosexuality within the blanket of sins on this list." With this statement hanging in the air, I (Tim) made a quick decision to "semi-out" Brandy. Brandy, a divinity student, was already "out" at Emmaus Way, but our young community is very transient at times and several in the discussion that evening did not know Brandy was a lesbian. Brandy and I had intentionally decided not to start the conversation with a declaration of her sexual orientation out of a general sense of fair play. We do not introduce ourselves at parties and social gatherings as "heterosexual white males," so we don't expect Brandy to make constant lesbian "admissions." We also thought it might be best to let the conversation develop naturally that evening. She was comfortable with me or others bringing up her sexuality and at this point in conversation, I thought it was best to even the playing field by sharing this reality with the whole group. We didn't want anyone to feel "set up" since the conversation had entered the delicate realm of moral critique.

In saying this, we recognize that something like "even the playing field" is never truly possible and maybe even a little naive or a luxury of the privileged. However, though our lives are too diverse and complex to reach complete honesty or equal knowledge, we recognize that knowing each other's stories is imperative for understanding and hearing each other. For example, in our group at least two in attendance have gay siblings, though few others knew this. This led us to see that the reality of our diverse experiences and relationships would inevitably become either the impetus to fruitful conversation or the root of failed dialogue.

This revelation inalterably changed the course of our conversation. Though we had introduced the evening by saying that one of the classic errors of controversial topics is to treat them solely as abstractions separate from specific human lives, Brandy's vulnerability erased any vestiges of this possibility. Our community, particularly those who did not previously know her sexual orientation, began to ask Brandy about her story and her perspective. Brandy was very quick to reiterate her challenge. In her words, "Being attracted to the same gender . . . I get nervous about this argument [that homosexuality is inherently immoral]. I don't see my sexual orientation as a struggle. The working assumption in Christianity is that my orientation should be something that I want to change, like stopping gossip. But me trying to be not gay is something that troubles me based on my personal experiences and my theology, particularly the assumption that if I'm not struggling with this then I can't be a good Christian." Brandy continued by telling the story of living as a Christian lesbian, the challenges this created in her family, and her experiences of isolation, rejection, and embrace due to her sexuality. Though this conversation led far from a bounded exposition of Romans 1, it was very much appreciated by the group. Following up with Brandy later, we did ask her if this felt like the "ask-a-lesbian hour." Ever gracious, Brandy had wanted to share her story and was fully aware of how significant this was for the community.

With any threat of abstractions demolished, the group was braced to ask hard interpretative questions. Adam, playing perfectly the stereotypical role of his vocation as a surgical resident, cut to the quick looking for some clear definition: "We are part of a community where we would all feel sad if you were excluded. But the real biblical questions are, is this a permanent list of sins of idolatry, or are there cultural elements on the list? Are we going to call homosexuality a sin?" Travis, who is married to a student in Brandy's class and is also a close friend of Brandy's, followed up with the characteristics we appreciate so much in him—personal honesty, kindness, and a biblical passion—by sharing his perspective and the hope "that we can be friends and disagree over this issue." Brandy and Travis have had the kind of relationship where they had already shared some of their differences.

Adam and Travis, then, began to push us to the final stage of our conversation, a dialogue on our readings and understandings of the text. But before sharing a bit on these opinions, we feel the need to interject a comment that came at the end of our session in order to do away with any romanticized views of our evening. Just as we were about to clean up, Joel hit us with a dose of honesty, challenge, and anger, wondering whether we had really tackled the text. Mincing no words, he remarked, "I think we ran from the text this evening. Maybe instead of congratulating ourselves [on what a great job we've done talking through these delicate issues], maybe next time we can talk about the text!"

Though we disagreed with Joel's ultimate summary of having avoided the text, there were some huge prophetic truths in his words. A community like ours can delight in "having conversations about the conversation." After Brandy's disclosure, the gracious tone of questions directed toward her (and others who have significant relationships in the LGBT community), the freedom some exercised to disagree, and the fact that our community was still intact, we were admittedly a bit euphoric. It really did matter to us that we could broach this controversial subject without spiraling into an all-out shouting match or losing half our congregants.

In retrospect, a conversation about the conversation was truly necessary. The previously mentioned tension between the texts on homosexuality and our contemporary questions or concerns certainly forces a conversation that extends beyond any specific text. The aftermath of our dialogue revealed a simple truism that every interpreting group must experience: that controversial issues and text are never single-event conversations. Realistic expectations are critical. The first conversation is the beginning of an ongoing dialogue.

From this point, our small community talked through Paul's Epistle to the Romans with respect to the issue of homosexuality.

Romans 1: "Unnatural Relations"?

Romans 1:26–27: Because of this, God gave them over to shameful lusts. Even their women exchanged natural relations for unnatural ones. In the same way the men also abandoned natural relations with women and were inflamed with lust for one another. Men committed indecent acts with other men, and received in themselves the due penalty for their perversion.

Upon first read, this passage comes across as straightforward (pun intended). These are very strong, seemingly unambiguous words that clarify and expound a broader statement on human idolatry in the previous verse ("They exchanged the truth of God for a lie, and worshiped and served created things rather than the Creator"). The images here are quite graphic and the condemnation offered unflinchingly. It is a scene that seems to be so pellucid that these verses contain, from some vantage points, the primary biblical denouncement of inappropriate, volitional female homosexual expression,[1] as well as reiterating the condemnation of male homosexual relations. Up front, at least in Dan's and my childhood traditions, the Bible's conclusion on the issue of homosexual relations seems to be clear.

But let us begin by offering a simple confession and introduction to the remainder of the conversation. As two heterosexual Christian males we must admit that these verses are a portion of Scripture that has never really presented us, on an individual level at least, with much fear or conviction. Whether or not Paul universally condemns homosexual relations here frankly does not make much difference for our individual lives, because it clearly is not a condemnation that touches our libido.

That said, as two pastors working to shepherd a congregation of people with a handful of gay and lesbian persons who are attempting to live faithful Christian lives, we are now challenged to take up these verses in order to study them with even more attentiveness. They are putting before us questions we have not engaged before (beyond abstract debate), if simply for the fact that they've not emerged in our own personal struggle. As a result, when we come to these verses as a community, there is more at stake because the community forces us to enter into a broader range of experience with this text.

This is not to say that just because there are people in our community who identify with Christ and affirm homosexual practices in certain contexts, these practices are automatically dismissed from criticism. Following Christ requires that we all embrace first God's form of life. Two of our favorite authors relate a phrase one of their Jewish friends is fond of using: "Any God who won't tell you what to do with your pots and pans and genitals isn't worth worshipping."[2] But the faithful testimonies of our community are forcing us to tend to this portion of Scripture with more care and inquisitiveness, learning not to render equivalent all forms of homosexual relations. There are many practicing homosexuals who are appalled at the idea of promiscuity and the licentiousness that may pass for normalcy in some gay communities, just as there are many heterosexuals who do not endorse a lifestyle of casual sex and one-night stands.

This has not been just our experience as pastors, but it has been the experience of our community as a whole. And it was this particular situation that birthed this conversation of Romans 1. That is to say, we must admit up front that we did not approach this passage as an objective third person with no interest in the results (and we are extremely suspicious of anyone who claims to do so). But our community broached this conversation because it was a conversation they were dying to have given the particular make-up of who we are and the community in which we live. Our understanding of community requires that we take seriously all the voices in our community and the full extent of our diversity. As a group of Christians seeking to follow Christ together, we continue to try to read and challenge each other with this text—and as you will see, that challenge does not always go in the direction one might initially think.

Following from the reading of this Romans passage, Adam, Travis, Dana, and several others at our dialogue pressed the straightforward interpretation of this passage in the most gentle and non-judgmental of manners. They all have close friendships in the LGBT community. The question was first posed to Brandy, who has a strong background in philosophy and biblical studies from a conservative Christian college and is currently studying at both Duke's Divinity School and the University of North Carolina's School of Social Work. Immediately, this changed the conversation because no longer was it a conversation about the LGBT community in general, about gay rights, or the idea of sexuality, but it was a conversation about sex among friends and fellow disciples trying to better understand how to faithfully live our lives. In response to the initial reading, Brandy was quick to challenge the notion that homosexuality in its totality, which feels like an entirely "natural" attraction to her, could be quickly placed under the tent of "unnatural."

As the organizers of the conversation, we were rightfully, we think, very wary of putting Brandy in the position of being "exegete-de-force" for the LGBT community, so Dan, Bill, and I (i.e., "the old guys" in reference to Bill and Tim and the three who have done the most pastoral reflection) did a lot of the talking in this segment of the dialogue, while realizing the irony of speaking about a community of which we are not a part.

This simple fact reveals one clear observation about this theological topic: the church has hosted so little open and honest dialogue on the subject that the laity, even the highly educated laity, know of few starting places and have heard few if any of the interpretative challenges. The dearth of interaction and dialogue on this issue, we think, is one of the main reasons for the hatred, fear, and division on this topic, as they tend to fill the void left by a church that refuses to talk about it. There is a deep-seated habit of denouncing homosexuality with little effort to explore the historical culture of the text or to make distinctions between orientation and activity or even to simply talk with those in their congregation who are gay.

But we know full well that it isn't just the conservative side of this conversation that has drawn broad assumptions about homosexuality. A couple years ago, at least ten people from our church attended a public event on homosexuality in the church sponsored jointly by Duke University and a consortium of "open and affirming" churches. We appreciated much of the content and all of the personal stories. Yet the tone of the event was anything but "open and affirming" to those who disagreed with the position of offering total blessing to gay marriages as well as encouraging the full participation of gays in the church. The meeting ended with the moderator praising the rare quality of the dialogue that evening. However, one of our community participants, who is sympathetic to the long history of hypocritical judgment and painful exclusion of gays in the church, grimaced and said that he would have been afraid to voice even a slight challenge in that environment. An exercise in its own brand of fundamentalism, the "dialogue" that night had not included even a single dissenting comment.

Prompted by this experience and the interactions within our community gathering (i.e., the exchange between those who see homosexuality as sin and the experiences of those who are gay), we realized we needed to tend to the conversation with care. And we knew we needed some help. We began to discuss with one another, in a move of catholicity, other secondary sources we had read on this passage. Consequently, this gave rise to four interpretive concerns: complications of culture, social possibility, genre/literary function, and mission, none of which are apparent in a first, quick reading of the text.

Culture

While many secondary sources raise, affirm, and reject these queries in much more extensive forms, we'll describe how our community engaged these questions and point you to some resources we have valued.

Tending to the passage with an eye toward the cultural context, one point we need to make is that the words of Paul are incarnate words, words shaped by the language and practices of his day. They are not disembodied words without a cultural context whispered by a God on high in a universal language about a universal experience to a mesmerized recorder. This is why we accept them as God's Word—that they are simultaneously appropriately incarnate to the specific cultural context and they are transcendent in that they speak with value to all people in all times. Yet the culture of the reader must also not be allowed to dominate the reading completely, for Paul does seem to have a particular decline into idolatry in mind here, a decline that leads in the end to sexual misconduct. However, in saying this we must recognize that our cultural context is not exactly that of Paul.

In the case of Romans 1, culture enters the text quite audaciously in the use of the modifiers of "natural" and "unnatural," terms that automatically point us to cultural standards and social mores. Our group was not the only one to notice this. Any cursory investigation of this text immediately discovers that there is a lively debate in the scholarship around just the meaning of these terms.[3] Furthermore, history and experience teach us that definitions of naturalness in regard to sexual ethics have been highly fluid over time. Polygamy, once a norm and an economic necessity if not a patriarchal ideal, has, in our radically divergent contemporary sensitivities, become illegal in most places and is considered "unnatural" if not downright offensive and reprehensible to most people in Western cultures.

Of course, this text begins with a broad statement of "general revelation." Romans 1:19–20 says, "Since what may be known about

God is plain to them, because God has made it plain to them. For since the creation of the world God's invisible qualities—his eternal power and divine nature—have been clearly seen, being understood from what has been made, so that men are without excuse," which can be taken to teach that there are transcendent, natural realities that all should be held accountable to recognize.[4] Joel was quick to set the stage for this issue in our conversation, saying the key "hermeneutical move is culture," from which commenced a lively discussion of the way culture affects our reading of the text.

Social Possibility and Historical Progression

Our culture conversation led us to a related issue of social possibility, which reminds us of an interpretative practice that should not be ignored or simply dismissed. The Bible, unless it is an inauthentic text, cannot be expected to discuss, defend, or advocate social categories to its original readers that did not exist at the time of its writing.

One sees this interpretative dilemma of social possibility in play, much to the frustration of many parents we knew when we served as youth pastors, in regard to biblical texts on premarital sex. There are many texts on promiscuity that offer relevant principles to the issue, but one cannot find a teaching text where premarital sex is the primary issue. This absence is due to the social realities of parentally arranged marriages at or before the age of puberty, the near universality of marriage that precluded a large population of unmarried, post-pubescent people, and the very minimal interaction between men and women outside of the family clan environment. Since sexual activity equated marriage, there was not truly a social category of premarital sex. Sexual activity outside of marriage usually constituted some level of forced sex, prostitution (usually associated with idol worship), or adultery. Hence, the Scriptures have much to say about adultery, rape, and prostitution but little to say directly about this unknown social category. There was plenty of promiscuity to go around; it just happened in a different social environment.

This hermeneutical principle is particularly important in the ethical, interpretative issue of slavery. Historical examination reveals that the

Bible is very progressive on this issue of slavery. The Old Testament and New Testament teachings both demand a practice of economic bondage that is more humane than the norms of the day. In these prescriptive texts on slavery and passages throughout the Bible on the created dignity of humanity, we find the powerful foundation to abhor the practice of slavery of all kinds. But the Bible never reaches the point of forbidding all forms of economic servitude. Society, in its historical development by the time the New Testament was written, had not reached a point where an economy without some forms of slavery existed. Therefore, the New Testament describes more ethical practices of economic bondage and the missional possibilities bondservants have to proclaim the gospel (see especially 1 Peter 2) but does not demand abolition at that point in history.

These two issues reveal that, in addition to being wary of social categories that exist in our culture but not in biblical times, we must make room for the historical development of social sensitivities in our reading of the Bible. It is impossible to read the text and embrace its many exhortations toward a redemptive social agenda without doing so. So when the Bible is consistently more progressive about an issue (as compared to its culture), we find the strong impetus of a continued progressive ethical imagination on the issue. In other words, when the Bible is consistently progressive on a social issue, we should consider greater progression and not consider the final ethic of the Scriptures in their history as the ultimate social stance on the issue.

For a more thorough examination of these hermeneutical issues, we recommend William Webb's *Slaves, Women, and Homosexuals*.[5] Webb's title reminds us of another interpretative sensitivity: one cannot change the rules in the middle of the game. He reminds us that a system of reading the texts that "works" for us, meaning it delivers a desirable outcome, cannot be fairly utilized for one issue like slavery and then jettisoned for gender or homosexuality. Consistency is obviously quite important.

This text in Romans reveals the Bible's blanket, universal condemnation of idolatry. (The replacement of Yahweh by a god made in our image or shaped by our expectations is, at some level, the definition of all sin.) The New Testament writers reveal a specific sensitivity about the heinous intersection of idolatry and temple practices including ritual prostitution and other promiscuities. Paul, writing in 1 Corinthians 10:20–21, puts this in the strongest of terms: "No, but the sacrifices of pagans are offered to demons, not to God, and I do not want you to be participants with demons. You cannot drink the cup of the Lord and the cup of demons too; you cannot have a part in both the Lord's table and the table of demons."

Earlier in 1 Corinthians 6:15–17, the strong linkage between idolatry and sexual immorality, including the enjoyment of prostitutes, is highlighted with unthinkable worship implications: "Do you not know that your bodies are members of Christ himself? Shall I then take the members of Christ and unite them with a prostitute? Never! Do you not know that he who unites himself with a prostitute is one with her in body? For it is said, 'The two will become one flesh.' But he who unites himself with the Lord is one with him in spirit."

This is the kind of sexual permissiveness (including homosexual practices that have been documented by many as a part of the ancient worship cults) that the Scriptures naturally forbid in the strongest of terms. Our group, though mixed in its opinions about this issue, found this to be a compelling arena for conversation. We were left with some uncertainty about the nature of the homosexual practice condemned in the Scriptures. Our questions of how the Scriptures might have engaged other practices—like monogamous homosexual relationships between consenting adults—that may not have been known to the church at the time the Scriptures were written seemed to us to be a critical place for ongoing dialogue.

Genre and Literary Function

Considerations of "genre/literary function" are new to our community. They are a bit complex, yet worthy of continued discussion. We were first introduced to this line of thought through the work of a local scholar, Douglas Campbell at Duke Divinity School, in his book *The Quest for Paul's Gospel*,[6] in which Campbell applies this trajectory of analysis to Romans 1. Campbell's argument is substantive, is extremely detailed, and merits a long examination far beyond our capabilities in this space. But to be savagely short, Campbell challenges some traditional readings of Paul's theological argument in Romans and particularly believes that the argument beginning at 1:18 contains portions of a theology that Paul intends to rebuke. If you explore Campbell's argument, you will find many sources of sharp tension between Romans 1:18–32 as it has traditionally been read and other portions of Paul's teachings.[7]

For the purposes of our dialogue, Campbell also raises an important question of genre for this text. It is possible that Romans 1:18–32 is a stylized "decline narrative" in the voice of theological opponents, a contemporary theology of Paul's day describing the world "going to hell in a handbasket" using familiar, graphic (pertaining to sexuality), and even hyperbolic idioms and language to illustrate this point.[8]

We all have a relative or two who talk this way—"The world ain't what it used to be—skyrocketing gas prices due to those greedy (insert oil-producing nation-state of choice), free spending, big-government Democrats or self-righteous, big-business Republicans ruining our government, all those teenagers having sex all the time at drug-filled raves, getting pregnant and passing STDs, and no respect out there for folks who really care." When I (Tim) was a kid, my uncle started a steel-fabricating business in his back yard, right next door to our home. I would often wander by at break time in search of a "fried pie" and a Yoo-hoo from the snack truck that appeared each day (to the uninitiated, the "roach wagon") and would hear a version of this speech at almost every visit. When we hear that uncle, aunt, or opinionated neighbor speak in this common form, we know there is an element of truth mixed in with its grandiose vision of doom and overly idealistic plan of hope. Does Romans 1 offer an example of a decline narrative that gives Paul a platform of critique to make his essential theological points? This is another worthy conversation.

Mission

Finally, our conversation turned to questions of mission. The Christian community has engaged LGBT questions primarily in the realm of doctrine. These issues have become, for many, the key arbiter in ongoing fellowship and the litmus test for one's belief in the authority of the Scriptures. As we are writing, the Religion News Service has reported that the Presbyterian Church (USA) has experienced its greatest drop in membership in thirty years. One of the key reasons is the departure of entire churches over LGBT issues, with "about 130 churches in total hav[ing] threatened to leave or hav[ing] left the denomination because of disagreements about homosexuality and the Bible."[9] In our evening conversation, many in our community preferred to also give voice to mission and compassion as a result of scriptural interpretation.

One of the stories Brandy told that evening involved her departure from a "Pride Week" event in Chapel Hill, the progressive, affluent college town that adjoins Durham. As she left the event early and walked alone to her car in a parking garage, she encountered five or six young men in their teens or early twenties who were clearly waiting to surprise a Pride Week attendee. Their greeting included throwing handfuls of stones and gravel at Brandy (obviously literal interpreters of the Leviticus 20 text). Instead of spending the evening studying for a midterm, Brandy spent the night in the emergency room being treated for potential damage to her retina in one eye. Many had remembered a clearly shaken Brandy coming to our worship gathering the next evening with an eye patch. But few had known the reason.

Such an act of violence and near-miss with tragedy without the gay subtext would have typically provoked open sharing and compassionate prayer in our worship gathering. But this was a story Brandy was not sure whether she should tell openly, and our community missed an opportunity to corporately embrace her.

This was clearly a time when a conversation over doctrine, even a friendly dialogue over our differences, would have been entirely inappropriate. The scriptural call in that moment would have been compassion, a freedom to unload a heinous story, and an arm around her shoulder at the Eucharist table. Especially in a contemporary setting where the origins of homosexuality remain debatable in the scientific and social science communities and where there is so much hermeneutical work to do, the call of mission is strong. There are many, many other circumstances when the dictates of mission, as derived from our passionate study of Scripture, should dance the lead over doctrinal certainty in this raging biblical debate.

Going Home

As we finished the evening's conversation, Brandy and Travis, both important leaders in our community, still disagreed and yet they still remain close friends. The subtopics of mission, genre, social possibility, and culture all produced vital entry points for continued conversations in our small community. As you have noticed, perhaps to palpable frustration, we did not produce either a definitive reading of Romans 1 or a community dictum on the issue of homosexuality.

Avoiding immediate conclusions is often a pastoral virtue. After almost twenty-five years of pastoral ministry and serving as an elder or a founding pastor for most of those years, I (Tim) have been in many dilemmas that required hard, uncomfortable decisions with the inevitable result of sharp critique from friends and community members. In each of these situations, the quality of the decision, regardless of how controversial, was a product of the quality of the dialogue that took place prior to its being made. One of the most common mistakes we've made is lacking the humility, or being too afraid to be honest, or moving on a decision (usually because of external pressures) when mission would best require that we wait, pray, and continue the dialogue.

As stated earlier, we are at the beginning of many conversations on the LGBT intersection with the church. But in the absence of a definitive pronouncement, our community made several kingdom steps on that evening. Romans 1 was reaffirmed and embraced as God's living Word for us. We were all convicted by our bouts of spiritual blindness and incessant idolatry, an obvious goal in this portion of Romans. Brandy's story was heard and our community walked away with a greater confidence that we could engage each other's stories and also enter into vital, life-giving dialogue even in the areas of our most passionate differences.

After this pub group, we decided to press forward with a conversation on homosexuality in one of our worship gatherings. On that evening, I (Tim) moderated a dialogue between Brandy and a theologically trained community member who is also a close friend of hers who disagrees with her biblical interpretation. It was a powerful night in the life of our community. Several local therapists use the podcast regularly as a part of their care on issues of sexual identity.

Our dialogue continues, and in that spirit, we thought it important to report some of our closing comments verbatim.

DANA: (responding to a question about the possibility of an ongoing, constructive disagreement) I disagree with family members on huge things and we still love each other.

BRANDY: I question how much I can expect from the community. Sometimes I can dialogue with those who disagree, but sometimes I also need people to stand up for me. Sometimes I need that, and I find myself going outside the church. But being gay and Christian really complicates my life with LGBT organizations.

ADAM: I have really benefited from being in a community of diverse opinions.

DANA: Thank you to Brandy for being so open. We are sorry for ways that we hurt you and don't know.

BRANDY: I'm so glad to talk about this.

ADAM: It was important for me to not be abstract on this issue, to be face-to-face.

BILL: We just can't assume. We need a forum to talk about what we wrestle with. We can't live in assumptions that we are all heterosexuals. We have to find ways to discuss our differences.

BRANDY: The assumption that everyone is straight, heteronormativity—I don't want to say, "Woe is me," but this is difficult.

DAN: (said with a wink and with one hand on the cooler of leftovers and one hand on the light switch) That's just because you don't know how hard it is to be a heterosexual white male.

Part 3

The Intersection of
Text and Community

9

Proclamation

The Liberation of Our Voices

I (Tim) would like to tell you that when I get in my car I always listen to National Public Radio, literary classics on CD, provocative podcasts, or brilliant, yet undiscovered, indie rock bands. But inevitably, when driving in the afternoons, I habitually tune the radio to catch fragments of Jim Rome's nationally syndicated "Jungle" on our local sports talk radio station. As a communicator, I am magnetically drawn to Rome's masterful use of sarcasm, wit, and street idiom in his "takes" on the sporting world. His listeners, the "clones," follow his lead with carefully scripted takes that push the envelope even farther in sarcastic taunts of other callers and sports figures. In jungle-speak, it is the tradition to end each call by declaring "War" on favored teams, issues, and sports figures (i.e., "War on the NY Giants" is a compliment). Rome is clever enough to allow the most biting words and opinions to be in the voices of his callers and fans (his mock protests of their most heinous opinions is powerful rhetoric on its own!).

The Jungle reflects much of the best and worst in cultural conversation. The presence of wit and sharply crafted opinion is only matched by the stark absence of dialogue. In our world of spoken opinion, real dialogue has become a prominent entry on the list of endangered species. In an environment where quick, pithy, and outlandish media quips dominate over prolonged, careful, and compassionate conversation, our speech is tending toward verbal warfare, each word a rapier of competition, one-upmanship, intolerance, anger, turf declaration, and self-protection.

Our society, though democratic and market-driven, is losing its skills for—and possibly its memory of—dialogue in a season when our cultural divisions have clearly widened (even though we are tempted to believe they no longer exist). I was recently watching a History Channel documentary entitled 1968—a graphic portrait of the tragedies and divisions of that watershed year in a decade of upheaval. In one scene, a police officer and a protester who were both involved in the Chicago riots outside the Democratic National Convention tried to describe this clash. They were barely able to agree on a single detail. At one point, the police officer was asked about any angst he might have experienced in the wake of the violence of the police directed at protesters. He matter-of-factly recounted that this was simply his job and that he went home and slept peacefully. The clear implication of the film was that we are still living in the same deep chasm of division exposed in 1968.[1] Some of us are sleeping, blissfully ignorant of the implications of monumental divides in our culture.

Linguistics scholar Deborah Tannen describes our communal lives as an "argument culture" in a book by that title.[2] She demonstrates how the language of warfare permeates our common discourse. When jumping into conversation, we "enter the fray" or "take a shot." In disagreement, we "fire volleys" to "shoot down our adversaries," who are often "half-cocked" anyway. The consequences of this language are not insignificant. Tannen warns how our metaphors become calcified in our language and that we become how we speak.[3] This breeds an attack and confrontation culture in media, art, religion, and politics, yielding real "casualties" (see, we can't avoid it either!).

Tannen offers as evidence the painful story of Dr. Robert Gallo, the co-discoverer of the AIDS virus. Articles written about Dr. Gallo in a media style that Tannen labels as "demonography" sparked a four-year investigation that he had "stolen the virus" from Luc Montagnier of the Pasteur Institute.[4] In this form of journalism, rather than questions being asked with suspended judgment, the reporting took the form of personal accusations, attack, and the assumed verdict of guilt. The media seems to declare war rather than chronicle a dispute in the scientific community. Though eventually exonerated, Dr. Gallo spent four years defending himself rather than fighting the AIDS pandemic.

Because our culture is replete with insidious and deep-seated divisions, the term *culture wars* has been used widely to characterize not only the current division in our society but also our mode of expression in an increasingly fragmented society. In an all-out linguistic game of survival of the fittest, it becomes easier and more efficient to destroy "the competition" rather than to engage in the discipline of careful dialogue. James Davison Hunter expresses the gravity of our negative communication:

> Arguably, this negative persuasion has become even more important, for in public discourse, "dialogue" has largely been replaced by name calling, denunciation, and even outright intolerance. In the words of the old adage, the contemporary culture war has become a contest that will determine "not who is right but who is left."[5]

The Absence of Dialogue in the Christian Community: Same Reality, Different Story

It isn't news that cultural divisiveness, animosity, a lack of civility in conversation, and the absence of dialogue have also taken deep root in the Christian community. The church has been tragically inimical and divided: we are socially divided between hemispheres (Eastern versus Western and Northern vs. Southern), and authoritatively divided between Roman Catholic and Eastern Orthodox traditions, and more recently between Catholics and Protestant affiliations. Given the significance of Christianity in our nation's social character, no one should be surprised that the fault lines of the current culture war also run through the fundamentalist/modernist controversy of the last century and the evangelical/mainline divide that still dominates the Protestant ecclesial landscape. Christianity, unfortunately, has a history of being a divided table, and many of us must admit that we have come to see the denominational world of North American Christianity as *normal*, such that, contrary to Jesus' prayer in John 17, division seems more comfortable than conversation and unity.

What may be news for many who take for granted the idea that denominations or congregations are monolithic, is the intensity of cultural diversity (in thought and practice) within specific Christian communities, even at the level of each individual fellowship. This diversity is often overlooked or ignored because it threatens the primary functionality and identity of our fellowships. On the surface, at least, the various denominations of the Protestant church in America have been largely formed around, first, doctrinal distinctions (hence, the forming of a new body or denomination), and then, volitional doctrinal agreement at the individual, congregational level. In a culture of denominations, these doctrinal assertions, though often whittled down to "essentials" or "core values," drive our primary procedures for enfolding new congregants, the content of spiritual formation, and accessing privileges within the body. The ability to join our churches, the freedom to marry with the blessing of the church or participate in the Eucharist, and many opportunities to serve as leaders and teachers are all tied to doctrinal assent.

It all sounds great—until we look a little closer and find that we really don't agree all that much, even on the essentials. This assertion has been an intuitive reality for us based on our thirty-plus years of pastoral ministry. Deemed as "safe" pastors by many in the evangelical churches in which we have served, we've had scores and scores of meetings in cafés, pubs, and the office with congregants who shared in hushed tones profound disagreement with the churches we served or what they assume to be evangelical consensus about topics like gay/lesbian issues, the particularity of salvation, gender and leadership, the existence of hell, and the Trinity. These appointments usually began with some version of, "I know I'm not supposed to believe this, but I think . . ."

There are many explanations for our differing theological perspectives and conceptions, and not all of them boil down to the perceived threat of relativism. We now inhabit a deeply pluralistic and de-territorialized world, such that the fences that tended to provide the illusion of complete theological unity have been broken down. With the technology to relay the experiences of other peoples and places instantaneously and the mobility to leave our familiar contexts at a whim, our parochial perspectives and experiences must now fit within a larger world of perspectives and experiences. The postmodern world has become, if anything, a nexus of competing stories where local perspectives collide with the generalized truths of other local communities. Naturally, theological rigidity and static thought do not fare well in this context, especially given the surfeit of recent scholarship sensitizing us to the terrors of colonialism. Our interest lies not in the origin of this situation but in our responses and their consequences. These responses have yielded a series of unintended tragedies that threaten the very nature of the gospel.

Unintended Tragedies

The reflex to reduce our statements of faith to the bare essentials in the face of the perceived threat of pluralism and postmodernity that strike at our sense of secure identity is itself one of the tragedies. Over the past decade or so our doctrinal statements have shrunk from long paragraphs on multiple pages to a few precise bullet points on a PowerPoint slide. The new catchphrases of our leaders have become "majoring on the majors and minoring on the minors," "letting the main things be the main things," and "fighting for the non-negotiables." For many participants, this development has been reasonable and welcomed.

But the tightening of our lines theologically has only served to buttress the myth of theological homogeneity within our churches. And this myth has engendered some unfortunate consequences. One of the most immediate costs has been the *homogenization* of most churches—as if we needed more incentive to do this. The more we gather around common ethnicities, nationalities, socioeconomics, educational backgrounds, and lifestyles, the more likely our belief systems will line up. Both Dan and I have had the privilege of visiting some financially impoverished communities around the world like the Korogocho slum in Nairobi, the city dump in Guatemala City, the shantytown of San Pedro Sula, Honduras, and the slums of Port-au-Prince, Haiti. We have witnessed remarkable embodiments of faith in each of these communities. In each of these places, we've wondered how many of the common theologies of churches in our culture, and even in our community, would hold up in this context. So many of us worship in fellowships where life has worked out nicely for almost everyone and where we attribute our good fortune to God as blessing, rather than the pure luck of birth or the results of excessive opportunity in a twisted theology that leads us to see ourselves as the chosen people of God, solidifying our disregard for those who suffer or face extreme deprivation. In these environments, many voices are lost, particularly those of the sick, poor, and marginalized.

Theologians Justo and Catherine González refer to these people as "neglected interpreters." They cleverly explain that our neglect of these interpreters results in a "Lone Ranger and Tonto" Bible. Drawing on the old western serial *The Lone Ranger* (though he was not truly alone), they describe the pervading and implicit portrait of white heroism. His Native American partner, Tonto, whose name actually means "dimwit," was silent and existed only as a foil to emphasize the real hero, the white Lone Ranger (although Tonto saved the Lone Ranger on numerous occasions). The Gonzálezes offer this verdict on the Lone Ranger Bible:

> There is then a type of "Lone Ranger" Bible study which, although not necessarily done in private, is done in the same sort of almost meaningless company which Tonto provided for the hero. This happens when our biblical interpretation fails to be challenged by others, either because they *share* our own perspective, or because, since they differ from us, we classify them as "Tontos" whose perspectives we need not take into account.[6]

Homogenization is devastating to Christian community. The Gonzálezes argue persuasively that we cannot truly understand the gospel or interact with the whole of the Christian tradition without proximity to the poor and the outsider, listening to their voices as interpreters of the text.[7]

Though it can ruin and skew our perspectives on gospel and king-dom, homogenization cannot ultimately rule the day. Our freedom of travel and the power of an information society are among many factors that nibble at our stereotypes and our insulation. Even in the height of the Jim Crow South, prejudices and stereotypes were eroded by social interaction and the prophetic voices of change. We face a similar situation in our burgeoning pluralistic and postmodern culture. There are simply too many available stories and influences to support an absolute isolation or a universal perspective. Even in the most homogenous Christian communities, we know or deeply suspect that there are many who differ on some of the most fundamental is-sues, and that the magnitude of those differences is significant.

However, our reaction to these heartfelt suspicions yields other unintended consequences. Forcing our faith out of the public realm and into a *privatized belief system* is a second such consequence. Christian piety and conviction becomes a matter for the conscience, the mind, and perhaps also the sanctity of one's home. Privately held beliefs presumably won't antagonize or shatter the myth of theological homogeneity. Such is the power of the myth that we would even con-sider this approach because our Christian faith is public, activistic, and holistic to the core. It cannot be confined by either the force of individual will or the strength of our picket fences. Jesus makes sure of it. He perceived himself to be the ultimate agent of change and radical redemption, saying, "Do not suppose that I have come to bring peace to the earth. I did not come to bring peace, but a sword" (Matt. 10:34). Jesus also connected his identity and our worship of him to expressions of care in the public sphere, proclaiming quite disturbingly, "Truly I tell you, whatever you did for one of the least of these brothers and sisters of mine, you did for me. . . . Truly I tell you, whatever you did not do for one of the least of these, you did not do for me" (Matt. 25:40, 45 TNIV). Jesus crossed the defined and comfortable cultural boundaries of his society in further acts of his comprehensive call to forgiveness by interacting with the Samaritan woman (John 4), dining with tax collectors and "sinners" at Levi's home (Luke 5:27–31), affirming the faith of a Roman centurion (Luke 7:9), and receiving the anointing of a sinful woman in the face of those who sought to enforce those old social customs (Luke 7:36–50). Making our faith into a privatized belief system is entirely inconsistent with the way of Jesus.

Another consequence is that we have unwittingly turned our churches into "don't ask, don't tell" environments. We are deeply suspicious that if we allow truly free speech in the theological and ethical realms, we will find a disturbing diversity that will threaten our identity as theologically homogenous and, as a result, all of the functions of fellowship that depend on the assumption of homogeneity. This becomes our motivation to discourage certain questions, to curtail speculative thought in theology, to silence our ideological and social prophets, to demonize certain trajectories of exploration, and to make some possibilities unutterable. The costs of "don't ask, don't tell" are almost incalculable. Sadly, in the wake of growing pluralism and diminishing secularism (the perfect storm of heightened spiritual interest and expanding avenues of spiritual exploration), these silencing environments have become the norm.

I (Tim) was recently privy to some of the background conversation of an international ministry struggling with internal theological diversity. At one point, one of their leaders exclaimed, "We certainly don't want our staff out there reading Brad [sic] McLaren books!" What a loss this would be. *Brian* McLaren is one of the preeminent missiological, pastoral, and theological voices of our time. He's also one of the kindest persons we know. Brian has never asserted that he had it all figured out or demanded that his audience agree with all that he says. His message has been an exhortation to courage, creativity, contextuality, and the bold hope that "we can be better" as Christians in the face of our cultural challenges. To squash his voice, even in jest, is a loss for the Christian community.

Emmaus Way is a more ideologically and theologically diverse community than many fellowships we've encountered. But we also feel the legacy of "don't ask, don't tell." Our first missional and ethical struggle centered on the issue of capital punishment. We had several people in our community who were—and continue to be—deeply opposed to this practice and regularly protest executions at Central Penitentiary in nearby Raleigh. On occasion they are arrested during their nonviolent protests (which involve prayer, singing hymns, and the reading of Scripture). In our worship gathering one evening, an invitation went out for any in the community to join them, with the warning that some have been arrested at these protests. This created quite a stir. Many persons approached us wanting to know when opposition to capital punishment had become the official stance of Emmaus Way. This is a vestige of the "don't ask, don't tell" legacy and the myth of theological homogeneity wrapped tightly together. These concerned people were so trained from previous experience that anything said from the pulpit, stage, or other vehicles of public communication had to have the full approval of the leadership that any such statements were, in effect, community policy. In several instances, we had to gently explain that we didn't practice that functional assumption. Affirming the importance of public expressions of faith, we understood that activism in the face of what was deemed an unjust policy was essential to the faith of some in our community. Their open expression of these convictions was not the final word of community policy but the invitation for a dynamic conversation to begin about the moral realities of this issue. In our posture, we would welcome open dialogue from multiple perspectives on capital punishment. In "don't ask, don't tell" environments these dialogues are forbidden. Public speech is the domain of conclusions that do not shake the illusion of homogeneity.

Finally, when dialogue is curtailed, the gospel, the good news of Jesus Christ, is diminished and eventually trivialized. The *reduction and trivialization of the gospel* is potentially the most egregious tragedy in this chain of unintended consequences. The gospel becomes the rapidly shrinking, lowest common denominator of assertions that we can state publicly without the threat of conflicting conversation, a bare-bones set of precepts we can act on boldly without division. This dwindling space that remains is becoming a frightening list of sentimentalities of entitlement or betterment that have little or nothing to do with the actual gospel. We end up with a version of faith that teaches trite theology in which we say, "If I'm faithful, generous, and good, God will surely bless my life." (Does the gospel really promise a better life? Many of the faithful find life to be far more difficult because of their convictions.) Or, "I know there's a good reason and purpose for this tragedy." (Does God really promise this knowledge or the certainty of this assertion? Does this line of thinking truly acknowledge the brothels, boardrooms, sweatshops, and governmental chambers in a world where greed, injustice, and cruelty operate as the dominant assumptions?) Or, "God helps those who help themselves." (Do we really even know how to help ourselves?) Or, "If we just have faith, God will show up and intervene." (What Christian leader or biblical interpreter can offer a cogent pattern of God's miraculous actions?)

We realize that some may object to this partial list of assumptions and sentiments. But we firmly believe that when the provocative issues and difficult questions that inevitably stir confusion, conflict, and creativity abdicate the floor, the banalities and simplicities are all that remain. So many of us pastors constantly complain about the fact that our people don't take their faith seriously. But is it any wonder when we've completely trained them not to do so by making many of the important arenas of their lives off-limits? The missional impact of this reality is devastating.

In our postmodern culture, universal proclamations of truth (metanarratives) and the objectivity of observers/learners are looked on with suspicion and replaced by an affinity for local stories, the contextuality of truth, and the subjectivity of observers and learners. In this environment, passion and authenticity in our conversations and affirmations become the highest ethical marks of discourse. In postmodern etiquette, we no longer make universal declarations, but rather honest and authentic personal descriptions of our perspective and tradition. Trite, trivial, and objective generalizations as the primary tongue of the church, when they are considered at all, become the objects of ridicule.

A single mom in our neighborhood understands these missional challenges all too well. Her teenage son has already experienced some of the harsh realities of racism and physical danger in his short life. These experiences provoke a range of sharp and honest questions. He wants to know some of the rationale for the assumed faith of his family. They worship in a fellowship where there is a great deal of enthusiasm about Christianity and the supposed outcomes of a faithful life, but little conversation about the justifications for this mood. He wants to know why they are so sure when his own life has yet to match their assurances. He asks his mom, "Would you really believe all this if you didn't just grow up in it?" His line of questioning strikes to those essential questions of credibility, authenticity, and even honesty.

He wonders if his church (and his mom if he dares the question) is being manipulated, is simply naive, or is being downright dishonest. There is not a lot of direct conversation about adolescent sexuality, drug use, and cruelty in his church. He wonders if these pleasant, attractive people know that the good kids aren't really all that good. Do they know how hard it can be to be a kid like him? He wonders why no one seems to be talking about this "important stuff" and he wants to know if the real reasons for this avoidance are ignorance or manipulation. Has certainty, the inertia of familial tradition, or the general optimism of upper-middle-class Americans made them all irrevocably blind? These are good questions. Missiologist Darrell Guder affirms this line of questioning, asserting that the contemporary church is in desperate need of conversion from a reduced gospel and the assumptions that extend from the nature of its reductions.[8]

A Different Way: The Sacrament of Conversation

Fortunately, there is a different way that can lead us out of the abyss of homogenization, privatized belief systems, and a trivialized gospel. This is the hard path of making conversation safe and sacred in the life of a community.

To this point, we have described many scenarios where conversation is discouraged, edited, or even feared, and have explained some of the consequences of curtailed speech in the life of a fellowship. What does the opposite look like? Our community, Emmaus Way, has explored this path and has found some of the delights, possibilities, and perils of allowing conversation to become sacred.

Every community spends its lifespan talking. It is what we do, all the time. As linguist Deborah Tannen implied earlier, our identity is found in our words. Our speech exists in a spectrum between cursing (the destructive potential of our words) and blessing (all of the sacred possibilities for our speech). We've all been deeply damaged by intentional and passive forms of cursing. We tend to recognize this use of language instantly, though undoing the havoc and pain it wreaks remains a colossal, if not impossible, task. We have all been in the crosshairs or part of the collateral damage of the winner-takes-all argument speech in our culture. But there are several practices and commitments that can make our conversation sacred as communities seek to live in the blessing end of the spectrum.

The Sermon Conversation

Our practice has centered on encouraging, protecting, and valuing a series of weekly conversations as sacred. These sacred conversations tend to spur many other less formal conversations that become part of a web of blessing speech in our community. Our first conversational practice occurs early on Tuesday mornings. Since the inception of Emmaus Way, a group of diverse people has gathered to discuss the coming week's sermon text. This group has transitioned in personalities almost entirely over the course of several years. But it has remained relatively diverse, passionate, safe, and creative. Our conversations have ranged from Spirit-empowered consensus on a text to times of sharp conflict. For those who know the seminary landscape in the United States, shockingly, there was a time when we had five seminaries represented in the conversation (Dallas, Southeastern Baptist, Gordon-Conwell, Duke, and Harvard).

There were many powerful products of this practice. For instance, every Sunday, the dialogue at Emmaus Way (and every choice of preaching topics when we aren't using the lectionary) begins with the authority of a "we" statement because it is the continuation of a conversation that began already on Tuesday morning. This typically yields a greater confidence in the dialogue leader than would have been the case if the preparation process had been done alone. The Tuesday morning conversation also establishes a range of meaning for our text that is highly relevant and specific to our community. This avoids negative "point reductions" where one voice demands "that the text can only mean this!"[9] Establishing this range of meaning affects the tone of the conversation as well as creates sensitivity to many of the delicate issues that could divide our community. As a result, these issues are often addressed more respectfully and openly as part of this intentional conversation.

This text dialogue ends in a formal sense after about two hours. But in a way it continues all week. As we continue to prepare the dialogue, e-mails and phone calls fly with recommended articles, ideas, and community illustrations. At the next week's text discussion, there is always a commitment to evaluate and critique the past sermon before moving to the week ahead. In this practice, scriptural interpretation feels like an ongoing midrash rather than an individual interpretative work with sharp stops and starts.

We believe that the perception of sharp starts and stops is one of the greatest impediments to creativity and theological exploration in the typical sermon, because it tends to teach the congregation that their job is something other than to live inside the text. One hour on Sunday is just not enough to bring our people into the world of the Bible. A pattern of stops and starts instead teaches our people to consult the Bible in the same way they do an owner's manual—only when something is broken—rather than continually having their lives shaped by living inside its narrative.

The Pub Conversation

A second intentional conversation occurs at our Thursday evening pub group. This conversation usually lasts a couple hours, but has been known to stretch out all the way to "last call." We typically use an article that is sent out early in the week via our listserv to function as the conversation starter. But the conversation comfortably moves through a variety of welcomed tangents and typically morphs into multiple sub-conversations throughout the evening.

There are two types of participants in our pub group: those who attend regularly and those who read the article regularly but never come to the pub. Pub group is related only tangentially to the weekly worship dialogue. Often the topics differ dramatically from the weekly sermon. But we ensure a connection between the two conversations because many of the text group members (which is smaller and limited in size) are pub group regulars.

The pub group has a variety of substantive benefits for our community. First, it is a regular open door. Unlike small groups that can have formidable barriers making it difficult for newcomers to attend, such as meeting at homes that might be hard to find or out of the way, our pub group is located at an easy-to-find, prominent location and is very accessible to newcomers. It is often more comfortable for people to walk into a pub full of strangers than a house full of strangers—there's something about that public, informal setting that helps people feel a bit more comfortable showing up alone for the first time. Many newcomers to Emmaus Way got their start in our community at the pub group.

In addition, the pub conversation raises the theological bar of conversation throughout the whole Emmaus Way community. We advertise the pub conversation as unabashedly theological, philosophical, and political. This allows us to test the limits of interpretation and some of the personal sensitivities related to specific topics long before the topic or particular text makes its way to our sermon dialogues.

For example, the present theological landscape has been significantly altered by new lines of interpretation over Paul's writing in the New Testament (called by some "the new perspective"), which, to generalize, emphasizes a more narrative, more political, less theological proof-texted reading of Paul's work.[10] For some in our community who have been taught a very static, theological apologetic to reading Paul and particularly the letter to the Romans, these new ideas and theological explorations could be quite intimidating and disturbing. But the pub group gave us the opportunity to read in community as well as post several articles on the new perspective. Several months later, when we did a dialogue series on Romans, the community was more prepared for these nuances in interpretation, and I (Tim) was more sensitive to their questions and possible points of confusion or unnecessary disturbance. As a result, the dialogue was challenging and engaging while also avoiding inappropriate levels of theological disequilibrium.

Finally, the pub group exists as an ideological and contextual sanctuary for our community. There is a safety implicit in the nature of the group such that ideas are readily connected to the life contexts and decisions of those present. The pub group is the ultimate foe of the "don't ask, don't tell" legacy in our community, because there really is a safe place where you can ask or tell. The existence of such a sanctuary permeates the ethos of the whole community. Obviously, from the middle section of this book, you've had an opportunity to experience some of the tone and bandwidth of this group.

The Sunday Conversation

A third intentional and sacred conversation is the sermon dialogue itself. Even before the sermon begins, there are often two groups of people who have interacted directly or indirectly with the text because of the week's previous conversations. We arrange the room to encourage participation. The conversation leader sits in an unthreatening manner on a swivel stool in the center of the gathering space. This ensures that the focus of the community is on the community rather than on a single authority. Sometimes we employ smaller conversation groups, and multiple conversation leaders are part of the process. Both of these practices feed the spirit of dialogue in our community. Each dialogue brings not only the momentum of the week's text group and pub group but also draws on the content of previous dialogues. We post a weekly podcast and provide blog space on our website so that those who are absent can stay connected to the conversation and add their comments. These also provide a means for those who don't like to speak out, even in small groups, to contribute safely.

Rather than taking away from the authority or power of the text, our dialogue works to enhance that power. When someone in the community gives voice to an idea, application, or possibility that is echoed by others, these points have much greater weight than if they had come from a single teacher or preacher. In addition to this regular chorus of echoes, a suggestion or assertion often comes from a source in the community with more credibility than the person leading the dialogue.

As individual teachers, we are always limited by our experiences, the focus of our training, and our life situations. These limits create natural boundaries to our credibility. How many sermons have you heard about poverty and injustice from preachers who have experienced neither? How many times have we as speakers tried our best to be sensitive to issues dramatically outside our realm of experiences? Authenticity is exponentially increased when these concerns come from the voice of someone with real experience on the topic.

Recently, we finished a dialogue series on the roles of the body and human sexuality in spiritual and community formation. This conversation was beautifully punctuated and extended by Sarah, a leader in our community, who through several stories added her distinctly feminine physical and emotional journey from adolescence to adulthood to the conversation. These stories about her family's and her church's awkward interactions about puberty and sexuality and their impact on her body image as a single adult were riotously funny and brimming with remarkable theological insights. The embarrassing drama of a cake decorated with blooming roses to be shared by her whole family (including her dad!) after her first period was certainly *way* beyond Dan's and my experiences! Her description of a natural non sequitur between her body life, given these experiences, and her life as a worshiper of God was a personal reflection that many in our community desperately needed to hear. Sarah's boldness and vulnerability extended the conversation in the sense of gender and added a texture of both angst and theological reflection that would have been starkly absent without her voice.

We have found tremendous blessings in these kinds of conversations and they have helped us learn how to talk to each other as well as listen to each other. But holding our practices up as inflexible templates to be replicated exactly in other communities contradicts our points regarding the sacred value of authenticity and context in community conversations. In another community, a pub might be the entirely wrong space for open conversation. The boundaries created by tradition and space in worship may provoke a community to discover different methods of creating a conversational feel to their worship gatherings. But even subtle adjustments and allowances for safe conversation on the text can have dramatic consequences.

I (Tim) once worked with a brilliant teaching pastor whose insight into the Scriptures was often unparalleled and served as an impetus to dramatic spiritual liberation to more than two decades of congregants. Interestingly, one undesired legacy of this friend's skill was that very few skilled teachers tended to develop around him. This was partially due to the immensity of his wisdom and creative insight. He was just one of those people who saw things that others missed. But this legacy could also be attributed to the utterly confident tone of his teaching and the fact that his sermons tended to conclude with one reductionistic, if brilliant and finely honed, unassailable point. In this manner, one of the most humble people I have ever met had inadvertently created a "ministry of the final word."

As our staff team worked together to unravel this legacy, we would often jokingly encourage him to lie by inserting into his sermons comments such as, "I struggled with this all week and I'm still not sure that I have it right, but here goes. . . ." Obviously, a lack of authenticity is not the right solution. In my friend's case, he needed to surround himself with equally confident, divergent thinkers and allow these people to impact the tone and content of his sermons.

Not every community can or should do what we've done at Emmaus Way. But as the story above demonstrates, sometimes subtle alterations to tone and process can foster the kind of sacred dialogue we are advocating even when the traditions of a fellowship won't allow for more dramatic interventions.

Transformations: Sacred Conversation Embodied

Breaking down the myth of homogeneity and developing practices that foster sacred conversation will result in a series of dramatic, missional transformations in a faith community. They also bring a kind of reciprocity to our understanding of the Scriptures. These conversational practices not only are modeled and encouraged in the biblical text, but also, when practiced, invigorate and even liberate our reading of the text. These transformations are the integrated results of sacred speech, but we'll parse them out and give them three names to expose a broader vision of the nuances of this change.

One element of transformation will be change in the *content and range of our conversation*. New words, ideas, and possibilities will begin to appear. We'll dedicate a later chapter to the impact of new words on our imagination, but the content and range of our speech will certainly expand far beyond the imaginary realm. Homogeneity, when it serves as a boundary, or in a protective manner, threatens and curtails numerous valences of speech. In our practice of sacred conversation, we've been delighted to see endangered forms of speech begin to multiply and flourish.

A growing volume of vulnerable and confessional speech is one example of a rebirth of significant but endangered speech that we often see. Confession is a remarkably necessary and healing form of speech. In an extreme irony, it is also quite common outside the bounds of the church. Set aside the image of the priest and darkened, closed-door confessional for a moment. Have you ever noticed how often we hear confessions, both simple and complex, throughout the course of a typical day? People confess perpetually their tardiness, laziness, angry or judgmental thoughts, lack of attention, bad habits, all forms of selfishness, and carelessness. We find ourselves saying, "You don't need to explain" all day long.

Perhaps this is the wrong response. People seem to desperately need to confess. Websites such as postsecret.com, where people post artistic, bold, and often-desperate confessions in anonymity affirm this pervasive need. When our communities allow or encourage "don't ask, don't tell" environments, confessional speech is one of the first casualties. Consequently, we find ourselves in faith communities that bemoan our lack of ability to tell the truth, all the while providing no practice of or space for truth telling.

Lament and strong emotive proclamations can also be on the endangered list. Many mission-driven churches with bold goals of expansion and significance in their local communities subtly outlaw proclamations of pain and attempt to maintain a positive, optimistic tone in all of their public discourse. This happens quite often even in fellowships that are ideologically distant from forms of prosperity theology. Many years ago, I (Tim) participated in a heated leadership meeting where a colleague critiqued another team member who had prayed vividly during the previous Sunday's pastoral prayer for the wounds of the community, including some direct speech about people struggling with addictions and suicidal impulses. The stated offense was "bumming out the congregation's enthusiasm and forward direction." His tone of lament did not fit with the upbeat optimism that some desired to present consistently from the podium.

On the opposite end of the emotional continuum, just as we were starting to form the Emmaus Way community, a young woman who was just being exposed to some of the freedom to express angst (and the volume of those expressions) in our fellowship let slip a "Praise Jesus" after some good news. She quickly blushed and asked if we were allowed to say that!

There are stronger forms of confessions, laments, and bitter emotions or questions directed at God that comprise a deeper and darker level of forbidden speech. These are the words we utter alone in the dark watches of the night. Though usually not appropriate for every audience, these are often the words we most need someone else to hear. Like most pastors, we've heard these visceral words of loss, anger, fantasy, sexual shame, despair, absence of faith, and indictment of God many times. Though we are privileged to offer blessing and intervention in these moments, the greatest blessing that is needed is the embrace of the community as an extension of God's mercy and understanding.

As we saw in chapter 6, the book of Psalms presents liturgies and templates of prayer in all of these forms of discouraged or forbidden speech. As we read them, we often wonder if the anger of Psalm 137 and the despair of Psalm 88 survive the tolerances of our communities. The Psalms strongly imply that the community of faith is to have an extreme range of content in its speech directed toward God. Sacred practices of dialogue and conversation lead us on this path.

A second element of transformation involves *the movement of conversation to accountable realms*. Unaccountable speech is most likely what James had in mind when he referred to the tongue as "a restless evil, full of deadly poison" (James 3:8). Most of us have experienced the maiming and disemboweling potential of speech—there are few weapons so deadly. In environments where conversation is limited or certain genres of speech are forbidden, some of our significant words tend to relocate themselves in unaccountable realms, where there are no resources to help the speaker, no measured sanctions for inappropriateness, and—when they are words of blessing—only limited recipients.

When among friends who do not challenge us, sharp words can remain unchecked. The blog and message board world offers an excellent example of the phenomenon of unaccountable speech. Too many times this sphere is filled with "bold" words hidden behind obscurity and anonymity. Just this week, I (Tim) randomly linked to the blog of a person I knew years ago who just that day had referred to me enigmatically as either "the most gracious person on earth" or "entirely full of . . ." you know what! Thinking I would never read his words, he was shocked when I posted a response that I was probably both at times! Lack of accountability certainly can breed sharp critique.

When we strengthen our reflexes and muscles of dialogue and practice the sacrament of conversation, our words become more accountable. We don't use that word as a way of creating limits. Rather, we want to relocate these words in a realm where speaker and listener challenge one another, so as to inform, appropriately critique, and spiritually form each other. "Don't ask, don't tell" fellowships also tend to be "off the record" communities where dangerous words, significant concerns, or words with great potential blessing are regularly lost in the shuffle.

Our community, at its most fragile inception, suffered because we did not provide accountable space for some significant critique. In Emmaus Way's first year, a group of highly creative, artistic, and expressive friends formed. They were among the primary patrons of our "art nights" (informal evenings in our loft when people would gather to work on art or even home projects, read books, listen to music, or simply share creative space in community), silent prayer vigils, and film screenings.

By our second year, some of these traditions had almost entirely disappeared. Our community had changed somewhat in constituency (especially with the birth of young children) and hence the availability of people for these events. Some significant pastoral needs that required significant time by the leadership had come up, and some logistical issues (particularly an arduous and frustrating search for space) further diverted leadership attention. The responsibility for some of these beloved traditions had been delegated from one set of leaders, who had redirected their energies to other arenas, to new leaders who didn't follow up quickly. As a result, there were frustrations, concerns about community change, and dislocated critique.

In our quarterly "Ekklesia" (an open meeting where we discuss our community life), we failed miserably by trumpeting the positives while not asking for concerns in this accountable conversational arena. By the end of this second year, all but a couple people from this group of friends had left our community. Critique and questions had not been expressed in a time and space when adjustments could have been made. Leaders, seeing our fellowship in an organic lens, and wanting the community to take responsibility for maintaining traditions, were frustrated that the ball had been dropped on some of these important gatherings. People in the community, assuming that important traditions were to be protected by leadership, wondered why the events they valued had disappeared. Feelings were hurt as the residue of inappropriate speech filtered through the community. Our leaders felt wounded and abandoned and were largely unaware of our failures until it was too late.

This is one of the common tragedies when critical questions and observations are embedded in unaccountable spheres. We spent one long afternoon unpacking this situation with one of the community members who remained and saw as a result the magnitude of this tragedy and the missed opportunities. So many wounds and damaging words could have been avoided. Emmaus Way's loss of valued and highly missional traditions could also have been avoided. The commitment to dialogue should not only help develop more spaces for accountable speech, but also the courage to use these spaces.

The relocation of inquiry is a third component of the transformation of sacred speech. The previously discussed movement of speech from unaccountable to accountable space is one example of conversational relocation. The language of accountability more naturally corresponds to words of frustration, critique, and failure. But there are many other forms of dialogue that can be relocated and bring about greater blessing in our communities. One such form is inquiry.

Inquiry is the heartbeat of Christian community and spiritual formation. Jesus offered the best and most obvious example of the importance of inquiry as he answered loaded questions with questions (for example, the teacher of the law's question of how to inherit eternal life provoked Jesus' questioning this man in the area of his expertise, the law, in Luke 10:25–37), used questions to motivate spiritual insight (to blind Bartimaeus in Mark 10:46–52, he asked, "What do you want me to do for you?"), and directed questions to expose spiritual hardness and blindness (to his opponents in Luke 20:1–8, he said, "I will also ask you a question. Tell me, John's baptism—was it from heaven, or from men?").

Despite the importance of inquiry, we would strongly suggest that many forms of Christian community and church are making a range of decisions that preclude inquiry. As we described earlier, the perceived threats of postmodernity and pluralism have served to motivate a tightening of our theological lines, resulting in a series of negative consequences. This restriction (what we named earlier as a reduction and trivialization of the gospel) pushes inquiry to the edge of our communities where it becomes unaccountable (where challenging and relevant questions are asked to people who can say whatever they want without consequence or challenge) or even inappropriately punitive ("You can't ask questions like that and be involved here!").

One of the results of the vast cultural shifts we now inhabit is that many "settled" questions of theology are being raised again with the fear and passion of new "cultural eyes." My (Tim's) kids attend a public art magnet school with a strong Lesbian, Gay, Bisexual, and Transgender student voice; they participate in athletics with friends from multiple ethnicities with dramatically divergent religious commitments; and they attend a church with radical differences in economic lifestyles. Our experience is really not that unique. Most families and friendships face gradations of new cultural situations and possibilities, all of which demand urgent and exciting theological reflection.

In the Christian community, lines of passionate inquiry are forming on the extent of salvation, the nature of God's sovereignty and intervention in human affairs, the atoning work of Christ, the ethics of warfare and the theological value of "collective security," ecological issues and the broad implications of acknowledging God as the Creator of our universe, and a whole range of sexual/gender questions. Many of these questions range far beyond the settled answers or established lines of debate in previous eras of theological conversation, and they range even farther beyond the boundaries established by our newly restricted theological essentials and non-negotiables. There is a vital conversation with unlimited missional possibility that we, unfortunately, are prone to ignore.

As it has always been, conversation is the pulse of human life and often the barometer of the threats and possibilities of human community. Allowing conversation and dialogue to become a sacred practice seems to be an essential act of mission in an increasingly diverse, transitory, and threatened world. And it is within this sacramental exercise of dialogue as the community of disciples gathered in Jesus' name that he promises to be present (Matt. 18:20).

→ 10

Ethics

Practicing New Creation

The sacrament of dialogue that we laid out in the previous chapter is the central practice of this book. In saying this we are making the point that reading the Bible as the Word of God requires that we need to do so in the right way, in community dialogue. It has been our assertion that a full reading of the Bible as the Word of God necessitates that we read it in community, that we facilitate dialogue, and that we listen to the many voices in our congregation as a means of opening the Scriptures for us.

While there is no doubt that "community" has become a buzz word in the last few years, we believe that reading the Bible apart from the context of a community doesn't make sense. As we pointed out in chapter 2, language only makes sense within the context of shared practices. It only makes sense within a community of people whose actions give the words meaning. For us, this practicing community is the church. And in the previous chapter we argued that it is the practice of reading and preaching in dialogue within this community that is central to hearing God's Word in our midst. This is not to say God's speech and revelation are restricted in any manner, or that the personal devotion or the authoritative sermon is categorically wrong, for we strongly believe that each of them is very appropriate and formative. But we also firmly believe that they must take place within and against the backdrop of a rich practice of communal dialogue. It is this dialogue, this ongoing exchange of the language of redemption, gospel, and the "strange new world of God"[1] that forms the space of the church and the community of those gathered in Christ's name.

Yet as we have said before, reading Scripture in dialogue is not the only practice of the community that helps us to understand the text. There are several peculiar practices of the church that facilitate how we make meaning out of the text. If this sounds circular to you, that's because that's exactly what it is. The art of interpretation—and it is more of an art than a science—is a circular process. Reading the text forms the way we live, while practicing the Christian life influences how we understand what the text is saying. So it is in the final portion of this book that we will speak to some of the most important practices that help to form the reading and dialoguing community. We will speak to the disciplines of the community that help shape us and our communal reading of Scripture. In many ways these are the practices that make faithful dialogue possible, and they are the actions that make the Word of God meaningful in our lives. Without them to complete the circle, it remains impossible to faithfully continue to read the Bible together as God's Word.

When we speak of the practices of the church, we are speaking of particular, regular activities that help to shape how we live in the world. Given that we are creatures of habit, it's good for us to pay attention to the types of habits we form. While we will turn our attention to the other practices of hospitality, mission, and cultivating our imaginations in future chapters, we will use this chapter to discuss the ethics of a Christian community. As we dive into this discussion, however, we realize that thinking of ethics as habits may sound a little confusing to some people. For many of us, ethics suggests the language of duty or obedience rather than habit. But we believe the understanding of Christian ethics as obedience to absolutes has limited our ability to form Christian disciples. So we submit that Christian ethics is the formation of habits that help us to live into the possibilities of new creation.

The focus of this ethic of possibilities leads us to a discussion of the practice of baptism. Baptism is one of the central acts of the church, one that teaches us to see our lives within a new creation. It is an ethical act that—in spite of the ways in which we have turned it into a private, personal statement devoid any real power—aims at nothing other than a restructuring and reordering of public life toward God. Baptism, and our continual remembering of it, is a practice that teaches us to be a peculiar people focused on possibility instead of absolutes, disciplining us to read Scripture together in ways that challenge the status quo with an image of what life with God could look like.

The Fragile Absolute

David James Duncan's novel *The Brothers K* chronicles the life of the Chance family living in Camas, Washington. The drama of the novel develops as Sarah, the devout Seventh Day Adventist mother, and Hugh, her washed-up husband and father of their four children whose promising baseball career ended before it really began due to an unfortunate mill accident, struggle through the mistakes and successes of trying to raise their family in a tragic, comic world. When Kincaid, the main narrator of the book, challenges his father for giving up on his love of baseball, Papa Chance, as he is affectionately known, sets out to make his comeback by building a shed to serve as a bullpen in the backyard. With the shed constructed and the pitching mound in place, Papa Chance, responding to his son's challenge, starts pitching again. At the beginning of the next chapter, entitled "Strike Zones," Duncan begins with an epigraph from John Gierach that states:

nothing is stationary
everything wiggles

Bathed in Duncan's witty prose, the chapter contains a discussion between Hugh Chance and his young son, Kincaid, both baseball enthusiasts, about the character of the strike zone. As Papa Chance puts the finishing touches on his impromptu bullpen, he leans an old canvas-covered mattress against the far wall to act as a catcher and backstop. But his attempt to paint a strike zone on the old mattress proves tougher than one might at first imagine—a lesson Kincaid was not soon to forget.

After staring at the mattress for longer than necessary, Papa Chance barks his frustration to Kincaid, saying, "It's nonsense to paint a strike zone at all!"

"Why?" Papa demands (asking a rhetorical question). "Why is a fixed strike zone nonsense? Think about it," he huffs. "Say we make our rectangle about the size of the strike zone on a six-foot hitter. This leaves out shorter and taller hitters. That's an obvious defect. But the deeper defect is, where the hell is the strike zone on a six-foot hitter? Where is it on any hitter?" Continuing his rant, Papa Chance says, "The reason no one can say where the strike zone is, is that the actual strike zone has almost nothing to do with the width of the plate or the size of the hitter. The real strike zone is located somewhere else entirely. . . . The strike zone that matters, the only one we've got to work with really, is the one locked up in the skull of the plate ump."[2]

Like the myth of a universal, objective strike zone, the field of ethics has tended to assume one universal and objective standard for all humans and every society. The laws of nature, we were told in the modern era, communicate to us both the standards for personal piety and the structure of any successful society. They are there for all time and for all people and dictate the correct response to every situation. When it comes to these disciplines there is only one right answer.

Yet this assumption has left many of us at the end of the modern era feeling lost in a world where medical knowledge seems to change on a daily basis and nuclear physics has begun to call into question everything we thought we knew about matter. When it comes to the social sciences, things have become much more unstable. We find that what we used to know about the rules of war, the rules of economics, the rules of political science, and the rules of personal action are no longer as certain as we once presumed them to be. We are beginning to find that the absolute rules we have painted, like Papa Chance's attempt to paint the strike zone, are too small, too large, and too unsatisfactory.

The Limit of Absolutes

One of the biggest problems of operating in a world of absolutes is that this belief in the rigidity of things trains us to believe that things are the way they have to be and that any attempt to break free of these norms is necessarily detrimental to the structure and fabric of a healthy society. We lose sight of the possibility that things can be different. Nowhere is this more evident than in the world of ethics and public life. Convinced that the only alternative to absolutes is the chaos of relativity, we have sacrificed the realm of possibility, choosing instead to remain within what is known and what is normal. Hence, we forgo the possibility of thinking that things can and indeed should change.

During the Great Depression of the 1930s and into the post–World War II era—which was also a time of continued racism and bigotry toward African Americans—Dorothy Day, a Roman Catholic activist and founder of the Catholic Worker Movement, began to live outside the "norms" of American culture. As an active response of love in the face of the racism of the time, Day invited black folk in need to live in her home. Similarly, she turned her focus to communal living in a world moving more and more toward individualization, and she set out to work on the problem of poverty by living with the poor and inviting them into her home. Even more, she began to speak up on behalf of workers who were being exploited, challenging the ethics of big business and corporate profiteering. These actions, saintly as they may seem, brought her into conflict with the presiding absolutes of mid-century America.

Having joined the International Workers of the World because of her convictions and having embraced many of Marx's assessments of capitalism while continuing to critique the oppression and atmosphere of all-out competition she saw vividly displayed in the scarred faces of the poor, Day's name was added to an FBI "list of dangerous radicals to be detained in the event of a national emergency."[3] Shockingly, these gracious acts of charity and her critique of American business practices—along with her call for peace—garnered her the suspicious eye of the hyper-sensitive, anti-communist FBI under J. Edgar Hoover. Hoover had even entered a personal note next to Day's name on the list of dangerous persons that read, "Dorothy Day is a very erratic and irresponsible person who makes every effort to castigate the Bureau whenever she feels inclined."[4]

The years of the second Red Scare and McCarthyism in the United States were years of absolutes. Any affiliation with anything that smelled or looked like Communism could have you cast out from respectable, safe society and under the surveillance of policing entities such as the FBI. Anything short of avid belief in capitalism was considered un-American, Communist, and treasonous to America and the American way of life—at least according to the strict political rhetoric of the day. In the case of Dorothy Day, the absolute fear of Communism put the US government in the odd situation of tracking as a threat to national security one of the very people who was seeking to help out the thousands of Americans trapped under racism, oppression, and poverty—that is, one of the very people working to make America better.

Now, legislators are beginning to recognize that strict regulations and absolutes often make change and new ways of doing business extremely laborious and difficult to implement. In no area has this been more evident in the past two decades than in the field of environmental protection. When ecological reports in the late 1970s began to sound the alarm on issues of pollution, global warming, and carbon emissions, few businesses were ready to comply with the regulations of the newly formed Environmental Protection Agency (EPA). As journalist David Bornstein reports, the then-assistant director of the EPA, Bill Drayton, began to rethink EPA regulations by "pushing through the 'bubble.'"[5]

Drayton saw that instead of regulating each individual piece of production with strict rules on each area of emissions, businesses could limit their overall emissions by focusing on the areas where it was easier and more cost-efficient to do so. The result was that businesses were less likely to fight the regulations of the EPA, which was now creating regulations that were less oppositional to business interests and therefore more successful in bringing about change.[6] By implementing this strategy, not only did businesses learn to see the deleterious effects of production, but environmentalists learned to see the process of regulations in a new way. As Bornstein notes, there were several people in the EPA's air pollution program who saw Drayton's bubble strategy as giving in to big business, and potentially as a threat to their own jobs.[7] Stuck in their own absolutist activism, these environmentalists were challenged to see new possibilities for reaching their overall goal.

Drayton's story is one small example of the way a strict adherence to "the absolutes" can actually work against the overall goal of creating good practices. When we become too tied to the current way of doing things, to a solidified code of conduct, to a bunch of absolute rules and regulations, the security of these rules and regulations leads us to take our eyes off of the larger picture. This often remains the case even when these rules and regulations no longer serve the purpose they were established to meet. Yet we are beginning to learn that absolute rules and regulations are rarely helpful in attempting to reach the end goal of forming a healthy society in an ever-changing world. Revising and reordering are often necessary for progress.

The Limit of Christian Absolutes

Probably no group has been more demonized and misrepresented by Christian churches in the past two thousand years than the Pharisees. The typical churchgoer knows when this group is mentioned in the Sunday sermon that the pastor must be preaching about works righteousness, religiosity, a lack of compassion, and legalism. Nothing could be further from the truth with regard to how the Pharisees viewed their relationship to Torah.

As more scholars in the past thirty years have taken a closer and more unprejudiced look at first-century Judaism, they have helped us gain a more authentic understanding of the faith of the Pharisees. In all reality, the Pharisees, like the other forms of Judaism in the first century before the destruction of the temple in AD 70, believed deeply in the graciousness of God. "Fundamental to Jewish piety was the view that God's grace preceded the requirement of obedience and undergirds both the life of Israel and also the entire universe."[8] Far from the arrogant and legalistic caricature most of us know today, the Pharisees viewed the law as life giving, not because they could perform it perfectly, but because it was a code for relating to the God who brought them out of Egypt and exile. "They thought that God had given them this law and bestowed on them his grace, and that it was their obligation within the loving relationship with God to obey the law precisely."[9] The law was a wonderful gift because it communicated to the people how to live with this gracious God who had pulled them out of the chaos of exile and promised to protect them. The law was grace, not burden.

While we have succeeded in making the Pharisees the whipping boys for our attacks on legalism, the law as opposed to grace, and works righteousness, it seems to us that Christians (even or especially "grace-focused" evangelical Christians) appear to be completely satisfied and more at home with a religion based on a litany of rules and absolutes than a life of experiment. Often, we seem more inclined to read the Bible as a manual for action or a compendium of moral truths for a black-and-white world, than to let it show us what life with God, life in Christ, might actually be. Rules are often just easier.

Yet many of us have become frustrated by the limited scope of what has been standard-issue Christianity in our culture. The reality of this form of Christianity came to light in an obvious fashion with the rise of the Religious Right, a brand of conservatism that has dominated evangelicalism since the end of the 1980s. Presenting a tightly packaged, simple and sure brand of what it means to be a follower of Christ, the champions of this type of conservative Christianity enlisted many loyal followers and gained much power and influence even on the level of national politics. By eliminating the complexity of the Christian life and reducing it to merely taking a "right" stance on a few hot-button issues, it appealed to a large portion of Christians concerned with what they took to be the ever-increasing moral depravity of the nation. It has been a brand of Christianity focused on absolutes, rights and wrongs, and fabricated on the premise that the world and our faith are fundamentally good or bad.

Many of us are waking up, however, to find that these absolutes have helped us paint a strike zone so tiny that not only are we finding it hard to breathe but we're also coming to realize that these lines of our faith are incapable of addressing the real breadth and complexity of the game. Reducing our faith only to those things that can be said universally and absolutely, we have settled for a form of Christianity based upon a list of rules with little place for creative or inventive following. In fact, for many of us, the positive expression of our faith has been confined to two main expressions: reading the Bible and prayer (two practices of faith when done honestly and often that do anything but reinforce a sense of human surety about absolutes!). The main problem here is quite simply the fact that we have reduced the faith. We've limited our Christian lives in such a way that even the most devout of Christians outside a monastery cannot live their faith for more than two or three hours a day (which we deem to be an extremely long devotional!). Is there any wonder why we have no idea how to bring our whole lives into conformity with Christ?

At this point, we understand if this critique on the role of absolutes, particularly ethical absolutes, has generated in you a growing concern over relativism. Yet we firmly believe that the bifurcation of ethics into the alternatives of absolutes versus relativism has been a dialogue captured by a fear that has come to cripple Christian ethics over the past few decades. Suffice it to say, we do not buy into this bifurcation. Instead we hope to assert—based upon our approach to Scripture—that Christian ethics ought, more appropriately, to be an *exploration* of the discipleship made possible in the resurrection of Christ.

Both of us have occasional opportunities to speak at youth retreats and various collegiate events. One thing we have learned in doing so is that one of the hardest tasks for youth and campus pastors to do in our age of Christianity is to convince the students that following Christ is something worthwhile. Our first instinct in assigning blame for this difficulty is often directed at the students. But the primary issue is not that students are bad kids or hellions bent on a love for evil. (Though make no mistake, we've worked with enough youth to have firm evidence for a strong doctrine of depravity and original sin.) It's not so much that these students don't like church or want nothing to do with God. Frankly, what we've found is that the majority of the time these students aren't anti-church; they're simply bored, uninspired, and unengaged.

And who are we to throw stones? We freely admit that we often find the normal expressions and expectations of Christianity to be extremely boring. Another congregational business meeting? Another couples' retreat on the secrets of a successful marriage? Another exciting word-for-word exposition of the book of Romans? Is this really as good as it gets for Christians? While we are not intending to downplay the role of these events in the life of the community or their usefulness for Christian living, we also find ourselves asking, "Is this really all we have to offer?" While we may jump on our students for their devotion to reality TV or their desire to spend more time with their iPods than their Bibles, we might need to take a closer look at the type of Christianity we're feeding them—for their boredom might be a sign of good sense and an indication that we're not handing them the real thing.

We believe that much of the problem begins with the fact that we've reduced the Bible to an endorsement of the status quo. We've convinced ourselves that it offers us a world in which God lays down the law with no shades of gray, and that every parable leads us to a nice and neat moral absolute—even when Jesus forgets to tell us what that moral absolute is. The wonderful problem with this is that when a community reads the text together, we very quickly find that the Bible simply doesn't read this way.

Just let one precocious and pesky teenager into the conversation and she'll confuse the whole standard ethical construction we try to take from the text. She'll soon point out that we find Jesus himself engaging in more than a few of the activities we think to be suspicious and shady. One minute he's partying like a rock star (all the old teetotaler arguments for the non-alcoholic nature of wine in Jesus' day now seem to be the fabrications of Prohibition religion), the next he's eating at a casino in Vegas. Then it's off to the dog races, and on a Sunday! He's hanging with the wrong crowd while dissing his mother and siblings. And to add insult to injury, he refuses to get married and settle down, even into his midthirties!

One of the main reasons Tim and I find the text refreshing— especially when we set it free from our own interests—is that it refuses to let us read it as an endorsement of our cultural or social norms or as a list of rules for living. That perspective on ethics and the life of the Christian community—not to mention the Bible—is simply too limited. It's not radical enough. We might even say, it's just not biblical enough. Instead it is reductionistic and boring, leaving no place for the experimental nature of learning to follow Christ.

The Ethics of Possibility Actualized: Baptism and the New Creation

The wonder of the Scriptures is that they cannot be reduced or even dismissed as a compendium of ethical absolutes. There are many occasions when we would prefer explicit ethical instructions free from any need or burden of interpretation. But the Scriptures vigorously resist this effort.

The historical nature of the Scriptures—the reality that the Bible was written and compiled at specific times in history—requires that even the simplest directives such as "You shall not steal" be interpreted contextually. Yes, stealing is always wrong. But what exactly is stealing? That is the work of the interpreter. After all, many of our tradition's most prominent theologians did not think that taking something out of need for survival was an act of theft. Yet today, we frequently put people who take food or water in jail for stealing. The Torah offers this apparently universal ethic without its writers ever wrestling with the complexities of copyrights, video and musical downloading possibilities on the Internet, or the ethical use of office supplies and corporate resources in a telecommuting, wireless world where the boundary between office and home is vanishing. Neither did they face the problem of trying to interpret the US tax code—especially for the self-employed!

Our appetite for simple social and ethical rules not only leads us to avoid the work of interpretation, it also tempts us to simplify other essential theological questions such as salvation. Why didn't God just give us a text with a straightforward, step-by-step set of directions for salvation? Why do we have the Bible with all of its beautiful and at times infuriating nuances, tensions, and diversities rather than a

neat booklet on the basic steps to salvation? Sure, we have the Ten
Commandments, or the Sermon on the Mount, and some verses in
Romans we can piece together to make a statement of faith. But
why all the other stuff? Why so much other verbiage to cloud out the
central, simple message?

The quick and straightforward answer to these questions is that
the Bible is a book that invites us into the life of God, a life that
presents us with new hopes, new ways of loving one another, new
ways of thinking of the world and what it all might look like when
it is restored to right relation with God. All the "other stuff" in the
text is not just filler, but part of the material those before us thought
integral for learning to live life with God. Its various books, letters,
prophetic oracles, narratives, and proclamations are scintillations
meant to expose our faulty vision of the world and to illuminate a
new creation under God's rule.

Though it may seem somewhat obvious when we say that the Bible
is meant to be read not by the unbeliever but by the baptized, that
is, by those who have passed from death into the life in the body of
Christ, it's a point worth making for how we approach Scripture. The
Bible is the text of the community of Christians, and it plays a central
function in our life together. It's not so much a step-by-step process on
how to get saved, but a thick, layered narrative that describes a new
way of life. And a new way of life is not something easy to describe
and certainly not something that can be reduced to a few central,
fundamental, absolute rules or steps. It's much larger than that; it's
much more creative, much more experiential. It's something much
more communal.

Similar to marriage, it is simply too simplistic to think of salvation
as a onetime, instantaneous, concrete step. While we do not deny the
fact that standing in a church on a spring day, exchanging the vows of
marriage before God and the community, means that you are in fact
married, any person in a marriage realizes that day was not the end
of things. In fact, in hindsight, the significance of that day seems to
reside more in the vows than anything else, because we tend to realize
later that we really had no idea what we were doing at the time. Any
couple who thinks they have reached the apex of their relationship at
the wedding is undoubtedly headed toward estrangement. And life in

The Intersection of Text and Community

the body of Christ is no different. Salvation is continued presence in the body of Christ, learning to receive, to live, and to improvise the actions and love of God as we go.

In his second letter to the Corinthians, the apostle Paul makes an extraordinary statement about what becomes possible when we begin to live in Christ. While it may be easy to miss in some translations, the NEB captures well Paul's thought. It reads, "When anyone is united to Christ, there is a new world; the old order has gone, and a new order has already begun" (2 Cor. 5:17). As John Howard Yoder points out, the extraordinary claim made by Paul is that "what is new is the whole world, or 'creation,' and not merely the individual (the 'creature' as we are more often used to hearing it rendered)."[10] Yoder goes on:

> It is not enough to say that each of us is individually born again and baptized, with the result that all the born-again individuals are collected in one place, commanded by God to love one another and plant churches, with no more reason for discrimination. Paul says more than that; he says that two peoples, two cultures, two histories have come to flow into one new humanity, a new creation. The order is thus the reverse of our modern expectations. There is a new inter-ethnic social reality into which the individual is inducted rather than the social reality being the sum of the individuals.[11]

Paul is saying that the death and resurrection of Jesus has made a whole new world possible—a whole new world of relations, ethics, economics, politics and, yes, maybe even science. It is this world, this new creation, this re-creation we come into through our baptism (our initiation into the new world) that we as a community must begin to understand.

One of our seminary professors, when speaking about the kingdom of God, would always make reference to the fact that more often than not Jesus in the Gospels begins to speak of it in parables. These parables often begin with the language of simile or metaphor. "The kingdom of God is like . . ." "It's as if a man who had much wealth went off on a journey . . ." "The kingdom of heaven may be compared to . . ." In speaking this way, Jesus seems to be communicating that we are going to have to envision something just beyond the limits of the world we live in, just beyond the world as we see it. He is forcing us to think more about the possible than the actual, more about how things might be than about how they are.

In *Philosophical Fragments*, Søren Kierkegaard asks the question, "Is the past more necessary than the future? Or has the possible, by having become actual, become more necessary than it was?"[12] This is a complex way of saying, "Is the world we live in, the universe, human history, and human life completely determined and bound by history? Is the way things might be completely determined by the way they are or could they be different?" It is the question of what is possible.

When we read the Bible, when we let it put before us the "strange new world of God," we find that one of our primary tasks becomes helping each other to envision this new world and to live into it. One of the main reasons we need to read the Bible in community and with one another is simply that seeing this new world and having the courage and strength to live into it is not easy. It's not easy at all. It means we are going to have to learn a whole new ethic while working to form a new society. Together, we are going to have to begin to think of how things could be, how they can be in the new creation, rather than focusing so much on what absolutes help us to survive in the world we see every day on the news.

Our Practice

At Emmaus Way, we work to make the practice of baptism accentuate the theme of new creation. Whereas some congregations may lean toward a practice of baptism that minimizes the mess created by dousing people with water, we try to make as much of a mess as possible. We try to use as much water as possible by baptizing in one of our local rivers, not so much because we think it is more theologically correct, but because we have found it helpful in communicating to our community that entry into these waters is entry into the chaotic waters covering the face of the deep at the beginning of creation (Gen. 1:2). By us simulating the disarray prior to God's ordering in creation, the reemergence of the person being baptized more vividly proclaims the entry into a new created order under the Creator.

Our culture is prone to taking death out of everyday life, hiding it
away in the multiple nursing homes and hospital rooms of our country.
To counter this, we use the practice of submersion to emphasize the
necessity of our full participation in the death of Christ in order to be
raised to new life. Without the resurrection there is no new creation
and there is no new life. Having been buried into Christ's death, the
person being baptized is then raised up in Christ's resurrection to a
new life in his body, the community of the church. Furthermore, the
full submersion of the person communicates a complete cleansing
from past sins in repentance. It boldly states that the washing of this
person means she can live a new life, no longer bound by the chains
of the past, family dynamics, cultural allegiances, or prior idols. The
change disturbs even the world around her and a whole new life is
made possible.

In each of these ways we take baptism to be a political and ethical
statement. It is the entry through death and resurrection, through
chaos and new creation, into a new community, a new world, a new
order. Similarly, our practice of voluntary baptism communicates that
this new creation is not something we make on our own, but rather
a response to the call and promise of the gospel. This new politic,
this new ethic is one of discipleship. It is a form of life that seeks to
follow after Christ in imitation of him—this is the good news that
he proclaimed and what he has called us to do. His life, not just his
death, has meaning for our existence as the people of God.

Closely linked to our practice of baptism is our practice of ministe-
rial commitment. On a quarterly basis, during the regular corporate
worship gathering, we offer the people who have been attending our
church the opportunity to participate in a "minister's liturgy." One of
the things we set out early to do was to avoid the language of "member" when speaking of those joining our church body, while realizing
the need for people to exercise their commitment to our congregation.
After much labor and thought, we crafted a liturgy that utilized the
word *minister* in order to convey our hope for those coming into the
center of the community. This liturgy functions as a collective credo
for our life together, reminding those who have publicly spoken these
words before as they continue to participate, and inviting those who
have shared in our community to make a public statement of joining

with us so as to take ownership within our community. Our desire was to begin to gather a community of ministers, all of whom understood themselves to be active participants in the work of God in our community.

One of the hopes of our minister's liturgy is that it draws a strong line between the Scriptures and other practices designed to embody the new-creation-life expressed in baptism. Hence, as part of the liturgy we promise to "cultivate the disciplines of: continual prayer; consistent and collective study of the word of God as found in the Holy Scriptures; participation in the daily life of the community; spiritual discernment; and authentic dialogue."

When we first unveiled the liturgy to the community, several people remarked that they fully embraced this ideal, but the disciplines of Scripture reading and prayer were common places of frustration and failure for them. We were quick to respond that many have only heard of these disciplines as personal, individual commitments. Honestly, many of us face times of pain, despair, or distraction when we shortchange these aspects of discipleship. But we meant this to be a community discipline. We would read and interpret the Scriptures—together. We would live in faith and the hope of a new creation—together. There would be times when each of us would be unable to muster courage, hope, and faith. At those times, it is the community that believes, hopes, and dreams for the individual. Particularly in the realm of the Scriptures, we understood that our community's practices and embodiment of the new creation proclaimed in baptism would greatly empower our reading of the text. And of course our reading of the text would constantly expand our dreams and visions of God's redemption and inform the daily possibilities we would be willing to venture in our lives as disciples.

We should quickly add that an ethic of new creation has not been an easy thing for us to embrace, nor has it come quickly. Yet we have found that many of our people have begun to live into their baptism in experimental ways. Many of them—and the two of us—are slowly beginning to see the world differently, to see a new creation, and to know ourselves as servants and ministers of that new world. We haven't had anyone sell all of his possessions; we haven't had anyone build an orphanage or gather all of Durham's sick into her home; but we have had a few folks in our church volunteer significant amounts of their time to help a young, single dad. We've had a few people leave behind very lucrative careers to do non-profit work because they were convinced that the gospel of Jesus pointed them in a new direction. We've had people who were lost in loneliness and despair see the light of God by sharing themselves with our community. We've seen schoolteachers suffer through the daily headaches of being underpaid, underappreciated, overworked, and mistreated, yet they continue to work with Durham's youth because the gospel has given them eyes to see the hope and health that education can give their students in need.

We are not a miraculous community by any definition of the word. But these are some of the ways that members of our community continue to practice their baptism—and they are miracles. Baptism, we believe, is not simply a sign, not simply an "outward proclamation" (which is a rather redundant expression if you think about it), but it is an initiation into a whole new creation. Being covered with the primordial waters of chaos (Gen. 1:2), the initiate is then raised to life in the Father, Son, and Holy Spirit, that is, she is raised to new life, to a whole new way of seeing the world as ordered by God. This sacred practice challenges all of us to live experimental lives in a world we see through the eyes of possibility.

Ethics and the politics that follow from it are dangerous business. They are particularly dangerous when blended with religion and even more so when this blending leads us to start speaking of reform and new order. As one of the fathers of modern political philosophy, Niccolò Machiavelli, pointed out, "[T]here is nothing more difficult to carry out, nor more doubtful of success, nor more dangerous to handle, than to initiate a new order of things. For the reformer has enemies in all those who profit by the old order, and only lukewarm defenders in all those who would profit by the new order."[13] Baptism is and continues to be a practice that makes a strong political and ethical statement, because it declares the advent of a new order.

Seeing the world as a new creation releases us to read the text with a freedom we cannot have when we are bound by our desire for absolutes. When we have been trained to see the world anew by practicing baptism, we can actually believe it's possible to turn the other cheek, to give to those who ask, to love one another, and to share our stuff in a world of scarcity. Furthermore, we recognize that practicing new-creation living allows us to read the challenges to experimental living in the text without quickly arguing them away or brushing them aside as idealistic nonsense. We learn to read the text as the Word of God that challenges the status quo, the kingdom of the world, with a new order and logic. And in doing so, we can take seriously its call to join in this new order.

→ 11

Hospitality
Setting a Subversive Table

Dan and I had remarkably similar childhoods. We were both members of rural Baptist churches (mine was Southern Baptist and Dan's was Independent Baptist) with parents who were highly engaged in leadership. We experienced some of the greatest possibilities of faith and disappointment in these similar settings. Unfortunately, both of us were deeply impacted by very negative experiences of hospitality by those who knew better.

For me, many of the visible failures of hospitality were oriented around racism and fear. Our church was deeply fearful. We were afraid of anything that might threaten our comfortable, rural isolation and entrenched way of life. The conflicted nature of hospitality in our community would look a little like a Heisman Trophy, with friends and extended families standing with one hand held close, beckoning observers to "come to Jesus," while the other hand pushes back, cautioning outsiders to stay away.

The breaches of hospitality in Dan's childhood involved theological fears. Dan's father took the crazy—but faithful—leap from a secure college professor's post teaching health and physical education at a fundamentalist university to follow a call into pastoral ministry in Florida. The task was hard, but after five years his fledgling congregation had grown from thirty to two hundred members. At that point, he received an ominous letter from his former employer. The letter, written to check up on rumors that had reached them, demanded a response to several questions. It read: "Please send a letter answering the following questions: (1) Do you consider yourself an Evangelical or New Evangelical, or sympathetic to the Evangelical movement? (2) Have you publicly preached or taught that you have no problem with people speaking in tongues? (3) Has [sic] your music and standards moved significantly in a more contemporary and leftward direction?"

In five years of pastoral ministry, Dan's father had faced many critiques, but the suggestion of being a left-leaning liberal in this letter was a new one to him. A notorious rule follower and instinctual conservative, he still doesn't know, even eighteen years later, how this school had discovered his "fall into evangelical debauchery" from five hundred miles away. But he does understand all too clearly the fear that motivated this type of institution to check up on former employees and church leaders. It was the same fear that was constantly directed toward new thoughts, ideas, expressions, and any other siren whose pleasant song might draw one further down these "slippery slopes." So great was this fear that his former employer, rather than warmly receiving the successes of one of its former leaders, threatened excommunication and retribution to those who pursued new paths.

Failed hospitality in the Christian community is all too common. To some degree, exclusions and insults based on appearance, socioeconomics, politics, theologies, race, or language can be found overtly and covertly in every church. We have worked and worshiped in churches where divorced people felt as though they needed to apologize—as if they were the only examples of moral failures. A new attendee at our pub group felt she needed to come out as a lesbian to us in the first thirty minutes of our conversation because she had been shunned so often before. She didn't want to embark on risking any friendships with those who had greeted her warmly only to see those people reject her once they knew her sexual orientation. We both have family members who won't attend church because they don't have the right clothes for their affluent local churches.

Most Christians can think of similar examples. But sadly, we continue to be insensitive to the existence of failed hospitality in the Christian community because we accept it as inevitable. So we feign ignorance about the consequences of this breach of hospitality. Yet it's impossible to overestimate the magnitude of this failure. This corporate sin obscures our understanding of the good news of Jesus Christ, mortally damages our telling of this great story, and perverts our experience of God's presence in our life and world.

The Common and the Sacred

Hospitality is the pulse of the biblical story. God's covenant with Abraham is boldly reaffirmed as a result of Abraham's offer of hospitality to three divine visitors (Genesis 18). In contrast, the gravity of the sin of Sodom and Gomorrah is epitomized by an unthinkable breach of custom as citizens from these infamous cities demand that these divine visitors be offered up for their sexual gratification after they entered the home of Abraham's nephew, Lot (Genesis 19).[1]

The Egyptians—particularly their rulers—failed in hospitality on a grand and epic scale. After having given sanctuary to the Israelites, who languished in starvation and drought, they abused and bound this whole people in the dehumanizing state of slavery. The exodus, God's intervention on behalf of his chosen people to bring them up out of slavery, stands as both the fulcrum of the Old Testament narrative and as an unprecedented act of liberation from human inhospitality.

The New Testament presents the incarnation of Jesus as the ultimate and universal exodus that restores humanity to the safe embrace of God. We are not reconciled in the abstract. We are literally united, by virtue of our unity with Christ, into God's life. There is little wonder, then, when you examine the story of Jesus' life and ministry, it is dominated by remarkable episodes of hospitality extended and hospitality received. He engages the marginalized and morally damaged such as the woman at the well (John 4:4–26); receives the wounded, sick, and lame (Mark 2:1–12); affirms the alien in word and deed (Mark 7:24–30, the Syrophoenician woman); tells parables and stories that assume and affirm hospitality (see the remarkable stories of Luke 14); receives all who come to him; and even feeds multitudes with meager resources (Mark 6:30–34 and Mark 8:1–13). Jesus exemplifies neighborly hospitality by coming to the aid of a beleaguered wedding host by turning water into wine (John 2:1–11) and demands the hospitality even of strangers, such as telling the tax collector Zacchaeus that he would dine at Zacchaeus's house (Luke 19:5). But perhaps his greatest lesson of hospitality is his reception of and unity with his Father's will (John 10:15).

The common and open table is one of most clear representations of Jesus' ministry. Many of his greatest and most shocking moments came at mealtimes (for example, his being anointed by a "sinful" woman at the table of his self-righteous enemies, Luke 7:36–50), and the Gospels record that many of his great teachings were associated with feasts and common meals. The early church was begun by women and men who had dined daily with Jesus, heard repeatedly his teachings on the subject, observed his dramatic "hospitality miracles," and followed as he extended grace across every social and moral boundary. Naturally, the infant church embraced this same tradition and elevated hospitality to a sacred expectation. Consider that of all the things Jesus could have left for his followers and disciples to do after he had gone, he chose to leave them with the practice of a communal meal. That doesn't seem like a whim to us.

As the early church met in small gatherings in homes, the table was central to their experience. One cannot understand the struggles and evolution of the first-century church or the narrative of Acts without this point of orientation. In Acts 2, the first Christians bind together their lives—many selling their possessions—and form the practice of a common daily meal. Acts 2:42 reports, "They devoted themselves to the apostles' teaching and to the fellowship, to the breaking of bread and to prayer."

The table is central to worship and the experience of the gospel. In this created space, the most mundane and common elements of the human experience become sacred. When Jesus blessed bread and wine, he took the incarnation to a profound level. God is with us, Emmanuel, in the most normal and essential of our tasks and experience—eating and drinking. Not only are these the acts that sustain our life, but they also sustain our worship by reminding us that we are limited, dependent, mortal, and created. In table worship, we align ourselves with an infinite Creator God and must align ourselves with each other.

The table in the first church did not function like pizza and Coke at a youth ministry event, something to get the kids into the building to hear the gospel, or a convenient transition between events on a program. Instead, to the gathered community of Jesus' followers in Jerusalem, it *was* the gospel. The meal represented the whole of their lives, aligned with the gospel. This theological worship reality is more easily recognized in cultures where meal preparations and consumption organize the bulk of the day. In a trip to rural Zambia a year ago—my (Tim's) first trip in a while outside our culture of convenience and abundance—I watched the women in our host village with awe and respect as they pounded grain for hours with huge pestles. Many would breastfeed their children while continuing this arduous task. The huge demands of preparing the evening meal required literally the entire day's work with no time for interruption.

The significance of the gathered meal and the essential social ethic of hospitality in Jesus' time and geographical context is profound. It makes greater sense when one considers that the denial of food or hospitality in nomadic cultures with harsh climates is paramount to passive murder. In Arabic the root words for *bread* and *life* are the same (*esh*). Civilization as we know it depends on the ability to store grain and bake bread. With the ability to bake and store wheat and other grains, human energy can be diverted to society building. But the roots of significance go deeper than this reality of survival.

In the days of the early church, the Greco-Roman meal occurred in three distinct social arenas: within the extended family (the *paterfamilias* system), in *collegium* (one's own social class), and in state-sanctioned feasts. The meals themselves, especially at the upper end of the social spectrum, could be quite elaborate with two distinct settings. The first setting—the meal proper—was the *deipnon* or *cena* (it also had multiple courses). A second setting, known as the *symposion* or *convivium,* functioned as a post-meal drinking party. Though this second phase could occasionally be sexually explicit or orgiastic, it would be best to envision it as the equivalent of men or women in recent centuries retiring for conversation with brandy or wine and cigars. In Greco-Roman culture, children were often included and the whole group engaged in philosophical speculation, dramatic recitations, games, and essential cultural education.[2]

Despite the strict dietary regulations that might cause one to assume Jewish meals deviated radically from these contemporary cultural forms, many scholars now assert that Jewish dining was greatly influenced by the Greco-Roman culture. They embraced the social rules of dining within class and family (hence, all the trouble that Jesus found and caused when it came to meals). They also maintained the two-segment dining custom. But the Jewish custom was to replace the content of the *symposion/convivium* with prayers of thanks for their food (*birkat ha-motzi*) and a series of prayerful benedictions for God's provision of food, their land, and the hope for the rebuilding of Jerusalem (*birkat ha-mazon*). They told their story and proclaimed their hopes at these meals. As Jan Michael Joncas summarizes, "Every meal would yoke the present, the past, and the future in the ongoing story of their relationship with Yahweh."[3]

The general cultural necessity of hospitality and the specific Greco-Roman and Jewish traditions offer a decisive backdrop to the practices of the early church. The Christ followers in Acts 2 were obedient to the social necessities of hospitality, continuing Jesus' norm of the common meal as the centerpiece of the redemptive story. They embraced Jesus' radical adaptations of an open social constituency at their worship meal and his blessing of the common meal elements as daily—and since meal preparation took so long, perpetual—reminders to live worshipfully in God's presence.

As the story progresses in Acts, we see the significance of hospitality as expressed in the worship meal extrapolated even further. Acts 5 brings a horrific story where a husband and wife, Ananias and Sapphira, "cheat the table," so to speak. They sell some land but they dishonestly hold back some of the profits from the fellowship. In dramatic fashion, they are both struck down dead. Besides offering the most frightening fodder imaginable for a ruthless tithing sermon, this story illustrates that the community and divine ties formed by the table were a life-or-death matter for the early church. God seemed to treat this failure as the worst form of blasphemy.

The growing church also faced its first great crisis at the table. Worshiping together around this common meal pushed the requirements of hospitality up a lofty organizational notch as the Christians shared their food and produce throughout the city of Jerusalem. It was essential to the social ethic of the Jews and obviously part of Jesus' gospel to provide materially for the economically disadvantaged. In the sharing of their provisions, apparently widows of Greek ethnicity were being underserved as compared to Jewish widows (Acts 6:1). The natural results of this issue would be suspicion, anger, and eventual division. The gospel that Paul adamantly described as salvation "first for the Jew, then for the Gentile" (Rom. 1:16) was metaphorically, materially, and socially at risk. The response was remarkable and visionary. The early church leaders appointed deacons, all assumed to be of Greek descent based on their recorded names, to supervise the distribution of food.

The table was significant enough to provoke one of the first layers of organization for the neophyte church. Perhaps giving us some insight into the seemingly harsh fates of Ananias and Sapphira, the table is the essential social program of the church. Luke, the author of Acts, makes it clear that when the hospitality of the table was properly administered, there should be no one within the community of faith left hungry.

A second great crisis in the life of the early church was also a table crisis. As the community expanded outside of Jerusalem, ethnic table practices began to clash in dramatic fashion. Strict Jewish dietary regulations collided squarely with the less prohibitive palates—particularly in regard to meat—of the Greeks. The market norms of the culture where meat sold in the markets had first been sacrificed in the local temples created problems for neophyte converts to Christianity. Jewish converts had long been instructed about the perils of association with idolatry and the ritual impurity that comes from improper eating (which surely in their minds would have included meat offered first in idolatry). The theological and social implications of this cultural crossroads were immense. Would Greek converts be required to convert to Judaism, or at least accept its dietary restrictions? The common table (modeled incessantly by Jesus) and the reality represented by the table (a church universal of Jews and Greeks) hung in the balance of this crisis. The real possibility of an ethnically divided table and hence an ethnically divided church loomed on the horizon.

This was far more than an inconvenience and an obstacle to evangelism. The good news of the gospel taught, and continues to teach, that there would be no ethnic division. In Christ, God's historic mercy to the Jews was being offered to all of humanity. Without the common table, the gospel was threatened in its very essence in both symbol and reality.

The early church recognized the gravity of the burgeoning division and moved quickly to counter it by calling its first major council. In the Council of Jerusalem (Acts 15), courageous steps were taken to repair a fragmenting table. The council decided that the dietary restrictions of the Jews would not be required for Greek converts to Christianity. In addition, the council made clear that although idolatry was strictly forbidden, the Jewish dietary requirements for ritual purity were no longer operative. The common worship table was protected, sustained, and required for all Christians in worship. In 1 Corinthians 8:1–11:1 one sees further development of this prescription applied to the issues of a local church. With these bold measures, the church clarified its identity as a community of people from all origins and ethnicities who were invited into the story of Israel and the life of God.

Jesus' table and the table practice of his followers were subversive to the core. They confronted the conflict at the heart of all of the damage sin has done in humanity. By teaching us that we are dependent on God's blessing and on community to survive, they confront our impulses of self-reliance and independence, which are the root of all idolatry. By bringing us into proximity with those who lack the essentials of life and demanding that we share from our abundance, they confront our greed. By requiring that human divisions cease at the table, they confront our racism and classism. This table practice is the platform of the gospel's social, economic, and ethnic revolution, a clear instance of the new creation we spoke of in the previous chapter.

Our examination of the table places hospitality at the very center of the gospel and offers a stark, even frightening, declaration of the gravity of failed hospitality in the church. Henri Nouwen uses the description "from hostility to hospitality" to describe what he calls one of the essential movements of spiritual formation.[4] His choice of words reveals a series of strong theological assertions. First, that damaged humanity rests in a state of hostility with itself and the rest of creation. Nouwen's second implication declares hospitality as a rejection of our hostility, a state that is reached only by the intervention of God and our practice of the gospel. Our examination of the place of the table in the gospel echoes Nouwen's point. The journey toward hospitality is a journey toward Christ.

Letting "Things" Get Out of Hand

Staff meetings at Emmaus Way usually fall apart—fast. Three of us are quick-witted iconoclasts who feed off each other, yielding quick verbal forays into what some (okay, most) might consider sacred territory. This is fun and somehow spiritually life giving for us, but less so for Jenny, our community lay leader. Raised in a family of sisters, Jenny is regularly tormented by her three self-appointed brothers (Dan, Wade, and me). Jenny often tells us she'll be late for meetings so we can get all of our sarcasm and "inappropriate" humor out of the way before she arrives. It never works. There is something about getting the three of us together in the presence of Jenny that sets our humor off. A good psychologist might recognize that all three of us grew up in male-dominated families—only one of us has a biological sister—allowing Jenny to fill that role of the sister we all love and respect but also feel biologically compelled to tease just a little. Whatever it is, there is some unique chemistry in this team of truly good friends.

When text and hospitality come together, things also get out of hand—in the best of ways. As we've written throughout this book, the term *text* means more than just the revealed, abstract, or disembodied Word of God. Inherent in *text* is a relationship of specific communities, their perspectives, history, gifts, and needs with the Word of

God. Hospitality is a discipline that allows the Bible to function as the Word of God, igniting this wonderfully out-of-hand relationship of community with the text.

As we move forward, we want to further illustrate how community practices with the Scriptures inspire and even necessitate the great spiritual movement that Nouwen so aptly described, the movement from hostility to hospitality. We can't stress the possibility of this point enough. A well-conceived and Spirit-guided community hermeneutic can drive us to the very heart of the good news that Jesus brings.

As we look for the formation of hospitality in a community and its individuals, it's good to remember the nature of hospitality. In chapter 3, using the same text from Henri Nouwen, we described hospitality as having two critical pillars: receptivity and honesty. Receptivity is the incessant willingness to receive the presence of others without demanding that they conform to your wishes, will, or standards. Nouwen reminds us that much of what we call hospitality is nothing of the sort.

In seminary, Mimi and I (Tim) were invited to meet a couple who were well known for their somewhat uncomfortable dinner parties. By report and experience, these dinners generally reflected two recurrent templates. One template was, "Let us show what we've got that you don't have yet and perhaps never will." These meals involved the hosts basking in the glow of marriage in front of their single guests, or showing off their expensive antiques, fine china, and other elaborate possessions as primers on style and taste to groups of significantly less-wealthy friends.

When the word got out on these celebrations of possessions and lifestyle, the guest list seemed to change from have-nots to the equally pretentious. With that change came template number two in which the dinners were polite competitions based on what one knew or had read or the quality of one's artistic taste. In this form, guests would bring favorite readings, samples of art they owned, or music they enjoyed. The subtext to this subtle competition appeared to be to affirm one's personal depth by conversation pieces that were ridiculously obscure and nearly incomprehensible in meaning.

Nouwen quips that bringing persons into elaborate homes, cleaned and decorated with the false pretense that no human actually lives in the space, and then intimidating or subjugating our guests with our beautiful possessions, good wine, unyielding opinions, and a seemingly infinite reading list is *not* a practice of hospitality. Instead, it is the construction of hierarchy and the subtle exercise of power—an attempt to get the upper hand.

Speaking of honesty, Nouwen affirms a practice of being truly present when we receive others. Kindness requires that we do not isolate guests in our homes or communities. We engage them and the gifts they bring (their lives, their stories, their needs). Honesty requires that we also vulnerably share our lives, our passions and our thoughts, with our guests. In contrast with the wealthy couple mentioned above, our friends Daniel and Lara Chase constantly demonstrate honesty for our whole community.

Dinner parties at the Chase household are loved by all of Emmaus Way. Daniel and Lara have lived in a co-housing arrangement for many years, so their home is already marked by diversity and generosity. Lara is an amazing cook, artistically gifted, and a remarkable organizer. Daniel has a sneaky sense of humor and is a tremendously loyal friend with a keen intellect. Despite the couple's many gifts, people are drawn to Daniel and Lara because of their honesty. Utterly unpretentious, they engage friends and guests with honest words about their joys and struggles. Their living room and dinner table are a haven for the weary and a redemptive space where guests are encouraged with truthfulness and vulnerability.

The discipline of hospitality is exercised when honesty and receptivity remain in tension by both being fully present, for true receptivity must be bathed in honesty. Hospitality in its purest form is making room for the other without eliminating the self.[5] When we survey the ecclesial landscape, we so often see Christian communities that stake their identities on one rather than both sides of this tension. Churches that practice honesty without receptivity are marked by a tone of judgment. Those who are highly receptive but avoid honest words of challenge sacrifice their prophetic voice on an altar of tolerance.

Like the other transformations and practices we advocate, the practice of gathering at the table to break bread teaches us the discipline of hospitality—an essential habit and virtue we need to read the Scriptures and to hear the Word of God. In turn, our hospitality fuels our interaction with the text. When a community reads and interprets, it must embrace hospitality. The biblical texts are provocative, personal, invitational, revolutionary, and sometimes frighteningly obscure. Every text, regardless of genre, be it a Gospel parable or an Old Testament narrative, requires a posture of receptivity to the divine as the readers fashion an openness and vulnerability to the voice and presence of God's Spirit. The previous rules of hospitality certainly operate here. We need to not only be open to receiving God's voice but also meet that voice with honesty—often a raw, untethered, visceral honesty. The Psalms stand as obvious examples and products of this form of hospitality, as we saw earlier. The divine hospitality required to read the texts about God's character and purposes gives birth to greater hospitality in our lives. Opening ourselves up honestly to the presence of God fosters receptivity to the voice of the other, the community in our lives. It is little wonder that the love of God and the love of neighbor are inexorably linked in the Scriptures.

The provocations and invitations of the Bible also collide with the different experiences and stories represented in a community and create infinite vectors of meaning and worship. As diverse people with contrasting stories, we have as many reactions to the reading of God's Word as there are people in the room. As we saw in chapter 5, the two of us will always read the story of the rape of Dinah (Genesis 34) as men. But we realize that the voices of women are essential to fully engage this text. Most importantly, this privilege of reading the Bible in community forces us to truly engage the stories of others. We begin to *need* the perspectives of others. And in this needing and yearning, the scope and passion of the Scriptures expand.

We have shared many examples of this process where hospitality enlarges the voice of the Scriptures in a community that then finds its commitment to the practices of hospitality emboldened. One recent Sunday, we had another of these shaping experiences. We had the opportunity to include Reino Hoy, a new ministry reaching out to the Latino community in our city, in our worship gathering.

This collaboration had its challenges. Our vision was to be bilingual throughout the worship gathering. With translation, all of the spoken elements of the worship would move at a different pace, especially our weekly text dialogue that often depends on quick responses and interplay between those who choose to speak and the dialogue leader. For speakers who depend on quick wit and a measure of responsiveness with an audience, this would certainly be a challenge.

Though some in our community are bilingual, our primary artists and musicians are not. Our guests did not have any artists to bring to this gathering. So Wade, our worship/arts pastor, had to struggle to find translations for some of the music we do and doubled his rehearsal time learning the Spanish lyrics to several songs. Thank goodness for the online availability of translations of the Bible and various liturgies that we draw from—but nonetheless, several folks in our community spent extra time translating English texts.

Our community is made up primarily of younger adults, which means we have only a handful of infants, toddlers, and early elementary–aged children. Reino Hoy has a slightly older congregation and many more families, so on the night of the shared worship gathering, our children's attendance more than doubled. Our workers for the evening were wonderfully flexible, but close to overwhelmed. There was even a request for a last-minute baby dedication from our guests that we struggled to squeeze into an already tight plan. You get the picture (and we're sure you've experienced this countless times): hospitality is always inconvenient at some level and often very challenging.

For our dialogue that evening, we had chosen the text of the parable of the unmerciful servant (Matt. 18:21–35). I (Tim) led the conversation for the evening along with Jean-Luc Charles, the associate pastor of a prominent African American church who has supported Reino Hoy. We shared several interpretative observations about this confrontational story of a man who had been forgiven of a vast debt by his master only to be unwilling to forgive a small debt owed to him by a peer. Despite having received great mercy from his lord, he has his own debtor thrown into prison.

One interesting observation concerned the role of the extended community of the lord's servants—who presumably work with both the man thrown in prison and the man who was unmerciful—in securing justice for the debtor thrown in prison. It is these other servants, and not the imprisoned man and his family who call out to the lord, demanding justice. This perspective led to a vigorous dialogue. We asked this very diverse community to describe injustices and wrongs that they found hard to forgive. Each community—Reino Hoy and Emmaus Way—heard stories that were outside their usual sets of experiences. Emmaus Way is predominantly white, and though certainly not blessed with lots of financial wealth at this point in our lives, we do enjoy the power and expectations of justice that come with education and being part of the majority culture. Though Reino Hoy is primarily working and middle class, they had many stories of fear of authorities and minimal expectations of justice from the powers-that-be. Questions about the role of the Christian community in the act of forgiveness and questions concerning our willingness to take risks to secure justice yielded rich and accountable responses in this ethnically diverse gathering. The text was enlarged and its voice became even more prophetic in this time of shared hospitality.

Our Practice: Introducing Text to Table

One of the beautiful paths that accelerate the synergy between text and hospitality occurs weekly for us at the table. Jesus' revolutionary practice of table hospitality and the early church's adoption of this countercultural norm was the ultimate archetype for the hospitality at the root of the church's Eucharistic meal. For us, the challenge of the table is not just a metaphor for a posture of hospitality or the motivation for many other demonstrations of hospitality. It is also central to our worship and our weekly encounters with the Scriptures. When we gather, we do not just gather to hear someone talk about the text, but we gather together to read and study as well as to celebrate the communal meal of our Lord. As a result, our textual dialogues are always aimed, shaped, and informed by the table, a table where we never really get to choose who shows up.

At times when we begin our gathered worship, we use our adaptation of the Jewish meal blessings we mentioned earlier (the *birkat ha-motzi* and the *birkat ha-mazon*; the pre-meal thanks for the provision of food and post-meal benedictions for God as Creator and provider, the provision of land, and the hope of the rebuilding of Israel). For us, these benedictions take the similar but contextualized forms of thanks for God's simple provisions, the affirmation of

God as Creator of all, a remembrance of God's redemptive covenant throughout history through the present to restore broken creation, and our yearning hope for the future completion of this restoration by resurrection and re-creation. The following is a succinct liturgy that we have used:

ONE
> *Barukh atah Adonai Elohenu melek ha-olam.*

ALL
> Blessed are you, Lord our God, Sovereign of the universe.
> *Barukh atah Adonai Elohenu* (Blessed are you, Lord our God), King of the universe, who brings forth bread from the earth.
> *Barukh atah Adonai Elohenu* (Blessed are you, Lord our God), who nourishes not only us, but all of your creation.
> *Barukh atah Adonai Elohenu* (Blessed are you, Lord our God), who is faithful in promise and gracious action to your people and creation throughout all of history.
> *Barukh atah Adonai Elohenu* (Blessed are you, Lord our God), for your mercy and redemption from now until the time when you complete your plan of restoration in re-creation and resurrection.

This liturgical call to worship explicitly describes how the expectations of the table and its implied radical declaration of hospitality frame our gathered worship as a table gathering. We strive each week to develop an intimate connection between the actual table and our text dialogue.

As we described earlier, our exploration of the biblical text takes the form of a community dialogue that we hope is marked by a number of hospitalities—hospitality to the thoughts and interpretations of our community and certainly hospitality to the voice of God spoken through preacher and community. In our typical worship template, this dialogue moves to liturgies of confession and absolution—sometimes music, sometimes the words of the historical church—and then the gathering at the table. Although this time can be solemn, silent, and formally served, our usual table practice resembles a family feast that draws upon our imagination of Jesus' and the early church's table gatherings.

The relief of absolution quickly bleeds into a rising crescendo of conversation, laughter, occasionally tears, and intimate moments of prayer in the corners of the small room while the community serves each other generous portions of bread, juice, and wine. We believe that the gathering of persons at the table is as sacramental as the food being eaten. Each week, we remind our community that our acts of serving each other the bread and wine and our conversations with each other are intentional acts of hospitality that bind us together as a community seeking to hear God's voice and follow God's redemptive path.

These hospitalities at the table flow naturally from the hospitalities of the dialogue. They feed each other. They teach us each week that we depend on each other to understand the text, to be empowered by the text, to embody the text, to worship God as Creator, and to have hope in God's mercy. Conversation becomes a sacred link between our community reading and interpreting the text and eating at the table.

When we first began to imagine what Emmaus Way might look like, we turned to the text in Luke 24 from which we derive our name. In this haunting Easter text, the risen Jesus joins two of his followers on the road to Emmaus. Their conversation turns to the great events of the weekend, the horrible execution of Jesus at the hands of his people and the state, as well as the strange, astounding reports of his resurrection. Jesus attempts to offer solace and hope through a grand explanation of the Scriptures.

Despite the truthfulness and power of his teaching, they still do not recognize him. But as they come to the end of their road, they offer a simple hospitality to the knowledgeable stranger, asking him to join them at their home for an evening meal. In the warm glow of their table, Jesus breaks and blesses the bread as he had done constantly with them in the common table practice of his ministry. Then and only then, after their extended hospitality, do they know him as the risen Messiah. In this story, text, hospitality, and table merge into a beautiful portrait and prophetic challenge to us. Our practices of hospitality liberate the text to the status of God's revelation, and it in turn forms us into a hospitable people.

→ 12

Mission

From Defense to Offense

Christianity is offensive—in both senses of the word. To be a Christian is to claim to bear good news for a world of people—Christians included!—in need. Christians have a mission—to go on the offensive as an aggressive attacking strategy, taking the message of the gospel into the world. Because of this missional offensive we step on some toes from time to time, becoming the other kind of offensive as a result. The aggressive evangelical proclamation of the gospel in our day and age has been looked on by some as undesirable, repugnant, and uncouth.

Yet we don't believe much of the time it is the gospel that garners this unfavorable response. We haven't found it to be the case that people are opposed to God or esteem themselves as too intellectual to believe in Jesus. From working in ministry for a collective thirty-five years, we have come to see that much of the repulsion to Christianity has more to do with the type of offense run by those who think it is their job to protect and interpret the text for everyone else. While we can be sure that there will always be those who will refuse to hear the good news of Jesus, just as they did during Christ's day, this doesn't mean we ought to go out of our way to sour the good news with the way we proclaim it.

No one more precisely pointed to the problematic posture of those bringing the Christian message over the past four centuries than the nineteenth-century philosopher and atheist Friedrich Nietzsche. Frustrated by what he deemed to be a "slave religion" because of its infatuation with other-worldly life rather than present realities, his all-out assault charged Christianity with, of all things, being simply too ugly. As Charles Marsh has so astutely pointed out, Nietzsche's calumny begins by pronouncing, "They must sing more beautiful songs for me to believe in their redeemer."[1] It is a telling commentary, even if it has been proffered by the person many theologians think to be a preeminent opponent of the faith. The failure of Christian mission, in our view, has been to some extent a failure to understand the offense of Christianity correctly. Like the protective hermeneutic, it is a failure tied deeply to a fear of engagement with others, a failure based on a bad understanding of hermeneutics, and finally a failure to understand the power of the good news of the gospel.

What we will assert in this chapter is that learning to read Scripture with a community hermeneutic can assuage our past failures and lead us into a new era of Christian mission. And yet, this mission continues to form us as readers of the Bible. It is our belief that by doing this we may learn to cease singing the songs of fear and defense and begin to play gospel tunes that will attract us all with their beauty.

Offense as Defense: Mission as Preemptive Strike

The best defense is a good offense. In the years following the attacks upon the World Trade Center and the Pentagon, our country decided this was the only way to react. It is a strategy we have been attempting to use in the war against terror with controversial success. While we had always known that the United States had many enemies around the world, we never thought they had the capability to attack us. But after the events of September 11, 2001, we had to rethink everything we thought we knew about the world we live in and the way we approached dealing with these opponents. We were awakened to the fact that not only were our enemies real, they were an imminent threat to our national security and could attack at any moment. We were awakened from our naive slumber to find ourselves in a dangerous world, vulnerable in ways we had never before considered possible. With the threat of another attack bearing down upon our nation, our administration decided that the best way to insure that we would not be hit again was to go on the offensive. Facing an unconventional enemy, we had to hit the threat before that threat hit us. In this age of terror, the only plausible defense is surely a good offense.

During the past five years we have seen the various effects this type of foreign policy has had on our world and our place in it. Americans have enjoyed a renewed sense of safety, though the constant presence of the Terror Alert (ever-hovering between the colors orange and red—who knows what that means?) from the Department of Homeland Security keeps us on edge just enough to maintain a healthy suspicion while traveling in the airport. Yet, the quest for safety has also motivated military interventions in Iraq and Afghanistan, and is currently threatening to lead us into Iran and maybe even Pakistan. Meanwhile, perception of the United States abroad has plummeted to new lows, encouraging new radicals to take up arms against our interests and multiplying the political states upon which we must keep a watchful eye. The philosophy of preemptive strike clearly has its advantages, but we are increasingly coming to see that it has many terrible disadvantages as well.

One comment we can make confidently about this tactic, prolifically noted by cultural critics of varying perspectives, is that it has succeeded in creating a culture of fear.[2] The very idea that we are now immersed in a war on terror communicates that we are in a battle with fear, even if we can never really put a face on it. Though as a nation we continually slip into short-lived states of amnesia, forgetful of the threat out there as we watch the BCS football championship or *Saturday Night Live*, we are reminded and awakened once again by the evening news, which is always quick to alert us to security breaches and the possibility of terrorist attacks. Fear dominates our culture even as we continue to devote billions of dollars to conquer it.

Our point is not so much to criticize the tactics of our country's administration (and yes, both parties are responsible for these tactics) in the years since 9/11, but simply to point out a certain type of offensive strategy: the preemptive strike and offense as defense. We bring this up because using the offensive as a form of defense also seems to have been the dominant missional strategy for evangelical Christians over the past several decades. It is a posture we have embraced with the same mixed success. While the Conservative Right has managed to garner an unparalleled level of power and influence, ushering evangelical Christians into a new day in the sun, more and more people are vocalizing their distaste for this type of good news. Though some will laud the increasing public presence of evangelicalism, what troubles us is not that evangelicals are boldly proclaiming our faith but that this proclamation, this mission, seems to be dominated by a defensive posture. In short, we seem to have embraced an "us" versus "them" mentality, in which we are convinced that we are good and as such are justified in condemning, eradicating, and attacking the evil people outside our group.

This defensive posture to "the world" is nothing new. In fact, it has been prevalent since the birth of American evangelicalism in the Great Awakenings of the eighteenth and nineteenth centuries as the church began to respond to the new ideas emerging in the Enlightenment. But what we are coming to see very vividly is that evangelical Christianity also developed in certain unhelpful ways in response to this threat. One of the main factors contributing to the "offense as defense" type of engagement with the world we find so ubiquitous in evangelical culture is the fact that we have accepted the lie of "subtraction theories" of modernity. These subtraction theories perceive the emergence of secular, modern, and enlightened (and these are, for the most part, synonyms) society to be an attempt to rid the world of Christianity, that one cannot exist in the presence of the other. However, we are coming to see that these types of narratives are far too simplistic in their understanding of the Enlightenment and the birth of the modern world. Charles Taylor has convincingly argued against these "stories of modernity in general, and secularity in particular, which explain them by human beings having lost, or sloughed off, or liberated themselves from certain earlier, confining horizons, or illusions, or limitations of knowledge."[3]

The lie of modern liberalism that many Christians have accepted as true is that the modern secular world emerged sometime between the mid-sixteenth to nineteenth centuries, when a few brave intellectuals and scientists got sick of the church wielding what they saw as its dark power over them, gathered their sense of themselves as individuals, and threw off the burden of God and the oppressive and unprogressive doctrines of Christianity in order to bring us into a new world of human flourishing and freedom. Following this line of thinking, the only alternative for Christians was to hunker down, circle the wagons, and secure the women and children against the impending outside threat of atheism seeking to raze faith wherever it may be found. To be Christian in the modern world, then, means to take up a defensive posture because your faith is under constant threat of attack by those seeking to liberate the world of any trace of religious expression, especially Christianity.

The repercussions of this story and the Christian defensive response can be clearly illustrated in the false narrative of American history in which the United States falls from its origin as a Christian nation. The heritage of this narrative is most evident today in the battle over prayer in schools or the inclusion of "under God" in the saying of the Pledge of Allegiance. The fact that our nation is more Christian than ever, as well as the real history of prayer in schools and the Pledge, seems to evade many evangelicals.

American evangelicals, while in one sense deeply historical in our attachment to the church of the first century, are notorious for our short and sentimental memories. We wonder how many of those fighting the "under God" battle remember that the words were not penned by the founding fathers of our country in their devotion to the God of Jesus, but were added to the Pledge in 1954 in order to foster religious patriotism as a valued resource against the pressures of rising Communist (and atheist) power in the dawn of the Cold War. "Under God" was never meant to be a proclamation of the good news of God's gift in Christ to redeem a lost world; it was a tool of political power to fan the flames of opposition to the second-largest power in our world at the time.

The evangelical energy directed to reestablish the saying of the Pledge in our schools seems to be paying off here in North Carolina.

Recently our public schools have reinstituted the saying of the Pledge every morning, a fact that was brought to our attention because a student we know ran into trouble when he refused to say the Pledge in class. A smart young man, he objected to this practice not because he hates America or wanted to be rebellious, but because he believed that the "god" of the Pledge was not the God he heard preached on Sunday, or spoken of in the Bible and revealed in Christ. This "god" was a god revived within a War on Terror to serve the purposes of a nation immersed in a battle with Muslim fundamentalists and who was being hauled out to fuel the flames of religious patriotism and jingoism.

Convinced that the world is a threat to our lives and existence, Christians have become overwhelmed by our own culture of fear. Who could forget the tragic events that took place at New Life Church in Colorado Springs on December 9, 2007, when a young gunman opened fire on church members after Sunday morning worship? We both remember watching the news coverage after the event and feeling compassion for the families that lost loved ones as well as the traumatized church community. It was a truly terrifying and horrible event.

But what also struck us as odd and problematic was the tremendous amount of praise showered upon the security officer who supposedly fired upon and killed the young gunman. (It was later discovered that this young man had actually killed himself, a possibility not even mentioned in the fanfare.) We must admit that it left us with a bitterly confused taste in our mouths, wondering what message it sent for Christians to employ security guards at our churches and for us to so publicly laud the killing of a threat to our people. We were left wondering whether we have not let an infatuation with security take control of us, having turned us into a people of fear. Protect our schools, protect our families, protect our churches, protect our investments, and our national interests. But in this search for security where has our mission gone? With all this emphasis on protection, what exactly are we giving? Is it any wonder that the world finds our message to be so selfish, so hateful, so ugly?

As a faith more recently defined by its fears, whether they be aimed at terrorists, scientists, evolutionary theory, pro-choice legislation, or gay rights, this brand of Christianity has embraced the tactic of preemptive strike. We have taken up the offensive in order to defend our American way of life, and we have come to find that this form of mission has in fact been very offensive to those we encounter—for all the wrong reasons. Because we have chosen to engage our culture and our world with an overwhelming sense of fear and judgment, we have succeeded in creating a Christianity of fear, a form of Christianity that has turned the beautiful good news into something repugnant.

What makes this form of Christianity ugly is its posture of suspicion toward the world and its sectarian stance. Put simply, it turns us into a church that has forgotten its mission to enter into the world to make disciples and to live new life together as witnesses to the good news. Engaging in a hermeneutic of suspicion saturated with fear produces a protective style of reading the text by constantly trying to remove anyone from the circle who will not come to the exact same conclusions as us. It is a form of reading that misunderstands the fragility of our existence. It trades the beauty of being creatures and followers of Christ dependent on God's sustaining Spirit for the repugnance of depending on our own inquisitions for establishing "the" faithful reading of the text. And it holds the Bible hostage as we work out its meaning among coteries of people who look, think, speak, and live on the same street as us. The result is an ugly, intense, and inwardly focused form of protectionism that aims at security, eyeing those on the outside with suspicion while engaged in a constant battle to maintain clear and strict borders. It is not beautiful because in the end it's foreign policy as usual: secure and protect the borders at all costs.

Offense as Defense Again: The War to End All Wars

The tactic of offense as defense has not been solely the missional strategy of conservatives and sectarians circling the wagons against the threat of a world bent on going to hell as quickly as possible. While the conservative strategy has somewhat succeeded in gaining them a place at the table of power, the last century was truly dominated by Protestant liberals. Yet these liberals, despite all of their promises, have not succeeded in painting a more beautiful picture for the future of humanity, as their missional exploits have only succeeded in making the twentieth century the bloodiest century in the history of the world. At the end of the day, it appears that one of the most violent and troublesome and truly revolting missions has been the liberal mission of the war to end all wars.

The hope of liberalism is also based in a fear, though it is the flipside of the concern for security in fundamentalism. It is a hope set on ridding the world of all violence by ridding the world of all fundamentalisms or anything that does not fit into the project of liberalism. One need only pick up a copy of Hobbes's *Leviathan* to find one of the primary sources of the modern, and often repeated, founding myth of the state of nature as war. Hobbes was convinced that if we were to get down to the bottom of things, we would find that the world is a place of all-out competition for limited resources. "A war of all against all" is the state of nature, a fact of life that without political and social structure would make it a state of "continual fear and danger of violent death; and the life of man, solitary, poor, nasty, brutish, and short."[4] And it was in a response to his fear of this state of nature that Hobbes set out to discover a method that offered protection by limiting violence.

It would become, with the additions of later theorists such as John Locke, a method based on individual rights and the myth of the personal choice of giving up these rights to the Sovereign for the sake of order and protection. Through organization and reason, humans could make things better, they could squelch some of the violence inherent in the state of nature and through cooperation lead us to a brighter future free of violence. And all of this would be possible through the logical application of scientific method to the whole of human existence. Science and technology would save us.

This is a dream liberals have had a hard time giving up. It is a dream that they have been willing to fight for, sacrifice for, and even die for. It is the grounding myth that has given birth to a full-fledged belief in technological advancement and liberal ideals as the salvation of humankind. Here, the method of science and liberal progress become the way of not only stilling violence but also solving every problem humans could encounter. The only stipulation is that you must buy into the program that everyone must be willing to give up his or her rights to the sovereign market in order to provide a future of peace and happiness.

Of course, this view quickly tends to elide the fact that there still have to be winners and losers by assuring us that capitalism will broker the best peace and prosperity for the most people if we just let it do its job. The only threats to peace are fundamentalists and extremists who are set on doing evil to the emerging utopia of technological and economic advancement. Hence, the war to end all wars becomes the "offense as defense" tactic played out in the conflicts of the past century, wars not fought over religion but fought in order to stop the spread of fundamentalist governments and fundamentalist believers (not always one and the same) as a threat to Western economic security. So while liberals quite rightly no longer fight wars of religion, they have become extremely advanced in their modes of fighting wars of liberty as a means of eliminating any and all threats to market stability and modern, Western, economic expansion.

In this way liberals have also failed to live the mission of the church, settling for something less than the beauty of Christ's message. The form of the liberal misunderstanding of mission, however, makes use of its one unique version of the preemptive-strike mentality by attempting to do away with any sect, people, or country standing in the path of its march toward future free-market universalism. Its repugnance springs from its failure to see that Christianity has anything significant to offer to the conversation that cannot be given by human creativity and scientific development.

Whereas the evangelicals feared modernity while co-opting its language of fear, the liberal coalition placed the claims of modernity at the center of its altar. Here the mission of the church, if there is any distinctive mission for the church left, does not take the form of Christ as a beautiful gospel for the world. Instead, it tends to trade this image of Christ for the likeness of Uncle Sam or Bill Gates as the promise of personal rights and economic success to guarantee a future of peace and happiness. Hence, any remainder of religion becomes merely an inward feeling that can help to assuage the daily vicissitudes of market exchange while bolstering the stability of the workforce with a personal piety that aims them toward being more efficient.

The narrative of Protestant liberalism's slide out of a mission and into a new mode of liberal imperialism is vividly apparent in the story of Harvard University. Founded in 1636 by Congregationalists of the newly settled colonies for the training of ministers, it took the early mottos of *"Veritas, Christo et Ecclesiae"* (Truth, for Christ and the Church) and *"In Christi Gloriam"* (For the Glory of Christ). Yet its mission of being an institution set on training clergy for the ministry in New England would eventually take a back seat to its adherence to the idea of a future under the dominance of liberal advancement. As George Marsden points out,

> From a traditionalist point of view what was happening at Harvard looked simply like the secularization of the college. Yet these developments were taking place not in the name of an attack on Christianity but under the banner of the expansion of its influence. At Harvard, in fact, this point was made in advance of other schools. Already in 1866 the Rev. Frederic Henry Hedge of the Harvard Divinity School reassured an alumni group that, even though the college had shifted from its original emphasis on training clergy, "the secularization of the College is no violation of its motto, 'Christo et Ecclesiae.' For, as I interpret those sacred ideas, the cause of Christ and the Church is advanced by whatever liberalizes and enriches and enlarges the mind." In effect, Hedge was declaring that whatever Harvard does simply *is* Christian.[5]

The process of acculturation would eventually culminate in the school dropping the *"Christo et Ecclesiae"* from its motto and settling simply for the word *"Veritas"* under the leadership of Charles Eliot in 1885. A truth no longer for the church and learned in Christ, it shines now as a truth of the expansion of the liberal ideal of market imperialism and elitism under the auspices of a dedication to human rights and knowledge. Set on a mission of liberal dominance, this brand of Christianity too has simply become ugly.

With regard to how it informs our reading of the text, this form of liberalism has led to solidification of the guild of biblical studies—that snobbish form of reading wherein only the Ivy League–educated are properly trained to read the text because they alone have the expertise to read it correctly and within the trajectory of the goals of a liberal future. Here an enlightened liberal—or professional—style of reading becomes the *modus operandi*, and while continually touting its dedication to freedom and the oppressed, serves as a continuation of liberal imperialism. The infatuation with professionalism within liberal hermeneutics fosters an imperialistic reading that feels the need to protect itself against the untrained brutes out there who may read the text without the proper lenses of liberal bias. In the end, we find here a method of reading that is no less repulsive because its mission is no less self-serving. A more aggressive form of offense as defense, liberal elitism uses the text to further its own project and to justify the removal of all "extremists" who might set out to read it against the imperialism of modern Western capitalism.

Mission as Offense

Sports fans will be familiar with the old adage: While offense may attract the crowds and win games, it is defense that wins championships. Yet it is exactly this mentality that has so damaged the mission of the church. We think that going on the offensive is the only way to practice healthy mission. In this way we want to respond directly to Nietzsche's critique of Christianity, by promoting a mission of attack in the form of singing more beautiful songs.

One thing that we believe a community hermeneutic allows us to do is to recovery a proper sense of Christianity on the offensive. While this may not be readily apparent at first, we think that reading the text together as a community can put us back onto the mission of the church. We must acknowledge that a church on the offensive is not a new idea, but it is merely a recovery of the traditional idea of the church militant that is deep-seated within the history of how the church has understood itself. Not to be confused with our modern use of "military," or the church as a martial society, the church militant was the church's way of speaking of its unique position in the present, as that place and time between the already and not yet. A term used to speak of the communion of believers on earth, it implied that the community was engaged in a struggle against sin—sin that we believe more often than not plays out in our desire to control, and for purposes of security prompts us to play God.

As the community of those following Christ on earth, as a people on the move, we find in reading together that our posture toward the world does not have to be one dominated by fear and separation, but can be one of open service by taking the good news to a world in need. In fact, it is this act of service and ministry that sets us apart, not our need to get rid of all extremists or the necessity of protecting the gospel from outside corruption. An important step, then, in learning to read the text together and in recovering our mission is for Christians to begin to give up our infatuation (dare we say idolatry) with security (regardless of whether that security comes from evangelical protectiveness or liberal imperialism). Our mission and our reading of the text are intimately tied to one another because they both require that we leave a defensive posture behind in order to embrace a truly offensive strategy.

In a spirit of transparency, we must admit that this is not a perfect strategy—we almost never get it right. We fail continuously at it, especially when it comes to teaching this posture and mission to our children and loved ones. But it is our aim. We confess that we constantly battle the fear of leaving the text open for the community and leaving our lives open in service to the world. We understand that the implications of this form of reading and this posture of mission require some extremely hard things, not the least of which is relinquishing complete control of our lives, the discussions that occur while interpreting the text, and ultimately, the safety of our children and families. We do not always succeed in this mission, but we think that this posture of openness and outreach, as a positive approach learned from reading in community, leads us to participate in God's work in a way that makes room for the Spirit's voice.

Offense as Offering: Mission as Prayer and Martyrdom

On a winter Mississippi night in 1970, John Perkins, a local civil rights leader, found himself driving to the city of Brandon because some students from a demonstration had been arrested by police on bogus charges. Perkins, who had seen his brother killed by the bullet of a white police officer in 1946, arrived at the courthouse to

the ominous welcome of a highway patrolman. Told by the patrolman to wait for the arrival of the sheriff, Perkins had no idea what
was about to happen to him. A few minutes later ten police officers
emerged from the building, dragged Perkins and his two colleagues
inside, and threw them in jail on charges of inciting to riot and possession of a concealed deadly weapon. Inside the jailhouse, the sheriff,
Jonathan Edwards, was waiting to get his hands on the civil rights
leader. Edwards and his men savagely beat Perkins for hours, at one
point even shoving a fork into Perkins's nose and twisting it down
his throat. The violence culminated in one officer sticking a gun to
Perkins's head, the click of an empty chamber sounding the end of
his cruel joke. It was a beating that left Perkins drifting in and out of
consciousness through the night.

Lying in a hospital bed a few days later, recovering from this brutal
act of racism, Perkins began to feel the hatred brewing in his soul as
the desire to reject his visions of reconciliation filled him. And yet,
at this moment the image of Christ on the cross fought its way into
his mind. With the image of the deserted, beaten, crucified Christ
uttering words of forgiveness for those who were killing him, Perkins
too embraced the Spirit of God, speaking the words, "I forgive them,
too." In doing so he found his way out of the "horror of hate," freed
to live life no longer dominated by the threat of violence and racism
in a Jim Crow South.[6]

Perkins has since continued to live a life dedicated to racial and
economic reconciliation. His has been a life freed from the *modus
operandi* of offense as defense and preemptive strike tactics. Instead,
he has been dedicated to humble service and love, even for those who
continue to oppose him simply because he is a black man. Following
Christ, he has been freed to take an offensive strategy of offering,
laying down his life in service of God's kingdom. Perkins continues
today to live a life with a beauty that aggressively proclaims the good
news of the gospel, refusing to bow to the tactics of fear or hatred
in order to find security.

Instead of leading the charge in a culture of fear or following along
blindly with the cultural trends and fads, Christians should be those
who are the least likely to let fear dominate our lives and the way we
interact with others. Our interactions do not have to be based on a

fear of death, a fear of losing our families, a fear of losing our homes or our wealth, for all of these things have been given over to Christ already in our baptism. In Christ, we have been given a certain type of mission, a mission that, as Nietzsche so gnomically put it, ought to sing more beautiful songs.

Because Christ has conquered death, and because we are able to enter into his victory by practicing our own death in baptism, we can encounter the world with optimism, allowing us to employ a rich community hermeneutic. This is not to say that we are to be naive or to carelessly think that all faiths lead to Christ. But it is to believe that we do not need to see others as a threat and therefore encounter others with a defensive posture. It is to recognize that God has opened up a whole new world of possibilities for us in Christ, recalling the new creation we spoke of in chapter 10. To paraphrase Stanley Hauerwas, it is to say that in Christ the kingdom of God has become the grain of the universe. And this means that when we interact missionally in the world we can do so with the knowledge and confidence that, against all odds and perceptions, God has already spoken on behalf of the new creation. With regard to mission, this means to understand that we now inhabit a post-secular age, that is, an age captured by the promise and righteousness of God in Christ.

In certain respects the world is ours to shape as we live into the form of Christ. No longer do we as Christians need to engage our world with an offensive that seeks to hold on to the way things were or to legislate against depravity—and really, we never did. Neither do we have to place our trust in technology or economic expansion to save us—we never did. We do not have to fear either the liberals or the fundamentalists, for it is not our job to keep hell from taking over (whether it looks like an agenda of all-out atheism or that of radical fundamentalists). But the political and social arenas have become the frontier of the church to invent new ways of doing good to our fellow humans, to think of new configurations that proclaim the goodness of God, to play with the way things are in order to find ways we might better embody the good news of God's kingdom.

Karl Barth, one of the most influential theologians of the twentieth century, when discussing the Christian's place in society, stated, "We shall maintain toward the world, toward men and ourselves, a grateful, happy, understanding patience—better indeed than do the others who know nothing of the opposition. We can permit ourselves to be more romantic than the romanticists and more humanistic than the humanists. But we must be more precise."[7]

It is this call to that which is far beyond the futile attempts at unity, reconciliation, and world peace proffered by our nation, our academies, and our nongovernmental organizations—the call to offer the good news of God to the world—that makes us resident aliens here. Learning to engage our world in a mission of self-sacrifice, leaving behind the spirit of fear and the infatuation with security, we can begin to act outside the lines, artistically giving new and beautiful expressions of our faith by offering ourselves for others as we proclaim God's act of redemption. As we participate in the mission of Christ, as we learn to bear the marks of Christ even upon our bodies, we will also extend that same fellowship (*koinonia*) to a world God desperately seeks to bring back into his life. Life with God, the whole world gathered into God's holiness, is, as theologian James McClendon reminds us, the end of the Christian message and mission.[8]

The mission of offering takes at least two related forms. Each of these two forms of offering we learn from a community hermeneutic while each of them serves to make that hermeneutic possible, and in each of them we discover our place in the mission of God to redeem a broken world.

In the form of prayer we remember constantly and continually to give the task of redemption over to God. We offer ourselves and all those around us to God. While in a prior chapter we pointed to the way in which we have limited the nature of Christian life simply to the activities of reading Scripture and praying, it was not to say that we do not take these practices to be integral to our lives as followers of Christ. But we are convinced that reading with a community hermeneutic also directs our prayer life in new and exciting directions. Just as we learn a posture of humility and dialogue from reading with our community, so we also learn to turn our prayer away from ourselves and our petty desires and begin to embrace its missional operation. This is not to say that we no longer pray for ourselves or our families or our friends, but it is to say that we continue to pray for these things with a cosmic perspective, offering them up to God in prayer for the sake of the kingdom. As we will see in more detail in our final chapter, prayer is an act of reliance on the power and promise of God. As such, it is one of the most powerful practices we have and yet one of the strangest things we do. And it is beautiful.

Second, mission in the form of martyrdom means that we constantly and continually offer our lives, yes, even our bodies for the sake of the gospel to those around us. It means that we continue to preach the good news of God's invitation to live with him to others even if they desire to take our lives because of it. We do this because laying down our lives is the way to victory; it is the path that leads to God's end for the world: redemption. That is to say, martyrdom is the offensive strategy because it is to follow the way of the cross.

In Christ's work on the cross, God has not only become reconciled with the world by doing away with sin; God has also definitively displayed the strategy for destroying the powers that have held this world in bondage. By taking up the cross and following Christ, we also participate in God's strategy for redeeming the world. In doing so, we learn to follow in the mission of Christ and we are conformed to the image of the Son (Rom. 8:29). We are made beautiful.

To remove any confusion, this is not to say that martyrdom is what we are seeking necessarily. We are aware of, and have even regrettably practiced at times, forms of self-aggrandizing messiah complexes. Mission can only take the form of martyrdom if martyrdom is not the mission. Martyrdom, as Barbara Brown Taylor reminds us, is for us just what it was for the saints through the ages: it is "what happened to them while they were living the fullest lives they knew how and trying to make that life available to someone besides themselves."[9]

The blood of those martyrs on which our church was founded and upon which it has been sustained was blood shed as a result of trying to reach out to the lives around them with the good news of Jesus. It was blood shed for the offense of love and service—and do not underestimate how offensive this may be to the powers that seek to maintain the status quo. To continue quoting Brown Taylor, "I don't think you can seek it [martyrdom] anymore than you can avoid it. I think it just happens sometimes, when people get so wrapped up in living God's life that they forget to protect themselves. They forget to look out for danger, and the next thing they know it is raining rocks."[10]

Martyrdom vividly displays to the world that we care more about them than they may ever care about us. In fact, it shows that we have such a dedication to the call and mission given to us in Christ that we are not willing to kill for it. To speak of martyrdom does not imply that we are passive. Not at all. But it is to say that we have become captivated by something more important than our own lives—the call of God to participate in his redemption of the world. But working for redemption is beautiful, dangerous business.

Yet it is only in the posture of openness produced in prayers of confession and offering our lives that we can find freedom from suspicion and the driving fear that we are going to lose the gospel message. This freedom changes our calling both in how we read the text and how we engage the world. Released from the false pretense that we are the keepers of the secrets and charged with the mission of possessing the truth, we can actually live our lives following the truth of Christ, and live that beautiful truth among each other in the way we read, as well as live for the world in humble service.

Our Practice

From the very first brainstorm sessions about Emmaus Way one thing was clear: we wanted it to be a missional community. While we were not sure what this meant or what it would look like (and we are still not sure entirely), we were convinced that it meant embracing our location and learning to live in service to the people who live here. In this respect, we wanted to be a church in touch with the pulse and issues of Durham. It became very important for us that our church not take on a "franchise" persona, but that it intentionally connect and reflect life where we are.

As a result, we did not feel the need to be project or program driven. Instead, we wanted to begin by taking a back seat to the community programs that were already taking place in the city and county, offering support and assistance where we could. In doing this, many people in our church expressed their fear of participating in events that may not clearly define or state the Christian message. What we found, however, is that our new offensive missional posture liberated us to work with and inside the broader community of Durham, while feeling the freedom to always articulate our reason for being there through the story of Christ. In some sense, it gave us a confidence to serve within Durham because it allowed us to see the places where God was already working.

One particular place where we have experienced this type of service and mission is in our involvement with a local grassroots political organization called Durham CAN. While we are well aware of the seeming apostasy of blending politics and religion, what we have found is that our missional instinct to establish proximity to our city and county have led us to see real issues in our community that needed to be addressed.

The beauty of local politics is both in the wonderful possibilities of making real change and in the fact that the normal bipartisan shenanigans we have all grown so tired of on the national stage don't seem to dominate the landscape. A tri-ethnic and bilingual conglomeration of Churches, Alliances, and Neighborhoods (CAN), this organization has offered us an invitation to participate in the outreach of other communities pursuing similar visions of the kingdom of God in our city. And even more so, we are allowed to speak about what we are doing in those terms. Hence, we've been able to serve through CAN, working with several African American congregations, Latino fellowships, and other denominational communities to address issues of housing, jobs, education, gang violence, and living wages.

Our involvement with Durham CAN is merely one of our missional partnerships. We also have a group that works with a downtown garden, using agriculture as a means to connect with inner-city youth, while discussing the process of food preparation and care for creation as a way to redeem the often-corrupted practice of eating. We partner with a nearby African American church working to help ex-offenders find housing and jobs and to offer them emotional and directional support. In each of these partnerships, while we never quite get it right, we have tried to foster a posture of missions that can see the kingdom of God where it is coming and greet it with joyous celebration instead of fixating on the possibility that the enemy might have found its way into our camp.

This is not to say that we believe the kingdom of God to be reducible to an earthly reality or that we do not tend to the uniqueness of Christ, but it is to say that we believe that procuring the survival of the church is not our job. Our job is to share, live, and celebrate the kingdom of God and trust that God will provide for our survival by continually sending God's Spirit. This is the type of missional life we think is beautiful and will be unavoidably attractive to those who desperately want to hear some good news.

In his novel *Orbit of Darkness*, Ian MacMillan paints the very stark picture of life in Auschwitz for prisoners during World War II. As the title gives away, it is a dark novel saturated with much despair and the ugliness of war. And yet, at the center of the many vignettes that compose its narrative there is a beautiful story of hope. In Penal Block 14A a group of haggard, sick, and exhausted prisoners stand waiting for the deputy commandant to speak to them. When he comes in, the deputy commandant announces to the prisoners that one of their block has escaped and that this prisoner on the lam has not been found. In reprisal, he states, ten of them will be selected by his random whim to die by starvation.

Amidst the gruesome selection process, to the shock of both the Nazi guards and the prisoners, a small priest steps forward, volunteering to take the place of a man who has just been chosen. It is a revolutionary act, an act that brings the Nazi machine to a grinding halt. His act of sacrifice has challenged the deadly power of the prison camp and given back to the prisoners the humanity that had been stolen from them. Locked in his cell, kept from food and water, somehow this priest continues to live, frustrating the Nazis and piquing hope within the prisoners. Eventually, MacMillan writes, the Nazis execute the priest by lethal injection—his very existence becoming too much of a threat to the stability of their project.

The novel paints the beautiful actions of the priest upon the macabre nature of Auschwitz as a means of communicating a lesson. MacMillan tells us, "Those who give up their lives, at least in principle, become more dangerous to the Germans than planes or tanks. They become the ultimate weapon."[11] In a novel replete with the horror of a world lost in war, murder, abuse, hatred, racism, and fear, the story of this priest stands out as something beautiful. It is a picture of Christ—a picture of beauty, and as such, a vivid display of the church's mission. These are the things we celebrate, and they are the songs that make our faith beautiful. This is the type of offensive we hope will become characteristic of a new age of mission.

The Impact of Mission on Reading

Reading the text must occur in a missional community. A church without a mission (1 Peter 2:9), just like an Israel without a mission (Exod. 19:6), doesn't make sense. Only with the perspective that we are on a mission to serve the world, to lay down our lives for its redemption, to take up the way of the cross as a strategy for proclaiming God's good news, are we able to read the text together and hear it as God's Word. Only formed in a posture of prayer and martyrdom can we seek to interpret the Bible and expect to hear the Word of God in it. Reading as a form of offering, the offensive way of redemption, will open us to see and read in the Spirit.

In this way, reading the Bible is a lot like reading music. Anyone who has had even an entry-level course in music realizes that reading music is an exercise that cannot be divorced from its performance. While a person may be able to theoretically explain the difference between a G sharp and a B flat and may even be able to locate these on the lines of a bass clef, this does not mean she can truly read music. To truly read music one must deploy an instrument to actualize the notes, to hit the notes with perfect pitch, and to join them together smoothly and eloquently. Expressing the music is half of what it means to read music.

In much the same way, mission cannot be divorced from the interpretation of the text. To read the Bible as Scripture is to perform it, to be called into its mission, to learn to sing its beautiful songs. A true reading of Scripture must live in its performance, and as a result we must be beautifully formed in order to know how to read its pages.

Practicing our mission in the form of offering, being shaped into the beauty of the way of the cross, allows us to interpret the Word of God in the Bible because, just like the singer who must actualize the notes on the page in her voice, we must actualize this Word with our lives, making them into beautiful songs.

→ 13

Imagination

Exploding the Bounded Set of Our Minds

We both grew up with huge, elaborately bound, ornate family Bibles prominently displayed on coffee tables in formal living rooms. The living room was a "no play zone" in our homes. Soccer balls, loud kids, and sticky fingers were universally excluded. This space served as a sanctuary for the nice furniture, adult conversations, and the entertainment of "company." The family Bible was not only the perfect complement for the formal decor, it rested open as an unwavering declaration of the rules of the room and a stern warning of the dire consequences that awaited any ball-kicking, loud-voiced, peanut-butter-and-jelly-laden kid who dared enter.

The Christian community often allows for Scripture to rest in a prominent space in our lives like the family Bibles of our childhood. We freely acknowledge its beauty. We offer due respect. We are very careful, even quite fearful, about messing with it or messing it up. Even when we don't ascribe a stern, austere tone to the text, we assume a specificity or even an inflexibility of message. Like the firmly bound Bibles of our childhood homes, the contents of the Scriptures are irrevocably bound in a specific set of theological prescriptions, ethical directives, and divine promises.

Of course, the Bible is shaped by the great historical narrative of God's work of creation, blessing, redemptive promises, and fulfillment of those promises. But we tend to see this narrative as standing within a bounded set of possibilities such that each vignette, each episode, and each character ultimately, if studied well, will *always* lead us to *the* right message. As servants in this quest to find the right meaning, we have become students of language, grammar, historical context, historical interpretations, and theological possibilities. For many, reading the Scriptures correctly leads to a precise interpretation or at most a limited range of possibilities shaped by our exegetical tools and the small space given by our theological systems. This is not necessarily wrong, but our search for the right message under the tutelage of our exegetical methods and theological systems often leaves no space or role for the imagination.

Imagination seems to be one of the very things we fear to bring to our reading of the text, and for good reason. When we think of imagination, we often think of the realm of fiction, fairy tale, folklore, and childhood fantasy, all things that seem to detract from our attempt to take the Scriptures seriously and to interpret them carefully. As such, imagination certainly does not seem to be something that should appear on the invitation list for entrance into the formal living room. After all, doesn't it present a problem for serious query, by interjecting rough and fantastical play with text, eventually breaking items that were once protected as valuable and sacred?

A couple years ago, we had the opportunity to hear the beloved Southern novelist and Duke professor Reynolds Price read from his recent book *A Serious Way of Wondering* at our local bookstore.[1] The subtitle of this work is *The Ethics of Jesus Imagined*, and its text is a literary performance of the "WWJD" slogan thousands of Christians wear on their wrists. At the center of the book are several brief stories Price imaginatively crafts, focusing on Jesus' response to three profoundly contemporary ethical dilemmas: meeting a gay man, encountering Judas Iscariot in the act of suicide, and a conversation with a woman caught in a sexual liaison with a man who is not her estranged husband. A scandalous trilogy to say the least. One of the remarkable aspects of the evening, however, was simply the author's repeated acknowledgment that his imaginative musings were forbidden by the church and established Christianity. In the book, Price offers this self-description:

> I'm what in all honesty I can only call an outlaw Christian. . . . I live outside the law of almost any church; and I cannot think my principles immoral, though of course I make a huge number of errors—from small to large—in my daily life. A few churchly friends have tried to persuade me that my presence in a congregation would be the practical way for me to join in efforts toward reforming at least some aspects of Christianity which are plainly in bald defiance of Jesus' life and work. Finally, I've been unable to agree. In loyalty to my mother's memory, and to my gratitude for its role in my youth and for its charities, I've retained membership in a particular church; but I haven't been there since her funeral.[2]

Not surprisingly, Price was honored as an outlaw even at this reading. At the end of the evening, while he signed the book of a local pastor, a woman also in attendance remarked loudly of her great surprise that any pastor would be in attendance, then spouted that she might attend a church whose pastor would listen to a Reynolds Price reading!

When we got to the front of the autograph line, we claimed our own place in the pastoral guild and commented that we believed the kind of serious wondering Price advocates is a skill that all Bible readers should hone. The author's surprise was obvious and well merited from his own experience since his own wonderings and wanderings were met with sharp rejections. Race was certainly one arena of life where Price was considered an unwelcome thinker. His imagination of a church undivided by race was unsettling, uncomfortable, and a menacing threat in the segregated South. He writes, "It's accurate, I think, to say that I heard no single word condemning or seriously questioning American, not to mention Southern, racism from the pulpit of my family churches or that of Duke University in my childhood and youth."[3] He continued to mention similar observations about the church's posture in regard to poverty and his own felt pain due to rejection in regard to his sexual orientation.[4] We wanted to request half an hour to share some of the remarkable transitions we have witnessed in the missional and ethical practices of the contemporary church, but we settled instead to respect his experience as a wounded prophet and thank him for the way his art had carried us out of our familiar perspective and into a new vision of Jesus' actions.

We do want to strongly reiterate our comment to Reynolds Price; imagination is an essential skill of any reader who loves and values the biblical text. An absence of imagination is partly at fault for the church's "flat-earth moments" throughout history. In addition to sound exegetical work, prayerful contemplation and bold expenditures of imagination are absolutely necessary to catalyze the practices of authentic dialogue, subversive hospitality, new ethics, and "offensive" mission that we have described in the previous chapters.

Our contemporary context specifically demands a commitment to the exercise of our imaginations. Few practices could be more missional at the moment. Walter Brueggemann's biblical expositions have been sterling examples throughout the last few decades of the beautiful possibilities that emerge when exegesis and imagination come together. For instance, in *Texts Under Negotiation*, he aptly summarizes the need for a radically changed intellectual environment. The Enlightenment and modernity had created a powerful interpretative norm for the Scriptures. In this era, universal truths were unlocked by objective, individual analysts who followed scientifically prescribed methods. Biblical interpretation followed suit.

Brueggemann describes this intimate, and sometimes unobserved, connection between modern culture and interpretation:

> Interpretation informed by historical awareness was such a close and appropriate match for our context of modernity for the past two hundred years that we have scarcely been able to notice that the connection is culture-bound and did not always exist.[5]

As the presuppositions of modernity fade, we learn not only that our once unquestioned methods were culturally influenced but that new practices are desperately needed in an emerging context. Brueggemann continues with appropriate urgency, saying, "We are in a quite new interpretative situation that constitutes something of an emergency."[6] He summarizes the changes in the interpretative climate as the growing acknowledgment of the contextual nature of knowledge, the primacy given to local contexts in interpretation, and dramatic ascent of pluralism and, hence, conflicting narratives of truth. These characteristics of the postmodern perspective on knowledge have been regularly chronicled, defended, and critiqued in recent years and it is beyond our purposes to pursue this much further. But Brueggemann's measured assault on "objectivity," one of the signature values of modern interpretation, is quite significant to our point. He offers this powerful demythologization of objectivity:

> We are now able to see that what has passed for objective, universal knowledge has in fact been the interested claim of the dominant voices who were able to pose their view and to gain either assent or docile acceptance from those whose interest the claim did not serve. Objectivity is in fact one more practice of ideology that presents interest in covert form as an established fact.[7]

This suspicious assertion about "objectivity's" service as a tool in the misuse of power reveals some of the deep footprints of an ascending postmodern consciousness that we bring to every act of interpretation.

Imagination rises as an urgent and essential tool of interpretation in this intellectual climate. Imagination acknowledges freely its own local and personal subjectivity and protects us from subjectivity masquerading as objectivity. We envision imagination not as an act of untrained daydreaming, but as the material re-conceiving of reality from a perspective that has been formed in the tradition of the Scriptures. In chapter 1 of this book, we gave our attention to many of the subjective biases that, often surreptitiously, shape our reading of Scripture. In chapter 2, we elaborated on the need to live inside the text and to inhabit the strange new world of God of the biblical narrative. In chapter 3, we explained how community exposes our biases, balances them with divergent perspectives, and constructively allows for our subjectivities to be servants in the task of allowing the Bible to become God's Word to all of us. This is all an act of tradition, but tradition itself is not quite complete for our reading of the Bible as the Word of God. The employment of imagination enlivened by God's Spirit is central to expressing our subjectivities, to hear God's voice in our lives, and to respectfully hear the voice of God in our communities and cultures. This faculty is what allows us to see how God's Word is being made real in our world.

Brueggemann adamantly defends this link between the discipline of imagination and our attentiveness to God's speech or spiritual transformation. He argues:

> People do not change, or change much, because of doctrinal argument or sheer cognitive appeal. . . . People do not change, or change much, because of moral appeal . . . people in fact change by the offer of new models, images, and pictures of how the pieces of life fit together—models, images, and pictures that characteristically have the particularity of narrative to carry them. Transformation is the slow, steady process of inviting each other into a counterstory about God, world, neighbor, and self.[8]

New models, images, and pictures of God, community, and mission are found in the space created by imagination, new views of life that pull us into seeing the ways in which things can be different than they are.

The Bible cannot be received as God's Word without imagination. Surely there exists a persistent fear that imagination will deconstruct our creeds and theological compass points and will lead us to find the evidence of Russian helicopters in Revelation, as Hal Lindsey did in his popular eschatology *The Late Great Planet Earth*.[9] To these fears, we offer the gentle reminder that the culture-bound elements of our theologies and church polities need to be regularly challenged, refined, and reformed.

Without the introduction of imagination, so much of the Bible—precisely because it is counterstory to the impulses and norms of our culture and character—dwindles to sentimentality, trite moralism, or mysterious imperative. Many of Jesus' words about the kingdom are obscure and confusing without imagination.

Down the Rabbit Hole with Lost Sheep

One particular story, the story Jesus tells about a lost sheep (Luke 15:1–7), is a parable that we intuitively recognize as near the center of Jesus' message. Yet unless it is engaged in imaginatively, it can read in our Bibles like a dull knife. Jesus is confronted once again about his table behavior, particularly his insistence on continuing to eat and fellowship with "sinners." In response to this salacious charge, he tells a story of a shepherd who leaves a flock of ninety-nine to find one lost sheep. The story ends in celebration as the lost sheep is found by the shepherd, which Jesus equates to the rejoicing in heaven over the repentance of even one sinner.

This parable has been a motivational centerpiece to Christian evangelism and a lovely portrait of a God who seeks us. But it is also a bit of a head scratcher. Though we are no experts in the bucolic trade, it doesn't look like a great model of shepherding. What real shepherd would leave a whole flock alone in a dangerous world to find one lost animal? Surely animals were lost on occasion, but putting a whole flock at risk—this can't be right. It doesn't seem that someone could pass their animal husbandry comps with such a philosophy. Reading the text closely, we find some obvious elements to the story that engage us. But on the whole, the parable leaves us with an odd sense that we're missing something or that the storyteller is experiencing a brain lapse and has begun to mix his metaphors.

Departing the context of shepherding, which is admittedly obscure to most of us, and replacing it with a contemporary situation doesn't really help all that much. Okay, we admit we might leave our iPods in a public space to make a quick dash to feed the parking meter, or we might even (heaven forbid!) leave one of *your* children alone for a second to go off in search of one of our own. But it's not likely that we would leave one of our own kids alone in the wilderness to go off in search of another Boy Scout who has inadvertently run off. Doesn't this common sensitivity offend the integrity of the story?

Our children are more valuable to us than anything else, and they are distinct. So when the story talks about leaving lots of sheep for one sheep—a sheep, by the way, that there is no guarantee of finding—the parable seems to come apart—even more so when we start to substitute more equivalent items into its framework. Would I leave my laptop in a public library to get my PDA? Would I leave my wife's engagement ring at a bus station to go find a necklace that once belonged to my mother? Would I even leave one of our kids in a dangerous situation on the mere hope of finding our other child?

Perhaps there were other shepherds involved or we are assuming too much danger for the remaining flock. Nonetheless, this story leaves us unsettled and far more likely to sternly lecture the shepherd than to join in on his celebration. We do know that if one of our kids pulled a stunt like this, there would be consequences involved.

However, when we free our imaginations to encounter the story, new possibilities and paradigms emerge. Imagination allows us to set aside our rational analyses of risk-to-return ratios and suspend our discomfort at the economic pragmatics involved. Imagination is the gentle voice that reminds us that we are trying to engage the story rather than planning to interview the shepherd for a comparable position. This path allows us to entertain the thought that this man is possibly a very poor shepherd.

Getting back to Jesus, maybe there was no hauntingly remorseful music and an emotionally charged altar call at the story's conclusion. His audience may have laughed, long and loud, when they heard the story. I can hear the taunts: "No wonder this clown eats with sinners, he doesn't know the difference between up and down and in and out, much less right and wrong!" My (Tim's) dad reserved a special term, *the village idiot*, for people who displayed lapses of good sense like this.

Imagination helps us find, consider, and even embrace the counterstory. And this parable is most certainly counterstory. Its foolish presupposition alerts us that we are being asked to enter an entirely different reality, a reality that has little resonance with the pragmatics, norms, and assumptions of our cultural world. Imagination prods us to consider the terms of the story, and every other story we've heard from Jesus, from a down-the-rabbit-hole, through-the-wardrobe, just-taken-the-red-pill perspective. Here we find a kingdom that makes the crowd's taunts about Jesus' directional foolishness become pure irony. In this place, up is down, left is on the right, and we find in by going out, just as we find our lives by losing them (Luke 9:24).

Imagination allows us to be swallowed by the story, taking the roles of all the characters like one of those crazy dreams where you are first yourself, then you are your mother, and then you are your dog, and then all of sudden you're in the boardroom but, unfortunately, without your clothes!

Jesus is describing a reality where foolish sheep who somehow leave the safety of the flock are found—every time. This could be a narcissistic, self-absorbed animal, who, thinking it must have been the other ninety-nine that have gone astray, does not even know he is lost. Yet, still he is found. This could be a nihilistic sheep, a disciple of Nietzsche, who not only does not care that she is lost but also refuses to accept the ontological possibility of lostness. Yet despite her intellectual protestations, she is found. This could be a hedonistic beast reveling in the idea of being away from the accountability of the group, living out his own personal Woodstock. Despite the vomit in his hair, a bad case of syphilis, and his obvious avoidance of bathing, he is gently put on the shoulders of the shepherd and taken back to the community he has rejected. Perhaps this is a sheep lacking in self-confidence, self-esteem, and basic life skills. She keeps getting lost or isolated from the flock and she never has the forethought to find out where everyone is going and is never able to find the herd despite the inevitable and large trampled path made by the hungry flock. She is not capable of getting home on her own and never will be. Presumably she is found, again and again.

Jesus is proposing a possibility where a single shepherd never wearies of lost sheep. He never plays the odds. He didn't learn the inevitability of collateral losses in the military. He did not get a prestigious MBA and become schooled in the logic of cost-to-benefit calculations. Carelessly and inefficiently, he simply goes out and finds sheep. Possibly, none of the lost sheep are penitent. The narcissistic sheep is angry. The nihilistic sheep is disdainful of the whole enterprise, considering it an act of narrative violence since the shepherd has imposed his perspective on the story. The hedonistic sheep is going through withdrawal and needs a fix. The incapable one is already wandering off the trail again. Yet this shepherd loves them, finds them, and seems content to host a perpetual party. With a relentlessly gracious will and inexhaustible patience, this exceptional shepherd is capable of finding lost sheep. We desperately need a shepherd like this (because those sheep do sound remotely familiar).

This is the counterstory of Jesus' kingdom. It does not make sense according to the norms of our world. What if this story infers a love and call of the gospel of a magnitude such that the listener might enthusiastically accept an economic downward mobility for the sake of those who are lost? Now that would be a counterstory in our accumulation culture. To get the counterstory, we have to imagine it.

We have to suspend the rules of rational thought and detach ourselves from cultural norms. Perhaps this is why Jesus tells stories like this again and again.

Luke will record another story just a few sentences later about a preposterous father who gives a rebellious, insulting son a huge portion of his ample estate "to find himself" and to seek a Burning Man-esque experience of riotous living in a far-off country. When he comes home, this father greets him like royalty, welcomes him back to the family, and puts the boy in the position to demand more of the family fortune. That's some dad![10] Jesus tells us about crazy farmers who sow seed with a frivolousness that seems to naively assume the seed will never run out, casting it on hard paths, rocky ground, and briar patches in addition to fertile land (Matt. 13:1–9). Jesus offers the repetitive challenge, "He who has ears to hear, let him hear" (Luke 8:8). This might just mean "Let he or she who has enough imagination consider this impractical, unprecedented, topsy-turvy, life-coming-from-death kingdom of mine."

Imagination is certainly a missional essential for the interpretative crisis of a postmodern world that deeply values story, nuance, perspective, and preference. It is also a required path for any generation into Jesus' great counterstory about the counterintuitive metanarrative of a God who wants to do the dirty work of redeeming soiled sheep.

Transformation: An Imagining Community

Interpreting communities inevitably become imagining communities, people who diligently listen for the voice of God in strange places and relentlessly pursue the counterstory. We saw the evidence of this assertion almost immediately after we founded Emmaus Way. As you have heard throughout this book, our insistence on the use of dialogue in our worship gatherings and the formation of numerous spaces where we expected the community to interpret text encountered general enthusiasm and occasional strong resistance. But quickly the accusations of abdicating the authoritative and prophetic office as preachers and primary interpreters dissipated in the face of creativity and as the community saw how their imaginative work brought them closer to the kingdom story.

In one of our first worship gatherings, Andei Williams (who sadly left us to become an English professor at Ohio State) took time off of her dissertation writing to compose a vulnerable personal connection to the faithless steps taken by Abraham to provide the heir God had promised (Genesis 16), entitled "Sleeping with the Handmaidens and Other Lapses of Faith." Another writer and high school English teacher, Rebecca Stevenson, carried us into our first Easter with an imaginative piece on the other thief on the cross who bitterly rejected Jesus that would have made Reynolds Price proud. These first gifts came because we blessed the impulse to imagine by creating ample space in our gathered worship for works of this type. Soon the gifts began to flow. Wade began to write music with a beckoning complexity that demanded an imaginative response from our community. One of his first works, written as he labored through a painful divorce, was a song on the darkness of Lent, allowing him to share his pain while blending it with the promise of redemption.

More recently, I (Tim) had an idea that generated a bold musical request. (Every artist in the world knows this is "dangerous" ground when non-artists like ourselves, who know little of the creative process integral to certain art forms, begin to toss out ideas!) We were trying to teach disciplines of prayer in our worship gatherings, so we wondered if Wade could set the Jesus Prayer to music.[11] After two long months of work and collaboration with a gifted friend, Dale Baker, Wade created an amazing piece.

Overcoming the great challenge of trying to craft a substantive piece of music for a prayer that is only two lines, Wade wrote a complex song that begins with beautiful but turbulent Eastern tones, inviting the listener to envision the cacophony and chaos of a first-century Palestinian market. The song moves with a vibrant flow of notes to a musical place of solitude, literally guiding the listener to the centering prayer experience of the Jesus Prayer.[12]

The majority of our imaginative work, however, has not been done by professionals. This past Advent, we had the opportunity as a community to participate in a project with Carole Baker, a local painter and the wife of our drummer, Dale, who maintains a passionate desire for the integration of arts and liturgy and offers workshops on this topic around the country. Carole had received an iconography grant to portray community impressions of Mary, the mother of Jesus.

Carole passed out one-foot-square cardboard panels and asked any who were willing to paint interpretative impressions of this saint. We created a painting studio in the front of our space and encouraged those in attendance to feel free to paint during our Advent worship gatherings. One of the willing artists was my (Tim's) then eleven-year-old daughter, Kendall. Kendall considered this time in the makeshift studio with other adults in our community her most exciting Advent worship experience ever, and she was able to create an interesting piece of biblical interpretation. As a pre-teen, the mouth for her is the ultimate symbol of self-will, rejection, and even rebellion. Like most kids her age, she receives most of her parental correction due to her words and expressions. So she interpreted Mary's words of willing, enthusiastic compliance to the angel's proclamation of the mystery of the incarnation, "May it be to me as you have said," by painting Mary without a mouth.

These examples are samples of our journey to accept the mantle as an interpreting community, and hence, an imagining community. Because they are our story, they are simply markers of growth and emblems of our faithfulness to these challenges. We don't intend to measure them against the works of other communities or promote them as the finest examples of the practices of art and imagination. Many other communities are on this same journey and they will find other ways to give voice to their imaginations. But the point we want you to get from our examples involves the organic causality between community interpretation and imagination. We want the text to become the community's in such a way that it inspires them to envision things anew, while bringing this imagination back to the text with them as they read together.

Sacred Practice: A Mosaic of Contemplative Prayers

In each of the chapters in this final section of the book, we have defended the significance of a recommended change in community life that can be the result of a commitment to community hermeneutics, described some of the actual transformations that are possible, and concluded by recommending an expanded definition of a practice (often a sacramental practice) that can reinforce and catalyze a community's commitment to live in the text together.

This final chapter will follow that same pattern by offering as sacred a practice we mentioned in chapter 12 that connects to the life of the community, not only with respect to its mission but also as an active expression of its imagination. In this case, the practice of prayer not only fosters imagination but also addresses what might be a lingering question or concern in our overall thesis. Turning our title image back into a negative, one might ask again, how does one prevent community hermeneutics from becoming a chaotic free-for-all where any reading of Scripture goes or where the majority rules? First, let's turn our attention to the practice of prayer and then we'll return to this important question.

Developing a passion and creating space for contemplative, physical, and mystical prayer can become a gentle, yet Spirit-empowered, impetus that incubates and accelerates the development of imagination particularly in relation to the biblical text. Times of extended silence and meditation not only teach us to mute our distractions and preoccupations, they also build the muscles of imagination. Those who regularly commit to silence in private prayer or public worship quickly understand that there is both a stamina and a tolerance that one builds for silence. Tracy Powell, a founding participant in our community, held silent prayer gatherings for a few of us. Novices to the practice would comment on how difficult thirty minutes of silence was, especially in a room of friends. Soon our ability to sustain silence increased and then ultimately morphed into a desire for silence. All reported that their silence was punctuated by times of daydreaming and even frivolous thought. But ultimately, our imaginations would willingly and excitedly submit to the discipline so as to then venture out in creative thought that was worshipful and constructive on many levels.

Body prayer, a discipline that we are slowly introducing to our worship gatherings, amidst some discomfort, demands that a participant take on a pose or posture that is often highly related to a petition that we eagerly desire to address to God (like a plea for mercy), an emotional state that we find difficult to frame into words (like unbridled joy or abject despair), or a profound wish directed toward a loving God (like a desire for courage, wisdom, or strength). These poses often shift our energies from the composition of words to the imaginative processes of receiving gifts from God or recognizing (in some cases one might even say "tasting") pleas and emotions embedded in our souls. The physical aspect of prayer, perhaps because it is unfamiliar to many of us or because it asks us to shed some inhibitions, tends to shake us from our often overdeveloped cognitive muscles and catalyze our imaginations.

Lectio Divina, the mystical and "divine" reading of Scripture, is another wonderful example because it exists very specifically in the space created by prayer, imagination, and text. There are many methods of this discipline, but the common denominator of each method is careful, quiet, and imaginative listening to Scripture in order to allow God's Spirit to highlight or elevate a single word or phrase above the rest of the text, allowing this word or phrase to challenge us morally and missionally. This discipline not only serves as a personal prayer form but has also been a powerful piece of our public worship even with large groups. Though it is a bit reductionistic to over-generalize this discipline from the lens of imagination, this is another practice (like body prayer) that at the very least challenges our overly dominant cognitive and analytic impulses when approaching the Bible.

There are many other relevant contemplative disciplines (and many excellent resources to learn them) that hone our spiritual gifts of imagination and accentuate its connection to the biblical text, but the practice of Ignatian prayer merits special emphasis. Ignatian prayer, the hallmark of the Jesuits (and named after their founder St. Ignatius of Loyola), emphasizes holistic, sensory, and imaginative reading of text and expression of prayer. A prime example of these emphases is found in St. Ignatius's *Spiritual Exercises*.[13] In *Exercises*, participants are often asked to prayerfully contemplate a single text for several days, even weeks.

Ten years ago, I (Tim) had the opportunity to take a three-month sabbatical to practice the Ignatian model of prayer. The Jesuit priest who was guiding my work would often keep me on the same text and portion of *Exercises* for days on end. At first this exasperated me, but ultimately I found out how repetition and sustained contemplation encouraged my prayerful imagination to soar. My journals during these weeks of repetition are filled with wonderful insights.

Participants are also encouraged to enter the text imaginatively by taking on a variety of roles and perspectives found in the story as well as through sensory reflection (imagining the tastes, sights, touches, smells, and sounds of text in contemplation). The passion of Christ plays a prominent role in *Exercises*, which are filled with contrasting perspectives and sensory material.

Exercises also recommend breath prayers, where participants synchronize their breathing with reading the text. They can breathe in and breathe out elements of a simple, repetitive prayer phrase (much like "the Jesus Prayer," which is often used in this manner) or alternate their breathing through longer texts. The physical component can center the imaginative process and, much like Lectio Divina, affirm a holistic experience with the text that can break participants out of their cognitive, analytical ruts.

This returns us to the aforementioned concern: how do we allow community interpretation to flourish as a commitment that liberates the text to be God's Word for us, rather than an impetus to infighting, the rule of preferences, dominance of the majority, and community chaos? The contemplative disciplines play a decisive role in minimizing this fear. One lesson we learned years ago in seminary that is often forgotten (especially by us) is that prayer and contemplation are inalienable components of exegesis. The creators of many of these now-ancient practices knew that well.

St. Ignatius and the Jesuits wrote about "testing the spirits." They understood all too well that the contemplation of Scripture opened individuals and communities to the influence of selfish desires inflamed by poisonous spirits. In *Exercises*, retreatants are asked to regularly test the spirits when they reflected on the Scriptures. The centerpiece of the Ignatian disciplines is reserved for the daily Examen. In the Examen, one examines her soul by asking a "question of desolation" (How have I missed the presence of God's Spirit and blessing of God's voice in this day?) and a "question of consolation" (How have I sensed and experienced God's presence in this day?). This discipline gains great power when it is employed daily. One begins to detect the greater movement of God's Spirit and grand themes in God's speech as well as the lingering toxins of our greed, anger, and lust, the desires to manipulate Word, friend, and enemy.

Earlier we mentioned one of Henri Nouwen's descriptions of spiritual transformation (the movement from hostility to hospitality). Another of the great movements of spiritual transformation he names is the transition from illusion to prayer that shares some similarity to the practice of testing the spirits.[14] In Nouwen's language, "Illusion" refers to the state of our lives when we are dominated by our own schemes, devices, manipulations, woundedness, and visions of grandeur. "Prayer" denotes a life that is blessed and molded by God's vision of our world and the work to redeem that world. The movement from illusion to prayer is a natural product of spiritual disciplines like solitude, acts of prayer, corporate worship, and most certainly the reading of God's Word. The postures of listening and alertness to God's voice, buttressed by many of these time-tested disciplines, allow community encounters with the text to become electric spaces of hospitality and Spirit-driven imagination.

A Blessed Free-for-All

We are passionate students of the Bible. We are even greater lovers of the "in Christ" community, the church joined to Christ in life and mission. When biblical text and interpreting, practicing, faithful communities intersect, there is an explosion. Abstract word becomes God's Word. These communities are inspired in proclamation, ethics, hospitality, mission, and imagination. In addition, the dynamic of God's redemption takes a firmer root in a world careening toward a glorious telos, an end where all glory is given to Christ, and the salvation of God's creation is made complete. Communities inspired by the text literally create space for God's redemption. And in this space, we continually drink from the well of God's Word.

We hope that you and your community find yourself in a free-for-all with the text. We hope you end up following the trails of divergent voices, multiple perspectives, differing biases, and unique callings, all under the powerful tutelage of God's Spirit. We hope we have quelled any fears and offered a compelling invitation to a hermeneutic that liberates both Word and church. May all our communities be transformed in the reception of God's speech. May we live in a rich dialogue with God and God's people, one that honors the dynamic voice of God.

Notes

Introduction

1. William T. Cavanaugh, *Theopolitical Imagination* (New York: T&T Clark, 2002). See especially the first essay, "The Myth of the State as Saviour," pages 9–52.

2. Phyllis Tickle, *The Great Emergence: How Christianity Is Changing and Why* (Grand Rapids: Baker, 2008).

Chapter 1: Boundaries and Biases

1. Justo L. González, *The Reformation to the Present Day* (San Francisco: Harper & Row, 1984), 30.

2. Stanley Hauerwas and William H. Willimon, *Resident Aliens* (Nashville: Abingdon Press, 1989), 33.

3. Robert Draper, *Dead Certain: The Presidency of George W. Bush* (New York: Free Press, 2007).

4. Walter Nigg, *The Heretics*, trans. Richard Winston and Clara Winston (New York: Alfred A. Knopf, 1962), 194, quoted in Donald F. Burnbaugh, *The Believer's Church* (Eugene, OR: Wipf & Stock, 2003), 43.

5. Adam Smith, *The Wealth of Nations* (New York: Random House, 1994), 15.

6. Jim Wallis, "Dangerous Religion: George W. Bush's Theology of Empire," *Mississippi Review* 10, no 1 (2004), http://www.mississippireview.com/2004/Vol10No1-Jan04/1001-0104-wallis.html.

7. Nick Hornby, *How to Be Good* (New York: River Head Books, 2001), 255.

Chapter 2: Recovering the Word in the Bible

1. We are indebted to several texts in their treatment of the Fundamentalist/Modern split in American Protestantism, particularly Nancey Murphy's *Beyond Liberalism and Fundamentalism*, which describes the philosophical continuity between liberals

and conservatives and their contrasting choices in the wake of modernity; George Marsden's *Fundamentalism and American Culture: The Shaping of Twentieth Century Evangelicalism, 1870–1925*, which gives an overview of the whole history of separation and the birth of the conservative Protestant movement in America; and Robert Wuthnow's *The Restructuring of American Religion: Society and Faith Since World War II*, which describes the end result of essentially a two-denomination America.

2. J. Gresham Machen, "History and Faith," *The Princeton Theological Review* 13 (July 1915): 337–51, quoted in Robert L. Ferm, ed., *Issues in American Protestantism* (Garden City, NY: Anchor Books, 1969), 275.

3. Ibid., 276.

4. Osha Gray Davidson, *The Best of Enemies: Race and Redemption in the New South* (Chapel Hill, NC: University of North Carolina Press, 2007), 115.

5. Dale B. Martin, *Sex and the Single Savior: Gender and Sexuality in Biblical Interpretation* (Louisville, KY: Westminster John Knox Press, 2006), 5.

6. For further discussion, see George A. Lindbeck, *The Nature of Doctrine: Religion and Theology in a Postliberal Age* (Louisville, KY: Westminster John Knox Press, 1984).

7. Martin Luther, "Sermon on Luke 2," *D. Martin Luther's Werke* (Weimar: H. Böhlaus Nachfolger, 2003), 1523.

8. Karl Barth, Geoffrey William Bromiley, and Thomas F. Torrance, *Church Dogmatics* (Edinburgh: T&T Clark, 1975), 111.

9. Richard Lischer, *The End of Words: The Language of Reconciliation in a Culture of Violence* (Grand Rapids: William B. Eerdmans, 2005), 63–64.

10. Walter Brueggemann, *Cadences of Home: Preaching Among Exiles* (Louisville, KY: Westminster John Knox Press, 1997), 26.

11. Stanley Fish, in Stanley Hauerwas, *Unleashing the Scripture: Freeing the Bible from Captivity to America* (Nashville: Abingdon Press, 1993), 20.

12. Lischer, *End of Words*, 54.

Chapter 3: Let the Chaos Begin

1. This is a story one of our friends, Chris Rice, told of a recent visit to Rwanda with a group of Duke Divinity students.

2. Frederick Douglass, *Narrative of the Life of Frederick Douglass: An American Slave, Written by Himself*, in R. Marie Griffith, *American Religions: A Documentary History* (New York: Oxford University Press, 2008), 215.

3. Ibid., 216–17.

4. Hauerwas, *Unleashing the Scripture*, 15.

5. We are indebted to Ramsey Michaels's work in the Word Biblical Commentary series for these insights into 1 Peter. (See J. Ramsey Michaels, *1 Peter* [Waco, TX: Word Books, 1988].)

6. This is really what Stanley Hauerwas meant when he threatens to remove the Bibles from the hands of individuals. He wants to place the text into the hands of the historical and contemporary practicing communities of faith.

7. John Howard Yoder, *The Priestly Kingdom: Social Ethics as Gospel* (Notre Dame, IN: University of Notre Dame Press, 1984).

8. Ibid., 24.

9. Ibid.

10. John Howard Yoder, *Body Politics: Five Practices of the Christian Community Before the Watching World* (Scottsdale, PA: Herald Press, 2001). See chapter 1 for a full explanation of this practice of binding and loosing.
11. See Henri J. M. Nouwen, *Reaching Out: The Three Movements of the Spiritual Life* (Garden City, NY: Image Books, 1986). In the first section of this classic, Nouwen chronicles the spiritual movement from hostility to hospitality and offers what we think is an ultimate benchmark in the understanding of hospitality. We will return to his thoughts in chapter 11.

Chapter 5: The Word in the Obscure

1. Peter M. Buston and Stephen T. Emlen, "Cognitive Processes Underlying Human Mate Choice: The Relationship between Self-Perception and Mate Preference in Western Society," *PNAS*, May 28, 2003, http://www.pnas.org/content/100/15/8805.full.
2. "Eighteen Percent of Young Women Experience Sexual Victimization," *Science Daily*, March 13, 2007, http://www.sciencedaily.com/releases/2007/03/070312231732.htm.
3. Phyllis Trible, *Texts of Terror: Literary/Feminist Readings of Biblical Narratives* (Philadelphia: Fortress Press, 1984).
4. Collin Hansen, "Entire Area Young Life Staff Out after Evangelism Mandate," *Christianity Today*, January 7, 2008, http://www.christianitytoday.com/ct/2008/february/1.13.html.
5. The first time I (Tim) heard Badley speak on this was at the 2002 Emergent theological dialogue on the Bible at Ecclesia in Houston. In personal conversations later, Badley cites Stan Walters's "Jacob Narrative" as highly formative to her teaching on the structure of this story. (See Stan Walters, "Jacob Narrative," in *Anchor Bible Dictionary*, ed. D. N. Freedman [New York: Doubleday, 1992], 3:599–608.)
6. Luke Timothy Johnson, "It's a Mistake to Search for the 'Historical' Jesus," Beliefnet, June 2000, http://www.beliefnet.com/story/27/story_2716_2.html.

Chapter 6: The Word in Pain and Joy

1. Richard J. Clifford, *Psalms 1–72* (Nashville: Abingdon Press, 2002), 123.

Chapter 7: The Word in the Familiar

1. Frederick Buechner, *Telling the Truth: The Gospel as Tragedy, Comedy, and Fairy Tale* (San Francisco: Harper & Row, 1977), 47.
2. For more information about Mike and this project, see gossmanpassion.com and mikegarrigan.com.
3. See http://reasontorock.com/tracks/watchtower.html for a full commentary on this classic folk anthem.
4. The Basics, "Ordinary Time," *Grow*, © the Basics, 2004, used with permission.

Chapter 8: The Word in Controversy

1. There are obviously many descriptions of prostitution. But one might ask how volitional prostitution was in the sharp patriarchy of this social context that held few,

if any, vocational choices for women no longer under the economic provision of a father or husband. And one must also remember that sex itself was hardly volitional for women in a patriarchy. Many of the biblical provisions are generous ethical demands for women and their families who have been defiled by men. Hence, this text stands out in its specificity particularly in regard to women.

2. Stanley Hauerwas and William H. Willimon, *The Truth about God: The Ten Commandments in Christian Life* (Nashville: Abingdon Press, 1999), 20.

3. See Richard B. Hays, "Relations Natural and Unnatural: A Response to John Boswell's Exegesis of Romans 1," *Journal of Religious Ethics* 14, no. 1 (2006): 184–215; and Dale B. Martin, "Heterosexism and the Interpretation of Romans 1:18–32," *Sex and the Single Savior*, 51–64.

4. These verses, taken in this manner, create their own interpretative challenges that we will address with the points made in the "Genre and Literary Function" section.

5. William J. Webb, *Slaves, Women, and Homosexuals: Exploring the Hermeneutics of Cultural Analysis* (Downers Grove, IL: InterVarsity Press, 2001).

6. Douglas Atchison Campbell, *The Quest for Paul's Gospel: A Suggested Strategy* (London: T&T Clark, 2005).

7. Ibid., 238–45.

8. Ibid., 246–53.

9. Daniel Burke, "Presbyterians Report Biggest Drop in Nearly 30 Years," *USA Today*, June 25, 2008, http://www.usatoday.com/news/religion/2008-06-25-presbyte rian-decline_N.htm.

Chapter 9: Proclamation

1. One graphic in the documentary demonstrated that the states carried by Democratic nominee Hubert Humphrey in the 1968 presidential election remain as the blue states in the contemporary blue state/red state political separation.

2. Deborah Tannen, *The Argument Culture* (New York: Random House, 1998), 7.

3. Ibid., 13.

4. Ibid., 12.

5. James Davison Hunter, *Culture Wars: The Struggle to Define America* (New York: Basic Books, 1991), 136.

6. Justo L. Gonzáles and Catherine G. Gonzáles, "The Neglected Interpreters," in Richard Lischer, *The Company of Preachers* (Grand Rapids: William B. Eerdmans, 2002), 251.

7. Ibid., 253.

8. Darrell L. Guder, *The Continuing Conversion of the Church* (Grand Rapids: William B. Eerdmans, 2000). See chapter 5, pages 97–119, for a full treatment on the issue of reductionism.

9. We realize you might reject this affirmation as a negative. So many say that they want to go to church and hear an "authoritative word." And certainly, authoritative words often go hand in hand with church growth. Certainty is one of our greatest values and demands from our fellowships. But we would respond quickly that a range of meaning does not preclude passionate affirmations of the gospel. A greater issue exists as well. In so many of the communities and municipalities in our culture, conflicting "authoritative words" are preached with an entrenched insensitivity to the reality, and contrasting words, perhaps on the same text, are being preached right down

the road. The roots of our divisiveness, lack of missional cooperative, and damaged authenticity of witness certainly emanate from this reality.

10. To reference the "new perspective," see E. P. Sanders, *Paul and Palestinian Judaism: A Comparison of Patterns of Religion* (Philadelphia: Fortress Press, 1977). See also James D. G. Dunn, *Romans 1–8* and *Romans 9–16* (Dallas: Word Books, 1988) in the Word Biblical Commentary series.

Chapter 10: Ethics

1. See Karl Barth, *The Word of God and the Word of Man*, trans. Douglas Horton (New York: Harper & Row, 1957), especially chapter 2, "The Strange New World within the Bible," 28–50.

2. David James Duncan, *The Brothers K* (New York: Doubleday, 1992), 125–26.

3. Robert Ellsberg, "Five Years with Dorothy Day," *America: The National Catholic Weekly*, November 21, 2005, http://www.americamagazine.org/content/article.cfm?article_id=4487.

4. Ibid.

5. David Bornstein, *How to Change the World: Social Entrepreneurs and the Power of New Ideas* (Oxford: Oxford University Press, 2004), 55.

6. Ibid.

7. Ibid., 57.

8. E. P. Sanders, *Judaism: Practice and Belief, 63 BCE–66 CE* (Philadelphia: Trinity Press International, 1994), 275–76.

9. Ibid., 446.

10. Yoder, *Body Politics*, 28.

11. Ibid., 30.

12. Søren Kierkegaard, Howard Vincent Hong, and Edna Hatlestad Hong, *Philosophical Fragments/Johannes Climacus* (Princeton, NJ: Princeton University Press, 1985), 72.

13. Niccolò Machiavelli, *The Prince* (New York: New American Library, 1980), 49–50.

Chapter 11: Hospitality

1. The societal custom of hospitality is so essential and pervasive that Lot responds with an equally unthinkable "solution"—offering his virgin daughters to the mob!

2. Jan Michael Joncas, "Tasting the Kingdom of God: The Meal Ministry of Jesus and Its Implications for Contemporary Worship and Life," *Worship*, July 2000, 333–39.

3. Ibid., 344.

4. Nouwen, *Reaching Out*, 65.

5. See *Reaching Out*, pages 65–109, for Nouwen's full treatise on hospitality, including receptivity and honesty.

Chapter 12: Mission

1. Friedrich Wilhelm Nietzsche, paraphrased in Charles Marsh, *Wayward Christian Soldiers: Freeing the Gospel from Political Captivity* (New York: Oxford University Press, 2007), 90.

2. See John Milbank, "Sovereignty, Empire, Capital, and Terror," in *The Future of Love* (Eugene, OR: Cascade Books, 2009), 223–41.

3. Charles Taylor, *A Secular Age* (Cambridge, MA: Belknap Press, 2007), 22.

4. Thomas Hobbes, Karl Schuhmann, and G. A. J. Rogers, *Leviathan* (Bristol: Thoemmes Continuum, 2003), 2:102.

5. George M. Marsden, *The Soul of the American University: From Protestant Establishment to Establishment of Nonbelief* (New York: Oxford University Press, 1994), 186.

6. Charles Marsh, *The Beloved Community: How Faith Shapes Social Justice, from the Civil Rights Movement to Today* (New York: Basic Books, 2005), 172.

7. Barth, *Word of God*, 303. We are indebted to Charles Marsh for bringing our attention to this quotation.

8. James Wm. McClendon Jr., *Doctrine: Systematic Theology* (Nashville: Abingdon Press, 1994), 2:443.

9. Barbara Brown Taylor, "Blood of the Martyrs," in *Home by Another Way* (Cambridge, MA: Cowley Publications, 1999), 127–28.

10. Ibid., 126.

11. Ian MacMillan, *Orbit of Darkness* (San Diego: HBJ Publishers, 1991), 249.

Chapter 13: Imagination

1. Reynolds Price, *A Serious Way of Wondering: The Ethics of Jesus Imagined* (New York: Scribner, 2003).

2. Ibid., 114, 117.

3. Ibid., 116.

4. Ibid., 117.

5. Walter Brueggemann, *Texts Under Negotiation: The Bible and Postmodern Imagination* (Fortress Press: Minneapolis, 1993), 1.

6. Ibid.

7. Ibid., 9.

8. Ibid., 24–25.

9. Hal Lindsey, *The Late Great Planet Earth* (Grand Rapids: Zondervan, 1970).

10. For a beautiful depiction of God's character in this story, see Henri J. M. Nouwen, *The Return of the Prodigal Son: A Story of Homecoming* (New York: Doubleday, 1992).

11. To learn more about the Jesus Prayer, see http://www.jesusprayer.org.

12. For "The Jesus Prayer" by Wade Baynham, see http://www.reverbnation.com/emmausway. This song is part of an online CD produced by Wade and the musicians of Emmaus Way. All proceeds from downloads go to an Emmaus Way fund dedicated entirely to the support of local artists.

13. For an excellent translation, see St. Ignatius of Loyola, *The Spiritual Exercises of St. Ignatius: A Literal Translation and Contemporary Reading*, trans. David L. Fleming (St. Louis: Institute of Jesuit Sources, 1978).

14. See Nouwen, *Reaching Out*, 113–60.

Tim Conder is the founding pastor of Emmaus Way, a missional Christian church in Durham, North Carolina. He has served for many years as a leader for Emergent Village. He is also a member of the board of directors for Mars Hill Graduate School in Seattle. Locally, he serves on the Dr. Martin Luther King Jr. Steering Committee and as a pastoral leader for Durham CAN, a grassroots political organizing community working for social justice in Durham.

Tim has authored *The Church in Transition: The Journey of Existing Churches into the Emerging Culture* (Zondervan, 2006) and was a contributor to *An Emergent Manifesto of Hope* (Baker Books, 2007). He is a graduate of the University of North Carolina and Gordon-Conwell Theological Seminary. He and his wife, Meredith, have two children, Keenan and Kendall. Tim can be contacted at timconder@gmail.com.

Daniel Rhodes is co-pastor of Emmaus Way. He serves as one of the editors for *The Other Journal* (theotherjournal.com), an online periodical that explores the interactions between Christian faith and culture. He also serves on the jobs team of Durham CAN, where he is an active member.

A graduate of Duke Divinity School, Daniel is currently pursuing his doctorate in theology at Duke University in Durham. He and his wife, Elizabeth, live in Raleigh, North Carolina. Daniel can be contacted at drhodes@theotherjournal.com.

Visit the authors' websites at http://www.freeforallbook.com or http://www.timconder.com.

>> Join the conversation. >>

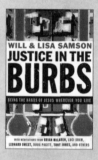

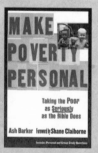